ArtScroll Judaica Classics®

a treasury of
chassidic tales
on the festivals

VOL. I

a treasury of
chassidic

by

Rabbi Shlomo Yosef Zevin

Translated by Uri Kaploun

סיפורי חסידים על המועדים

tales

on the festivals

A COLLECTION OF INSPIRATIONAL CHASSIDIC
STORIES RELEVANT TO THE FESTIVALS

Published by

Mesorah Publications, ltd / New York

in conjunction with

HILLEL PRESS / Jerusalem

FIRST EDITION
First Impression ... November, 1979
Second Impression ... August, 1980
Third Impression ... September, 1983

Published and Distributed by
MESORAH PUBLICATIONS, Ltd.
Brooklyn, New York 11223

In conjunction with
HILLEL PRESS, Jerusalem

Distributed in Israel by
MESORAH MAFITZIM / J. GROSSMAN
Rechov Bayit Vegan 90/5
Jerusalem, Israel

Distributed in Europe by
J. LEHMANN HEBREW BOOKSELLERS
20 Cambridge Terrace
Gateshead
Tyne and Wear
England NE8 1RP

A TREASURY OF CHASSIDIC TALES — ON THE FESTIVALS VOL. I
© Copyright 1981
by MESORAH PUBLICATIONS, Ltd.
1969 Coney Island Avenue / Brooklyn, N.Y. 11223 / (212) 339-1700

ISBN
0-89906-912-6 (Hard cover)
0-89906-913-4 (Paperback)

סדר במסרבית
חברת ארטסקרול בע״מ

Typography by Compuscribe at ArtScroll Studios, Ltd.
1969 Coney Island Avenue / Brooklyn, N.Y. 11223 / (212) 339-1700

Printed in the United States of America by Moriah Offset

Table of Contents

There is a well-known statement by Rabbi Acha in the Midrash (*Bereishis Rabbah* 68:9) which may be paraphrased as follows: "The patter of the servants of our forefathers is related in greater detail than the Torah taught by their descendants. For the story of Eliezer the servant of Avraham and his quest for a bride for Yitzchak is recounted over several pages, and is repeated, while important laws of the Torah are often indicated by a single letter."

This statement, which illustrates so powerfully the pre-eminence which the Torah accords the words and doings of our forebears, strikes one anew as one presents to the English-speaking public a further volume of stories of tzaddikim. This thought was evidently shared as well by the many thousands of readers who received with enthusiasm the preceding two volumes of *Suppurei Chassidim* — on the Torah. And for this reception I should like to give thanks to HaShem.

In our generation, when all at once everyone — mystics, agnostics, philosophers, cultists of various hues — have (as it were) discovered Chassidism, and are publishing books on the subject indiscriminately, it is more than ever necessary that the earnest reader be given, as an antidote, an unbiased and authoritative presentation of the chassidic story as originally told. Whereas every authentic chassidic story was intended to deepen awareness of HaShem and love for his Torah — and in this aim Rav Zevin indeed succeeded in his anthologies — modern "chassidic" stories are all to often slanted to achieve the opposite, and to project a hero who is independent of HaShem and His Torah. The Talmud rules that a *sefer* Torah written by a *min* (a person whose beliefs are suspect) is invalid. Now on the face of it a *sefer* Torah is impossible to twist away from the true path, as it is merely a copy of an existing Scroll. How much more vulnerable, then, is a story, where the in-nuendo of a single word can distort the whole point of the story; how much more certain is it to be *pasul*, invalid, if written by a *min*. The present work, however, written in warm, classical Hebrew by one of the giants of our generation, is proudly presented to the English reader with the confidence that every single story in it has a point, and that the objective of the author — to deepen awareness of HaShem and the love of his Torah — has been faithfully conveyed.

That the stories are here presented with authority and authenticity is due to the skill and loving attention lavished on this work, as on previous works of Rav Zevin in English, by Mr. Uri Kaploun, whose services I was fortunate to obtain, and with whom I hope to collaborate on many other worthwhile projects.

It is also a great pleasure to pay tribute to Rabbi Meir Zlotowitz and Rabbi Nosson Scherman of Mesorah Publications, whose encouragement in this project has been of great help, and to Reb Sheah Brander, whose graphic skill makes all books in which he has a hand an aesthetic delight.

Finally I offer the traditional prayer which is uttered when finishing a tractate of the Talmud: "Just as I have been found worthy of completing this work, may I be found worthy by השי"ת of beginning and completing other works" — in order to increase and enhance the knowledge of the Torah.

Meir Holder
HILLEL PRESS

Jerusalem/2 Adar Sheni, 5741 (1981)

Note: A biographical sketch on Rav Zevin appears in volume one of *A Treasury of Chassidic Tales on the Torah*, pp. xii-xiv.

✍ Translator's Foreword

"In each and every generation," the Sages of the Mishnah teach us, "a man is obliged to regard himself as if he personally came out of Egypt."

This sublime command, which is widely known through its appearance in the *Haggadah*, was of course originally expressed in Hebrew. Now one of the uncanny marvels of the Holy Tongue is that its words are spelled not by any arbitrary conglomeration of syllables, but by a divinely-inspired internal harmony of letters, each combination being meaningful in its own right. Thus it is, for example, that the Hebrew word for Egypt, מִצְרַיִם, is composed of the very same letters as is the word מְצָרִים, signifying "straits." And herein lies our lesson. For to merely imagine oneself as having come out of Egypt would be barren play-acting, a sorry festival indeed. What the Mishnah is telling us is that each individual is commanded not only to recall a national exodus at a certain historical period from a geographical Egypt, but *to effect a personal exodus*, at any given moment in his life, from the straitjacket and shackles of his own private House of Bondage — the psychological hang-ups, the self-imposed spiritual malnutrition, the petty pursuits — that prevent his soul from reigning free and supreme within him. This, then, is the Egypt from which a man must liberate himself.

Though this command is in effect through every day of one's life, yet there are times at which its fulfillment enjoys the especial encouragement of Him Who gave the command.

A hint of this is to be found in the *Megillah* which is read on Purim: וְהַיָּמִים הָאֵלֶּה נִזְכָּרִים וְנַעֲשִׂים — "*And these days are recalled, and realized.*" On this the Baal Shem Tov comments: "Whenever they are recalled, they are realized." That is, every year when Purim comes around, for example, the same divine salvation disguised in the workings of nature which then shone forth, shines forth again. A person needs but to observe the recurring day with ever-increasing spiritual sensitivity, for his soul to be illumined by the light of that first fateful Purim. So, too, Pesach every year is a particularly propitious season for a man to make the effort to free himself from his own House of Bondage — for he will be helped. Similarly, for those who are prepared to stand humbly at the foot of Sinai, Shavuos is a time when the Torah is given afresh every year. And so on, around the cycle of the year.

❀ ❀ ❀

After all the hard work that they have put into preparing their home for Friday night, many thousands of English-speaking families have ב״ה been glad to bring to the table week by week one of the two volumes of *Sippurei Chassidim* on the Torah. Its task: to help these hard workers breathe a soul into the waiting corporeal frame of *gefilte* fish, gleaming tableware, and the family's innocent small-talk.

Like those two volumes on the Torah, the present two-volume anthology of chassidic stories on the festivals appears as the result of a happy collaboration with Reb Meir Holder of Hillel Press, Jerusalem, and Rabbis Meir Zlotowitz and Nosson Scherman of Mesorah Publications, New York. And it is now my hope that like the earlier volumes in their field, these volumes too will help those who observe the festivals — as well as those who do not yet observe them — to regard each *Yom Tov* as it comes, not merely as an occasion for erudite historical recollections, but as a "happening": a personal Day of Awe, a personal exodus from Egypt, a personal standing at Sinai. This calls for creative reading. As an aid to this end, therefore, the next volume will אי״ה include an exhaustive listing of sources, succinct biographical notes on the leading personalities with an index of the stories in which they figure, and a subject index — all covering the four volumes of the series.

❀ ❀ ❀

Three times a year the old grey stones of Jerusalem's walls strain wistfully to hear the long-promised murmur and rumble of pilgrims thronging from afar. Three times a year the tired old stones strain almost visibly to see those pilgrims, breathless but wide-eyed, as they clamber over the hilltops that surround the Holy City, and behold for the first time the Temple Mount in all its rebuilt splendor. Three times a year — in a year not distant — Jerusalem is yet destined to echo to the rhythm of their tramp, and clamor, and songs of thanksgiving.

And among those who will greet them at the gates of the City, may my dear parents שי׳ be counted. To them this anthology is dedicated.

U.K.

Jerusalem/9 Adar Sheni 5741 (1981)

ᴇ§ Author's Introduction

[The following note introduced the original Hebrew edition of
Sippurei Chasidim al HaMoadim on its first appearance.]

The introduction which prefaced *Sippurei Chassidim al
HaTorah* [the English edition of which is entitled *A Treasury
of Chassidic Tales on the Torah*], delineating the aims of the
stories, applies with equal validity to the present anthology
which is set out according to the festivals of the year. This collection resembles its predecessor also in the criteria used in the
choice of stories, in the manner of their arrangement, and in the
style of their presentation to the reader. I therefore think it apt
to preface the present volume with the same Introduction.

❈ ❈ ❈

Chassidic stories lead to many destinations. There are those
whose aim is to show how the hand of God is revealed —
often supernaturally — through the wondrous workings of
tzaddikim. Their message: וְרָאוּ בָנָיו גְּבוּרָתוֹ, שִׁבְּחוּ וְהוֹדוּ לִשְׁמוֹ —
"As His children beheld His might, they extolled and offered
praise to His Name." Others seem rather to highlight the role
of the tzaddik in these wonders, as if to echo the dictum of the
Sages: צַדִּיק גּוֹזֵר וְהַקָּבָּ"ה מְקַיֵּים — "A tzaddik decrees; the
Almighty fulfills." Yet others conceal a moral, pointing to the
reward that is bestowed upon the righteous, and the retribution
that awaits the godless. Some stories set their sights on a didactic target, in particular those which dwell on the uprightness
and holiness of tzaddikim in their exemplary dealings with
their fellows and in their enviable rapport with their Maker.
There are stories in which a point deserving of contemplation is
taught — whether directly or indirectly — through an original
scholarly insight, such as a novel interpretation of a Biblical
verse or Talmudic teaching. What captures our attention in
some of the narratives is the spiritual and psychological
motivation that steers the actions of tzaddikim and chassidim
alike. In other stories these same protagonists fascinate us by
their wit, intellectual prowess, or sage understanding of human
nature. Then again, the very backdrop to a story is sometimes
as attractive as its personages or its action, allowing us a peek
into the ethos and lifestyle of a vanishing age in a faraway

world. And indeed, in certain of the stories one can savor many of the above ingredients, if not all.

The chassidim of bygone generations disapproved of stories which merely recorded miraculous feats, for these are things which are rather to be tasted than consumed in quantity. Such stories used to be seen by the school of Pshischah as suiting the spiritual sophistication of pagans. They would take the innocent phrase from the Evening Prayer — אוֹתוֹת וּמוֹפְתִים בְּאַדְמַת בְּנֵי חָם, which, in the context of the plagues inflicted upon the Egyptians, refers to "signs and miracles in the land of the Hamites" — and drily rephrase it to mean: "Signs and miracles belong best in the land of the Hamites ..." Reb Menachem Mendel of Kotsk likewise underplayed the role of miracle stories in the growth of the man of faith. There is a verse in *Psalms:* אֲבוֹתֵינוּ בְמִצְרַיִם לֹא הִשְׂכִּילוּ נִפְלָאוֹתֶיךָ, which in fact means that "Our forefathers in Egypt paid no heed to Your wonders." Reading this verse on a less literal level, Reb Menachem Mendel understood it to imply that it was not the miracles that refined the faith of our forefathers in Egypt.

This attitude can in fact be traced back to the Talmud, where the following is related: "There was a man whose wife died, leaving him an infant, and he had no money with which to hire a wetnurse. A miracle was worked for him, and he developed breasts like those of a woman so that he was able to nourish his baby. Hearing this, Rav Yosef exclaimed: 'How great is this man, that such a miracle should be wrought for him!' Said Abbaye: 'On the contrary — how blameworthy is this man, that the natural order of Creation should be disturbed for him!'" A similar view is evident in a comment by Rashi: "The further a man can keep his distance from miracles, the better." Indeed, even concerning a miracle that does not defy the natural order of things, the Talmud says that a person for whom a miracle is performed has this privilege subtracted from his account of merits.

In the teachings of *Chabad* Chassidism we find the following: "The miracle of Purim, it is true, was clothed in the ways of nature through the story of Achashverosh — but for this very reason it is clear that the divine light then manifested was derived from a lofty source indeed." It is apparent, then, that it is more praiseworthy to listen to the voice of God as He walks about the garden of everyday life in the natural world than to witness miracles that burst the bounds of nature. So, too, writes Reb Shlomo Zalman of Kopust, relating this exposition to the two classic categories of divinity — the four-letter Name (compounded of the letters *yud-hei-vav-hei,* and here referred to as *Havayah*), which represents God as an infinite, transcendent essence, and the Name *Elokim,* which signifies His connection with the finite, created universe, through His seeming self-limitation in nature. Reb Shlomo Zalman, then, writes as follows: "Yisro had long known of these two divine Names. He knew well that when the Name *Havayah* rules supreme, the laws of nature are suspended altogether, and that when the Name *Elokim* holds sway, nature comes into its own. Accordingly, when he heard from afar of the miracle of the splitting of the Red Sea, he assumed that the divine Power had utterly withdrawn from the confines of nature — and did not see this as remarkable. When, however, he came to Moshe Rabbeinu who told him that the conduct of the laws of nature through the Name *Elokim* had not lapsed at all, he was overcome with wonderment, and exclaimed: עַתָּה יָדַעְתִּי כִּי גָדוֹל ה' מִכָּל הָאֱלֹהִים." [The plain meaning of this verse is: "Now I know that God is greater than all gods." For the purposes of his interpretation on the plane of *derush,* however, the rebbe of Kopust understood the last word of the verse — *ha-elohim* — to refer not to gods, but to *Elokim,* God. The verse thus reads as follows: "Now I know that even when the Name *Elokim* is the perceptible force in the natural universe, the Name *Havayah* — *through it* — yet reigns supreme."]

Typical of this outlook is the story told by Reb Yosef Yitzchak of Lubavitch (passed away in New York, 1950). During the imprisonment in St. Petersburg of Reb Shneur Zalman of Liadi, he was taken to the Senate one night via the River Neva for cross-examination. On the way there he asked the official who was taking him to stop the boat for a short while so that he could recite *Kiddush Levanah,* the prayer which is said during the waxing of the moon. Since the official refused, the Rav said: "If I wanted to, I could stop the boat myself." The official was adamant, and the boat stopped of its own accord. When the Rav later requested the favor again, the official obliged — in exchange for a blessing which the tzaddik gave him in writing.

"When I was a child," commented Reb Yosef Yitzchak, "I used to wonder: Since the rebbe had already stopped the boat by himself, why did he not go ahead and say the prayer instead of requiring the favors of that gentile? But as I grew older and studied Chassidism, I understood that the rebbe had no choice but to act as he did. For a mitzvah should be performed only when it is clothed in nature, and not in supernatural miracles."

(See "The Blessing in a Gold Frame", on page 263 of the present volume).

Notwithstanding all the above, the fact remains that both the Jerusalem and the Babylonian Talmuds are replete with innumerable accounts of miraculous deeds wrought by the *tannaim* and *amoraim* of ancient times. Some of these have been anthologized in recent generations, as have been the many extant accounts of supernatural feats performed by the post-Talmudic Sages, from the period of the *geonim* until modern times. The careful reader will observe, however, that in the main, these stories were told not as miracles or wonders for their own sake, but as vehicles for conveying a certain moral or educational message.

Moreover, for all their reservations about mere miracle stories, tzaddikim and chassidim have always valued highly the telling of stories — particularly those proceeding from reliable sources — that illustrate the ways in which saintly men have lived their lives and served their Maker. This evaluation is expressed by Reb Menachem Mendel of Lubavitch (the author of *Tzemach Tzedek*) in a *derush*-level reading of the well-known passage in the Passover *Haggadah* which begins וַאֲפִילוּ כֻּלָּנוּ חֲכָמִים. The straightforward translation of that sentence is simply: "Even if we were all wise (חֲכָמִים) and understanding (נְבוֹנִים), and we all know (יוֹדְעִים) the Torah, we are still obliged to recount the story of the Exodus from Egypt." Reb Menachem Mendel bases his interpretation of this verse on the three nouns which lie at the root of the above three Hebrew words: חָכְמָה, בִּינָה, דַּעַת. These latter three words, better known by their acronym חַבַּ"ד (Chabad), represent the demand of that school of Chassidism that the love and awe of God be generated by intellectual means. Reb Menachem Mendel's *derush*-level reading of the passage is thus as follows: "Even if we have fulfilled the demand that God be served through the intellectual effort required by the *Chabad* system, it is still a mitzvah for us to retell chassidic stories. Moreover, the very act of recounting them enable us to free ourselves from the worldly straits (מְצָרִים) which confine each of us in the psychological bondage of his own individual מִצְרַיִם, his own personal Egypt."

The same tzaddik wrote: "When one hears a story of a good deed from one's rebbe, one becomes bound to the rebbe's faculty of action; when one hears a Torah discourse from one's rebbe, one becomes united with his faculty of speech; when one listens to one's rebbe singing a *niggun*, one cleaves to his faculty of thought. The bond with one's rebbe is thus on the levels corresponding to each of the three names for the soul — *Nefesh, Ruach, Neshamah.*" And his grandfather, Reb Shneur Zalman of Liadi, recalled: "When we used to hear a Torah discourse from the rebbe — Reb Dov Ber, the Maggid of Mezritch — we saw this was the Oral Law, and when we heard a story from his mouth, this was our Written Law."

Reb Shlomo of Radomsk writes in a similar vein — "A story which retells the deeds of tzaddikim is Torah" — and borrows support for his statement by a novel reading of a familiar Talmudic dictum. In explaining the seemingly excessive coverage allotted by the Torah to the lengthy account which Eliezer the servant of Avraham gives of his movements, the Talmud says: "The conversation of the Patriarchs' servants is loftier than the Torah as studied by their sons." Reb Shlomo explains: "This is so because the conversation — the storytelling — of the servants of the Patriarchs *becomes* the Torah of the sons." In a verse from *Psalms,* Reb Shlomo found a similar teaching: הַלְלוּ עַבְדֵי ה' הַלְלוּ אֶת שֵׁם ה'. The straightforward construction of this sentence gives the following translation: "Offer praise, you servants of God; praise the name of God." However, instead of seeing the first half of the verse as a call to the servants to God to praise Him, Reb Shlomo treated "the servants of God" as the *object* of the first verb in Hebrew, so that the first clause reads: "Praise the servants of God." The verse as a whole could thus be taken to mean that the praise of God consists of the praise of his servants, the tzaddikim.

"Through telling stories of tzaddikim," concurs Reb Nachman of Breslov, "one draws down the light of the *Mashiach* into This World, and repels from it all manner of darkness and tribulations." And in another place he writes: "It is given to him who is in Eretz Yisrael to tell stories of true tzaddikim, and thereby to cleanse his thoughts." Reb Shalom of Belz found the merits of such storytelling hinted at in the verse from Malachi which opens with the words אָז נִדְבְּרוּ: "Then they who feared God spoke, one man to another; and God hearkened, and heard it, and a book of remembrance was written before Him for those who feared God, and took heed of His Name." Reb Shalom took the verb נִדְבְּרוּ literally, in a passive sense, so that the verse means: "Those who feared God *were spoken of* after their passing by one man to another; to this God hearkened, and heard it; and a book of remembrance was written before Him — both for those of the departed who feared God, in that 'their lips speak on in the grave' by virtue of the stories told of them, as well as for those who took heed of His Name, that is, those who tell these stories." And the final word on the subject comes from the Baal Shem Tov himself, the founder of Chassidism: "To speak of the praises of tzaddikim is as praiseworthy as meditating on the loftiest mysteries of the Divine Chariot."

It can fairly be said, then, that the doctrines of Chassidism are the *halachah* of Chassidism, and the stories of chassidim are its *aggadah*. Its *halachah* speaks to the intellect; its *aggadah* speaks to the heart. Its *halachah* delves earnestly into abstruse scholarly questions involving the knowledge of divinity, the mystery of creation, the descent of the divine light, the hidden truths of the Torah, the secrets of the mitzvos, and the profoundest enigmas and tortuous byways of the human soul. On the one hand this *halachah* of Chassidism bursts its way into the highest heavens, directing its words ever upward; on the other hand, it plunges to the depths, revealing the sanctity of creation in the innermost essence of the material existence that constitutes the universe. The *aggadah* of Chassidism, with its stories of the roadbuilders and trailblazers of the movement — the tzaddikim, their lives and deeds, attitudes and attributes, their customs and conduct, their words and their wonders — this *aggadah* of stories rouses the heart, revives the soul, and breathes the spirit of life into the driest of bones.

❀ ❀ ❀ ❀

The narrative literature of Chassidism is rich indeed. In addition to the hundreds of books that have been compiled, and the tens of thousands of stories that have been handed down in writing, an oral tradition lives on, rebbe to rebbe, chassid to chassid. From these written and oral sources the present writer has chosen and arranged (in the whole series) almost nine hundred stories. He has neither adapted them to suit his taste nor tampered with the facts as related, whether in content or in detail; he has simply aimed at rewriting them in an intelligible style. The stories chosen were those in which he found a moral or didactic point, regardless of whether they involved some supernatural wonder or not. Finally, he set them out according to the weekly Portion of the Torah (in the earlier volumes), or according to the festivals of the year (in the present volumes), assigning each story to the verse or occasion that best suited it. That is not to say, obviously, that he exhausted all the resources which could have served his aim, for have our Sages not taught: "You are not obliged to complete the work"?

There may well be such as will raise objections to some of the stories included, but it seems to the author — rather: the compiler and editor — that in each of these stories there is something instructive to be found. Not that this "something" will be seen in the same light by all readers, for a single story can sometimes reflect a subtle variety of hues and shades. On the first story, for example, the rebbe of Gostynin commented: "We may be expert in assessing the value of gold and silver and gems — but to appreciate the true worth of a Jew is way, way beyond us." Another may be impressed chiefly by the esteem in which tzaddikim and chassidim hold the mitzvah of saving a life. A third may prefer to contemplate the spiritual cataclysm which overwhelmed that soldier when "the Jewish spark inside me flared up," and motivated him to act as he did. And yet a fourth may find the center of gravity in a different direction altogether: the privilege of healing children is one of heaven's ways of rewarding a man; one would have to be rich in merits to be allowed to attain a level such as that ...

This variety of reaction applies not only to a story with a whole plot of its own — in which case, too, some reader might perhaps enjoy it simply for its narrative value. It applies even to a brief story, boasting neither the suspense of a plot nor the mystique of the fanciful. Consider, for example, *Brevity is the Soul of Wit*, on page 617 of the second volume of stories on the Torah. One reader will simply be interested to learn the interpretation it offers of the words in *Deuteronomy*, עַד תֻּמָּם. Another will note the sharp-witted brevity characteristic of Reb Yaakov Yitzchak of Pshischah — a discourse of exactly two words, with no explanations offered. A third reader will perceive the continuity of style within the school of Pshischah, for the disciple and eventual successor, Reb Simchah Bunem, finds the two succinct words both ample and eloquent. And what may impress a fourth reader is the demand of that disciple that others too determine the essence of that novel teaching, unaided. In the words of Reb Simchah Bunem to Reb Henich: "Here, you're a clever fellow. You work out the rebbe's meaning — yourself!"

In keeping with the narrative nature of this anthology, well-loved snippets of chassidic lore and teaching — no matter how quotable — were not included, unless they were connected with an incident of some sort.

S.Y.Z.

Jerusalem/Teves 5717 (1956).

ראש השנה

rosh hashanah

⋪ No Move is Futile

Even if one solitary Jew is exiled among the alien nations, it is as if all of Israel were exiled there (Midrash).

הָאֹבְדִים
בְּאֶרֶץ
אַשּׁוּר
וְהַנִּדָּחִים
בְּאֶרֶץ מִצְרָיִם

Those who are lost in the land of Assyria and the outcasts in the land of Egypt [Isaiah 27:13] (Musaf)

The son-in-law of the Baal Shem Tov, Reb Yechiel Ashkenazi, was known by the Yiddish nickname "der Deitsch'l" because — as his Hebrew surname also indicates — he hailed from Germany. He was the father of two celebrated sons; Reb Moshe Chaim Ephraim of Sudylkov, the author of *Degel Machaneh Ephraim*, and Reb Baruch of Mezhibuzh. His own father was both a pious and wealthy man, whose sons were all men of scholarship and refinement.

One day he called them together and said: "I am going to give each one of you a certain sum of money. You have my permission to travel wherever your hearts lead you, and if a proper match should be proposed to any one of you — with a young woman who is known for her good deeds, and who was brought up in a fine family — then you are free to settle for that *shidduch* and marry. I make only one condition: that in five years' time you all meet here in my house, so that I may see what has come of each of you."

Each son set out in the direction of his choice, and Reb Yechiel eventually found himself in the hometown of the Baal Shem Tov, where he married Adel, the tzaddik's saintly daughter.

Almost five years elapsed, and Reb Yechiel went to take his leave of his father-in-law, explaining that he planned to make the journey home in fulfillment of the commandment of honoring one's father. When the Baal Shem Tov gave him his blessing for a safe journey and a safe return, Reb Yechiel asked him to bless him that he would return in time for Rosh HaShanah, for the summer months had already come. The tzaddik gave no answer. Three times he asked, and three times received no reply. Realizing now that he would definitely not be back in time for the New Year season, he took the precaution of preparing a *shofar* for the journey, for who could tell where he would spend the Days of Awe?

The appointed day arrived, and from all the points of the compass the sons converged on their father's house. He prepared a festive meal in their honor, and invited all the scholars of the town to share in his day of joy. When the meal was under way, he asked the eldest son to grace the gathering with a learned discourse. After him the second son demonstrated his prowess in scholarship, and then the third, and so on. It was now the turn of Reb Yechiel. Throughout the preceding dissertations, unlike the other guests, he had shown no signs of attentiveness, but seemed to be busy instead eating and drinking. When his father now asked him to speak, he claimed that he had nothing to say. The father let him be, and proceeded with the younger brothers. And as each of them showed what he was capable of, Reb Yechiel continued as before. The guests were of course stupefied; they did not know that the Creator can be served through eating and drinking, and that the loftiest *yichudim* may be effected through this means.

After they had all gone home the father called Reb Yechiel aside, and told him in anguish: "My son, you disgraced me today before all those guests. Not only is it clear that you alone among all your brothers have not grown up to be a Torah scholar: on top of that it seems that you have even become a glutton."

And the poor man broke down and wept.

"Be not grieved," Reb Yechiel consoled him, "for in the course of these years I have grown no less than my brothers. Perhaps you would like to arrange another festive meal tomorrow, to which you could invite the same guests, and then I will show you what I have gained. Believe me, father, you will derive no less satisfaction from me than from all your sons."

The next day, when all the distinguished guests were again in their places, and the eldest brother had risen to deliver another learned discourse, Reb Yechiel rose from his chair, approached him, and passed his hand before his face. The speaker was at once thrown into confusion.

He left his dissertation in the middle of a sentence, and ראש
began instead to confess all the sins of which he had been השנה
guilty from his youth until that day. After a few moments he regained his presence of mind, and spoke no
more.

Reb Yechiel returned to his place, and his father asked
the second son to deliver some *divrei* Torah. Exactly the
same happened as before, and it was once more repeated
with the third son. The guests were left speechless with
wonder.

It was then that Reb Yechiel told them of his father-
in-law, the saintly Baal Shem Tov, one of the tzaddikim
upon whose righteousness the world stands. For the first
time in their lives they heard of the way in which the
Baal Shem Tov served the Creator, and as they listened
thirstily, the heart of Reb Yechiel's father too was glad.

It was already the month of Elul, the last month before
the New Year, so after some days the sons went their
separate ways. The ship which was to take Reb Yechiel
to his home was caught in a fearful tempest, and it was
drawn by the turbulent sea far from its intended course.
Only on the eve of Rosh HaShanah did the sea calm
down, and at long last the ship was able to drop anchor
in a quiet haven near a strange city in a distant land — a
city in which no Jew had ever lived.

Reb Yechiel realized that it was on his account that the
storm had raged. It was clearly God's will that he spend
Rosh HaShanah in this remote spot, instead of sharing in
the prayers of the congregation in his hometown, and he
accepted his suffering with loving patience. Setting foot
on the alien terrain, he rented himself a room near the
seashore, so that he would be able to immerse himself in
the sea as in a *mikveh*. This he did in preparation for the
afternoon prayer of the eve of the holy day, which was
followed by the evening prayer of Rosh HaShanah. And
needless to say, these were prayers uttered in devout ecstasy. His very heart cried out and wept — for this was
the way of the Baal Shem Tov and his disciples.

The passersby stood still, amazed. The man inside the
house who cried out in there all alone must certainly be
out of his mind. In the morning they saw him make his
way down to the sea, and then after he returned they

again listened through the window to the unaccustomed sounds. He prayed the morning service, blew a series of thirty blasts on the ram's horn that he had brought for the purpose, and then built up to a climax of awesome ecstasy in the *Musaf* prayer.

Just that morning the king of that country decided to go out in his carriage for a ride. Surprised by the unaccustomed sight of a crowd near a little house by the seashore, he approached and asked what drew them there. Being a learned man, he gathered from their description that the stranger inside the house was no madman, as they had assumed in their ignorance. He warned them not to harm him in any way, because he was no doubt a believer in some faith unfamiliar to them, and this was his mode of service. He then called for the chassid, who in answer to his questions told him where he came from and how he had reached those parts. When the king invited him to continue their conversation in his palace, he promised to do so the following evening. And indeed, as soon as the two Days of Judgment had come to a close, he was received most cordially at the royal palace. So pleasing did the king find his company — and his prayers of the day before — that he asked him if he could bring three hundred Jews like himself to settle in his land.

"Your Majesty," replied Reb Yechiel, "for two reasons I am unable to fulfill your wish. In the first place, I am no minister nor governor that I should be able to order any man to leave his home and to settle in your land. And secondly, if it were indeed God's will that Jews should live in these parts, then Divine Providence would have ordained that they be led here even in iron shackles, against their will. Since, however, not one Jew lives in the land, it is clear that this is the Creator's will — and it is thus impossible that your request be fulfilled."

This answer found favor in the eyes of the king, who thereupon gave him his farewell blessings.

In due course the chassid found his way back to his home, where he went at once to see his father-in-law, the Baal Shem Tov.

The tzaddik greeted him affectionately, and said: "In the place which you visited, a vast number of holy

sparks were hidden. Had you not arrived there, a certain ראש
number of our brethren would have been obliged to be השנה
led there at some time — even in iron shackles, against
their will. But since you were there on Rosh HaShanah,
and through the sheer potency of your prayer you succeeded in elevating all of those exiled sparks to their
divine Source, there is now no longer any need for any
other Jews to live there in order to accomplish that task
— and, indeed, no Jew will ever live there, until the coming of the Messiah."

❧ How Strong is their Faith!

A barber's apprentice once passed by the house of עֶרֶב
Reb Levi Yitzchak of Berditchev on the eve of Rosh ראש
HaShanah. His head was uncovered, and — in further הַשָּׁנָה
defiance of the requirements of the Law — he flaunted a *The eve*
shock of wavy locks which had been carefully groomed *of*
over his forehead.
Seeing him through the window, the tzaddik called *Rosh*
him in and said: "Why do you cultivate those locks?" *HaShanah*
"Because my line of business brings me in touch with
nobles and squires," said the young man, "so I have to
make myself presentable."
"Listen here," said the tzaddik. "I'll give you a gold
ruble if you cut off those locks. After all, wearing your
hair according to the fashion of the gentiles is an in-
fringement of the commandment in the Torah: וּבְחֻקֹּתֵיהֶם
לֹא תֵלֵכוּ — 'You shall not walk in the way of their
laws.' "
"No!" said the youth.
"Very well," said the tzaddik, "then I will give you
three rubles."
The youth did not agree — and remained insistent,
even when the offer reached twenty rubles.
"If you cut off your locks at once," said the tzaddik,
"I promise you a share in the World to Come."
No sooner did the youth hear these words than his
hand dived deep into his pocket for his scissors, and
within seconds he had cut off his wavy locks.
"Master of the Universe!" exclaimed Reb Levi
Yitzchak. "How strong is the faith of Your People, even

the simplest among them! How many weary hours of toil and trouble must such a young man endure until he earns one solitary gold ruble! Why, twenty rubles is for him an undreamed-of fortune... And yet, what he was not willing to do for twenty gold rubles he did for a share in the World to Come, even though he has never laid eyes on it!"

⋙ In Earnest

The following incident was recounted by Reb Zvi ("the Beadle") of Rimanov.

"It was dawn on the eve of Rosh HaShanah," he said, "and my rebbe, Reb Menachem Mendel of Rimanov, was leading the congregation for the penitential *Selichos* prayers. He surprised all the worshipers by pausing as soon as he had said these words: אִם אָמְנָם שָׁבוּ כֻלָּם בְּלֵב וָנֶפֶשׁ לַחֲלוֹתֶךָ — 'If in truth they have all returned to you, seeking you with all their heart and soul...' They assumed that the tzaddik had no doubt paused in order to meditate on the lofty mysteries of the Names of God. But among those present were three great men — Reb Naftali of Ropshitz, Reb Yaakov of Premishl, and Reb Zvi Elimelech of Dinov, and it was they who told the other worshipers that they had been mistaken in their assumption. The tzaddik had not been meditating on the Divine Names at all: he had simply decided not to proceed with his prayer until he had succeeded in imbuing each man present in his synagogue with the power to return to God in earnest, *with all their heart and soul.*

On a later occasion Reb Zvi was told that one of his own chassidim had missed the communal *Selichos* prayers on the morning of Rosh HaShanah eve because he had overslept. Reb Zvi called for him and said: "You should know that I too was one of the worshipers present on that occasion. From this you can work out for yourself what you lost this morning by not joining us all for the same *Selichos* prayers!"

⋞ Nothing More Ambitious

R eb David Moshe of Chortkov told the story of a
difficult moment in the life of his grandfather.

"When my grandfather Reb Shalom of Probisht was
once at the home of his father-in-law Reb Nachum of
Chernobyl," he said, "it so happened that while Reb
Nachum was leading his congregation in the last
Minchah service of the outgoing year with his accustomed ecstasy, my grandfather sensed that he himself
had suddenly slipped from the lofty levels of divine service to which he had raised himself over the years. He
found it quite impossible to worship in the way that a
tzaddik commonly worships. He was sorely grieved.
Why should this have befallen him at a moment like this,
when every other Jew was now praying with his highest
degree of devoutness? He made every effort to recapture
his accustomed fervor, but in vain. Finally, after
prodigious exertion, he succeeded somehow in making
his way through the prayers with nothing more am-
bitious than a consistent attentiveness to the meaning of
the words he was uttering — just like every ordinary
worshiper does.

"As soon as he reached the end of his prayers Reb
Nachum approached him and exclaimed: 'My son! What
eloquent reverberations you set up in the heavens just
now with your afternoon prayers! Do you know that
thousands of erring souls were elevated through your
words?' "

⋞ The Only Way I Can Help You

I n a township not far from Premishlan there lived a
wealthy man of violent disposition who got it into his
head that he should be chosen to lead his townsmen in
prayer on the Days of Awe. None of them were pleased
with the idea, but on the other hand they were afraid of
what might happen to them if they were to defy his will.
So they put their troubled heads together and decided to
send a delegation to ask Reb Meir of Premishlan for
some wise counsel. The tzaddik replied that since the

chazzanim from all the surrounding towns were accustomed to paying him a visit before Rosh HaShanah in
order to request his blessing, their self-appointed prayer
leader would no doubt want to follow suit. When he
came, therefore, the tzaddik would size up the situation
and decide how to act.

When in due course all the *baalei tefillah* of the district
came to Reb Meir to receive his blessing before undertaking the weighty responsibility of leading their
brethren in prayer, the tzaddik first spoke to all the
others and sent them off happily on their respective
ways. It was now the turn of this pretentious boor.

"As you know," began Reb Meir, "the Torah speaks
of three kinds of prayer. There is תְּפִלָּה לְמֹשֶׁה — 'the
prayer of Moshe Rabbeinu'; there is תְּפִלָּה לְדָוִד — 'the
prayer of King David'; and there is תְּפִלָּה לְעָנִי — 'the
prayer of a pauper.' Now Moshe Rabbeinu was indeed
'heavy of mouth and heavy of tongue' — but he was the
father of the prophets and the teacher of all Israel. King
David — why, he is called 'the sweet singer of Israel.'
And as for the pauper, his heart is humble, and we know
from *Psalms* that 'a broken and contrite heart, O God,
You will not despise.'

"Now the *baalei tefillah* of our days who lead their
congregations in prayer likewise fall into these same
three categories. There are those who are not very
musical, but they are righteous — so their prayers are accepted like 'the prayer of Moshe.' Then there are those
who are perhaps not quite so righteous, but in their
melodiousness they 'exalt God with their throats' — so
their prayers are accepted like 'the prayer of David.'
Finally, there are those who are neither righteous nor
musical, but since they are poor and their hearts are
humble, their prayers are accepted like 'the prayer of a
pauper.'

"Now as for you," concluded the tzaddik, "we cannot
say that you are especially righteous; nor can we say that
you are musical; and neither (thank God) are you a
pauper. So if you want to lead your townsmen in prayer
on Rosh HaShanah, I will have to pray that you now attain one of these three levels. There is no need for me to
explain to you that to ask heaven to make you a tzaddik

or a great singer all of a sudden would be a vain prayer. רֹאשׁ
The only way I can help you, therefore, is by asking הַשָּׁנָה
heaven to make you poor, and then at least your prayer
will be תְּפִלָּה לְעָנִי — 'the prayer of a pauper'...''

"No, sir!" exclaimed the man in alarm. "I definitely
don't want to lead the prayers anymore!"

◄§ Echoes

It was the custom of Reb Menachem Mendel of לֵיל
Lubavitch on the first night of Rosh HaShanah to רֹאשׁ הַשָּׁנָה
deliver a discourse on the philosophy of Chassidism, fol- *The night*
lowed by words of encouraging exhortation to his disci- *of Rosh*
ples. *HaShanah*

When he had completed his discourse on the eve of
Rosh HaShanah in the year 1847, he turned to his congregation and said: "Today we have to make ourselves
ready to greet Him Whom we address in our prayers as
אָבִינוּ מַלְכֵּנוּ — 'our Father, our King.' A father likes to see
a pure heart; a king likes a clean garment."

The tzaddik went on to explain that the divinely-
appointed task appropriate to the New Year season was
for every man to purify his heart, and cleanse his
"garments," for this word in chassidic usage (לְבוּשִׁים)
signifies the soul's three means of self-expression —
thought, word and deed.

"Every man is accompanied by two angels," he continued, "and when after the evening prayers of Rosh
HaShanah they hear each person wishing his neighbor
with a pure heart לְשָׁנָה טוֹבָה תִּכָּתֵב וְתֵחָתֵם — ''May you
be inscribed and sealed for a good year' — they soar aloft
and appear as defense attorneys in the Heavenly Court,
where they plead that the well-wisher be granted a good
and a sweet year."

Reb Menachem Mendel concluded his own words
with the blessing: לְשָׁנָה טוֹבָה תִּכָּתֵבוּ וְתֵחָתֵמוּ — ''May you
all be inscribed and sealed for a good year."

❧ ❧ ❧

The above episode was recounted by Reb Yosef
Yitzchak of Lubavitch, who added that his grandfather
— Reb Shmuel of Lubavitch, the son of Reb Menachem

Mendel — had recorded that "that year was indeed a good year."

"For my grandfather," commented Reb Yosef Yitzchak, "this was the first Rosh HaShanah after his *bar-mitzvah*. And on that occasion he heard what delight was caused On High by the enthusiastic tumult of New Year wishes exchanged by a few hundred worshipers who prayed that year in the 'little hall,' as well as in the 'big hall' that was set up in the grounds for the vast numbers of chassidim who converged on Lubavitch to spend the Days of Awe with the rebbe. Now it is explained in the Kabbalah that there is a difference between the way things are heard from the World Above *before* the age of *bar-mitzvah*, and after it. And it was in the first year *after* he had attained the age of thirteen that my grandfather Reb Shmuel heard that delight in the World Above which is an echo of the wholehearted blessings exchanged in the World Below."

⋙ What Would the Angels Say?

During the last year of his lifetime, Reb Yaakov Yitzchak (the Yid HaKadosh) of Pshischah visited his rebbe, Reb Yaakov Yitzchak (the Chozeh) of Lublin, a little before Rosh HaShanah. When he was preparing to return home he went to take his leave of the Chozeh, and mentioned that he would like to say something of a private nature. As soon as they were left alone in the room, the Yid HaKadosh told his rebbe that while he was studying *Sefer Raziel HaMalach* he saw that he would be obliged to leave This World immediately after Rosh HaShanah.

"Then stay back with us for Rosh HaShanah," said the Chozeh, "and we will keep you back in This World."

The Yid HaKadosh, however, took his leave from his rebbe and set out for home.

On the way he repeated the above exchange to the disciples who accompanied him, and added: "But do you think that the rebbe lied, God forbid? Not at all! He would in fact have kept me back in This World, but I would have had to part with the spiritual attainments

that I had gained — and I have no interest in life without ראש
them." השנה

When the first night of Rosh HaShanah arrived, he
said to his elder disciples: "I have heard it announced in
heaven that one of us — either I or the rebbe — must
leave This World straight after Rosh HaShanah. And the
Heavenly Court gave me the choice as to who should
depart, and who should live on. I chose that it should be
me who should die. Now I know that if I were to remain
alive I would on no account allow the rebbe to leave This
World — but I was ashamed of what the angels would
say, for they do not know that I have this power. And
then they would say to each other: 'What do you say to a
disciple like this, who sends off his rebbe from That
World, and wants to stay alive himself?' "

◆§ A Futile Prayer

> If a man pleads for that which is past, this is
> called a futile prayer (*Mishnah, Tractate
> Berachos*).

In the year 1856 Reb Shalom of Belz fell ill. It was the
month of Elul, the last month of the year, a short time
before Rosh HaShanah. The tzaddik asked that a
telegram be sent to Reb Chaim of Zanz, requesting that
he intercede on his behalf in heaven. At that time a certain merchant happened to be in Belz, who had business
connections with a wealthy chassid called Reb Yosef
Schiff of Tarna, and since he knew that Reb Yosef
planned to travel to Zanz for Rosh HaShanah, as he did
every year, the telegram was sent to his home in Tarna.

On the morning of the eve of Rosh HaShanah Reb
Yosef duly arrived in Zanz, where he immediately told
Reb Chaim of Reb Shalom's illness and of the telegram
which he had received. Reb Chaim gave no answer. At
midday he raised the subject once more, but there was
still no response. And so it was again when he tried a
third time. Reb Yosef marveled at this. How could the
tzaddik of Zanz pay no attention to the illness of Reb
Shalom?

His query was answered only after Reb Chaim had

told him the following story.

"On the first night of Rosh HaShanah every year," began Reb Chaim, "Eliyahu the Prophet used to appear to Reb Elimelech of Lyzhansk and reveal to him what was happening in heaven. When this visit took place as usual in the year 1772, the Prophet Eliyahu told him that the world depended at that moment on the prayers of three great tzaddikim — and he named them. Reb Elimelech was most surprised not to hear among them the name of his rebbe, Reb Dov Ber of Mezritch. But his query was later solved. For in that year, on the nineteenth day of the month of Kislev, the soul of the Maggid of Mezritch ascended to the World Above."

From this story Reb Yosef understood that there was nothing to marvel about in the fact that Reb Chaim had not responded to his request that he pray for the recovery of Reb Shalom of Belz. And indeed the news reached Zanz soon after — that on the twenty-seventh of Elul, two days before Reb Yosef's arrival there, Reb Shalom of Belz had passed away.

⋙ Knowing One's Place

Better is one hour spent in This World in repentance and good deeds than all the life of the World to Come (*Mishnah, Tractate Avos*).

Reb Shlomo Zalman of Kopust, the grandson of Reb Menachem Mendel of Lubavitch, delivered a discourse one Rosh HaShanah eve that dealt with the dynamics of souls and spiritual worlds which exist on a mystical level far beyond the reach of most mortals. In keeping with his custom, the discourse was delivered before the evening service; the congregation of chassidim would then pray together in the *shul*, while he would enter an adjoining room to worship alone. On this occasion, his exposition of chassidic teachings brought them to such a peak of inspired ecstasy that as soon as he had completed it, his disciples began spontaneously to sing a soulful medley of meditative *Chabad* melodies — for chassidim know songs that have no words, yet speak

eloquently of their *dveikus*, the yearning of their soul to רֹאשׁ
cleave to its Maker. הַשָּׁנָה

When after singing they at length completed their
prayers, one elder chassid — Reb Aharon of Liozna, who
was then visiting Kopust — waited at the door of the
room in which the rebbe was praying. He wanted to be
able to exchange with him the traditional greeting:
לְשָׁנָה טוֹבָה תִּכָּתֵב וְתֵחָתֵם — "May you be inscribed and
sealed for a good year!"

In due course the rebbe came to the door, and when he
saw his chassid, he exclaimed: "Reb Aharon, what a
precious thing This World is! For in the World to Come
one can speak only of the spiritual level which one is at,
and not above that level; while in This World one can
speak of levels as lofty as one likes."

But to this he appended a warning against the self-
delusion that such high-sounding talk can engender:
"Except, of course, that one must be careful not to be a
fool..."

ⰾ§ Clean Hands

R eb Shmuel Abba of Zichlin was leading his
congregation through the twenty-fourth *Psalm* during the prayers of the first night of Rosh HaShanah, and
reached the verse which, in answer to the question,
"Who shall ascend the mountain of God?" — replies: נְקִי
כַפַּיִם וּבַר לֵבָב — "He who has clean hands and a pure
heart." At this point, though, he startled all those present by repeating these four words over and over again.
Then he cried out the words "Clean hands!" at the top of
his voice, and ran about among the assembled chassidim,
shouting: "Clean hands, not a thief!" — until he saw that
one man slipped out of the synagogue. The tzaddik then
returned to his lectern, resumed the chanting of the
Psalm, and completed the evening prayers. The chassidim were wonderstruck. What was so special about
this verse on this night? And what was it about the man
who slipped out that had stirred up this tempest?

Two nights later, at the close of the two awesome
Days of Judgment, everything became clear. On the day

before Rosh HaShanah, this man had paid a certain gentile a business debt he owed him, and had been handed a receipt for the amount. The gentile had left the room for a moment, leaving the money on the table. This man had then succumbed to temptation. He had pocketed the money and hurried from the room before the gentile had time to return. Since the place where he had done his business was near Zichlin, he had decided to join the congregation there for Rosh HaShanah.

The gentile returned to the table, and finding neither his money nor his debtor, immediately dispatched messengers to trace him — but to no avail. At the close of Rosh HaShanah, however, while the debtor was on his way home from Zichlin, he was caught by the local police and arrested. And since he realized that Reb Shmuel Abba already knew what he had done, he sent a messenger to Zichlin to ask the tzaddik to do him a favor. The tzaddik instructed the messenger to tell him to confess at once, and to restore the stolen money to its owner.

The messenger thought otherwise, and said: "But if he does not confess, perhaps they will not believe the gentile, whereas if he confesses and returns the money, they will certainly take him to court and throw him into prison for a few years!"

"In our Torah," said the tzaddik, "we find that for a theft one is obliged to pay twice the value of the stolen object, and sometimes four or five times its value. But we find no mention of imprisonment for theft. Let that man return the money he has stolen, and not be apprehensive of imprisonment at all — but only on condition that he return the money at once, without any delay whatsoever."

And so it was. The man confessed, returned the money, and was freed.

◆§ O King

Year after year, without exception, a chassid called Reb Meir Mirer used to travel to spend Rosh HaShanah with his rebbe, Reb Mordechai of Lechovitch. One year the pressure of business brought him to Leipzig, where he was obliged to remain over the Days of Awe. He went

to one of the local synagogues for the *Shacharis* prayers, ראש
but when he recalled how every year at this time he spent השנה
these auspicious hours in the presence of his rebbe, he
was overcome by such a melancholy that he stood still in
his place, as insensitive as a stone, unable to open his lips
in prayer.

Then suddenly there resounded in his ears the voice of
his rebbe from faraway Lechovitch. He was leading his
congregation in prayer, and he cried out: ... הַמֶּלֶךְ — "O
King Who sits upon a lofty and sublime throne!"

The chassid in Leipzig cast off his melancholy. Once
more his heart was alive and his brain alert. A great light
had been showered upon him, and he recited all the
prayers of Rosh HaShanah with the fervor to which he
was accustomed when he had been in the company of his
rebbe.

After the festivals he traveled to Lechovitch, and when
he entered the rebbe's study to receive his greeting, he
was surprised to hear the tzaddik quoting from the Book
of *Esther:* וְנִשְׁמַע פִּתְגָם הַמֶּלֶךְ — "And the decree of the
king shall be heard." But then the rebbe went on to explain what he meant by this quotation: "When a Jew
says הַמֶּלֶךְ — 'O King!' — it can be heard even in Leipzig."

◄§ The Fearless

And no razor shall come upon his head (*Haftarah*).

When Reb Shalom Ber of Lubavitch used to read
aloud the *Haftarah* passage from the Prophets on
Rosh HaShanah, he would wear his *tallis* so far over his
head that it would cover as well the *machzor* from which
he read. And while reading the chapter which tells of the
promise of the birth of the Prophet Shmuel, his eyes
would flow with tears. On Rosh HaShanah in the year
1905 he paused a moment after reading the words וּמוֹרָה
לֹא יַעֲלֶה עַל רֹאשׁוֹ — "And no razor shall come upon his
head." His lips continued to move, but no voice was
heard — and then he resumed the reading of the passage
aloud.

Now that year Lubavitch was plagued by the antics of the anti-religious forces of the Left, who sought by means of threats and brute force to close down the *Tomchei Temimim* yeshivah which Reb Shalom Ber had founded in the township in 1897. The rebbe's brother, Reb Zalman Aharon, became friendly with one of them, and through him found out what they were conspiring to do.

Reb Zalman Aharon was by nature fearless, and an illustration of this quality was once recounted by his nephew Reb Yosef Yitzchak, the son of the rebbe. Reb Zalman Aharon lived in Lubavitch, in a building which once housed the *shul* of the first rebbe of the dynasty to establish himself in the township — Reb Dov Ber of Lubavitch, the son of Reb Shneur Zalman of Liadi. This synagogue was so long that people used to say that someone who started his morning prayers with הוֹדוּ at one end would reach the conclusion of the prayers — עָלֵינוּ — by the time he had arrived at the other end.

Late one night someone woke up Reb Zalman Aharon to tell him that a fire had broken out not far from where he lived.

"When the fire reaches that wall on the other side," he said, "wake me up then."

And he turned over and was soon fast asleep.

On this occasion, however, when the plots of the Leftists became known, he was clearly perturbed.

"These people we must consider seriously," he said to his brother, the rebbe. "They are outright scoundrels, and can do us serious damage."

"To be afraid of them does not come into consideration," said the rebbe. "On Rosh HaShanah I said explicitly: וּמוֹרָא לֹא יַעֲלֶה עַל רֹאשִׁי — 'No fear shall come upon my head' [in paraphrase of the words from the Book of *Shmuel*]. As for money, we may have to throw them a coin."

Reb Zalman Aharon was impressed by the simplicity of his brother's answer. And when he left the room, Reb Yosef Yitzchak asked his father the rebbe what he had whispered so quietly on Rosh HaShanah during the reading of the *Haftarah*.

"The verse as it is written says מוֹרָה, meaning

'razor,' " said the rebbe, "but when I read it I had in mind רֹאשׁ
מוֹרָא, meaning 'fear'. So that is why I read it again הַשָּׁנָה
silently."

◆§ The Master Key

The Baal Shem Tov once instructed his disciple Reb תְּקִיעַת
Wolff Kitzis to study the kabbalistic *kavanos* on שׁוֹפָר
which he would meditate while blowing the various *Blowing*
blasts of the *shofar*, in readiness for the prayers of Rosh *the Shofar*
HaShanah in his synagogue. Reb Wolff studied the
mystical significations of the Divine Names associated
with this mitzvah, and made notes of them on a sheet of
paper which he put away in a pocket, so that he would
be able to read them while blowing the *shofar*. The Baal
Shem Tov was not pleased by the fact that he had committed these secrets to writing; the sheet of paper slipped
out of its pocket and was lost.

The awesome moment drew near. Reb Wolff searched
his pockets in vain, and was obliged to blow the *shofar*
without knowing which divine mysteries to meditate upon. This grieved him no end, and he wept with a broken
and humbled heart.

After the prayers the Baal Shem Tov said to him: "In a
king's palace there are many chambers, and each door
has its own particular key. But there is one implement
which can open *all* the doors, and that is — the ax. The
kabbalistic *kavanos* are the keys to the gates in the
World Above, each gate requiring its own particular
kavanah — but a broken and humble heart can burst
open all the gates and all the heavenly palaces."

◆§ The Shofar of Our Liberation

The inner circle of elder disciples of the Baal Shem Tov
— the חֶבְרַיָּא קַדִּישָׁא — maintained a special house outside the town, where they would retire to discuss his
teachings immediately after each discourse he delivered.
One year, on the first day of Rosh HaShanah, the tzaddik expounded the mystical meaning of the words from
the prayer book: תְּקַע בְּשׁוֹפָר גָּדוֹל לְחֵרוּתֵנוּ — "Sound the
great *shofar* for our freedom." He then closeted himself

in his study, and the holy brotherhood proceeded to their
retreat outside the town.

At that time a certain sixteen-year-old youth used to
live in the house of the Baal Shem Tov, the son of a
scholar by the name of Reb Yitzchak Dov. Because of his
age he did not join the disciples, but remained in the
house. On this occasion, having heard the discourse of
the tzaddik, he began to imagine that the Messiah was
going to arrive on that very day. From moment to moment the thought took hold of him with growing intensity. No one was able to calm the exhilaration of his ecstatic spirit, and it was even feared that his soul would
fly from his body. He decided to run to the brotherhood
and to tell them of his thoughts: perhaps with them he
might find peace for his soul. He ran wildly through the
streets of the town, never stopping to answer the
bewildered townsfolk who cried out to ask him what had
happened.

He reached the meeting-place of the venerable disciples, but when he entered breathlessly, he was stupefied
to see that they were all sitting around the table, utterly
speechless — for to them too it seemed clear beyond all
doubt that the *Mashiach* was about to come. He quietly
took a place amongst them. But when the stars came out
on the following night, signifying the close of the solemn
two-day festival, the beautiful thought vanished from
them all, and they mutely returned to the township.

ᴥᔆ *Not on Purpose*

In his old age Reb Elazar Rokeiach of Amsterdam made
the voyage to *Eretz Yisrael* and on the way, on the first
night of Rosh HaShanah, a fearful tempest broke out.
The ship sprang a leak. Afraid for their lives, the passengers tried desperately to bail out the water. The aged
scholar meanwhile sat tranquilly in his cabin, engaged in
holy meditation.

Seeing the water rising rapidly, his two traveling companions cried out to him: "Can't you see that we are in
dreadful trouble? The ship is soon going to founder, God
forbid!"

"If that is the case," he answered enthusiastically,

"then prepare yourselves to be in my cabin punctually at ראש the first glimmer of day. Have our *shofar* ready, so that השנה we will be able to fulfill the commandment which belongs to this day."

And so they did. But as soon as the tzaddik blew the *shofar*, a wind came from above, the turbulent breakers calmed down — and the grateful passengers thanked the Creator for having spared them.

❀ ❀ ❀

"Do not think," commented Reb Simchah Bunem of Pshischah, "that Reb Elazar intended the blowing of the *shofar* to act as a *segulah* which would serve to quieten the storm. Such a thought did not even occur to him. But when he was told how great was the danger in which they stood, and realized that according to all the laws of nature it was impossible for them to be saved, he was overwhelmed by a deep desire to fulfill the mitzvah of blowing the *shofar* once more before his death. And so holy a man was he, that the mitzvah saved them all."

⊷§ *Pillars of the World*

E very year, as the New Year season came around, Reb Eliezer of Dzikov would tell this story which he had heard from Reb Shalom of Belz.

One Rosh HaShanah, when it was time to blow the *shofar*, Eliyahu the Prophet and another old man appeared to Reb Elimelech of Lyzhansk, and told him that in the Heavenly Court the voices of the prosecuting angels were prevailing. The world indeed was about to be cast into turmoil and destruction — if not for two men then alive who supported it, and saved it from collapse.

"And who is this venerable guest who stands here beside you?" Reb Elimelech asked Eliyahu.

"Why, this is the Patriarch Avraham," replied the Prophet.

"And who are the two men who support the world?" Reb Elimelech asked further.

"One of them is Reb Shmelke of Nikolsburg," said Eliyahu.

"And who is the second?" asked Reb Elimelech.

"You are not worthy of being told that too," replied the Prophet Eliyahu.

After Rosh HaShanah, Reb Elimelech set out to Nikolsburg to offer his greetings to Reb Shmelke, who said to him as he opened the door: *"Shalom Aleichem!* You no doubt know that if not for the two of us the world was at the point of collapse."

And only then did Reb Elimelech discover that he was the other pillar.

◆§ Why Do You Weep?

There is a verse in the Book of *Lamentations (Eichah),* which says: כָּל עַמָּהּ נֶאֱנָחִים מְבַקְּשִׁים לֶחֶם — "All her people sigh; they seek bread." There is another, unrelated verse in the First Book of *Shmuel,* as follows: מַדּוּעַ לֹא בָא בֶן יִשַׁי גַם תְּמוֹל גַם הַיּוֹם אֶל הַלָּחֶם — "Why has the son of Yishai (Jesse) not come, neither yesterday not today, to the bread?" In these words Sha'ul is simply inquiring after the whereabouts of the young David; in other contexts "the son of Yishai" signifies the Messiah, who will be a descendant of David, the son of Yishai.

Now it once happened that Reb Shmelke of Nikolsburg walked into his *shul* on Rosh HaShanah when it was time to blow the *shofar,* and in a voice choked with tears, said: כָּל עַמָּהּ נֶאֱנָחִים — "The entire congregation is sighing and weeping, but (Dear God!) what are they crying *for*? It is only because מְבַקְּשִׁים לֶחֶם — *they seek bread...*"

And on the next day, the second day of Rosh HaShanah, he again joined his congregation just before the blowing of the *shofar,* and with tears in his eyes asked: מַדּוּעַ לֹא בָא בֶן יִשַׁי — "Why has *Mashiach* the son of Yishai not yet come? It is because גַם תְּמוֹל גַם הַיּוֹם אֶל הַלָּחֶם — because *yesterday and today,* on both days of Rosh HaShanah, people are praying only *for bread,* instead of lamenting the exile of the Divine Presence."

◆§ The Loftiest of Intentions

One year Reb Levi Yitzchak of Berditchev spent a long time in search of a man who would be worthy of

blowing the *shofar* in his *beis midrash*. Rosh HaShanah ראש
was fast approaching, and though many righteous folk השנה
sought the privilege, vying with each other in demon-
strating their expertise in the abstruse kabbalistic secrets
associated with the *shofar*, none of them were to his
taste.

One day a new applicant came along, and Reb Levi
Yitzchak asked him on what dread mysteries he medita-
ted while he was performing the awesome mitzvah.

"Rebbe," said the newcomer, "I'm only a simple fellow; I don't understand too much about the hidden
things of the Torah. But I have four daughters of marriageable age, and when I blow the *shofar*, this is what I
have in mind: 'Master of the Universe! Right now I am
carrying out Your will. I'm doing Your mitzvah and
blowing the *shofar*. Now supposing You too do what *I*
want, and help me marry off my daughters?' "

"My friend," said Reb Levi Yitzchak, "you will blow
the *shofar* in my synagogue!"

◂§ *The Weight of a Curl*

During the earnest days preceding Rosh HaShanah —
when Jews make their annual stocktaking while saying the penitential prayers of *Selichos*, and when the
Heavenly Court weighs an entire year's evidence in
preparation for the trial of all mankind — Reb Levi
Yitzchak of Berditchev saw that the Accusing Angel was
preparing to press ominous charges against the whole
House of Israel. Moreover, Reb Baruch of Mezhibuzh
wrote him a brief letter, telling him that this year in particular he would have to stand on guard and invoke the
mercy of heaven for his brethren. Reb Levi Yitzchak
began at once to seek out some special *zechus*, some
mitzvah of such outstanding merit that it would tip the
scales and silence the arguments of the prosecuting
angels.

One morning, therefore, as soon as he had completed
the *Selichos* prayers, he slipped out of his synagogue and
made his unobtrusive way to one of the twisted alleys in
the quarter where the poor folk lived. He sought, and
lost his way, and searched again — until he saw a radi-

ance that illuminated the thatched roof of a dilapidated
cottage. This, then, must be the place he was seeking.

Entering through the low doorway he saw a young
woman sitting alone, her hair modestly covered by a
kerchief. She was reading *techinos*, the Yiddish supplications that pious women would offer up to heaven
when their hearts were heavy. She was alarmed at the
sight of the tzaddik, for she knew it was his custom during this season of penitence to visit the houses of sinners
and to arouse in them a desire to repent. If he had now
called on her, she must clearly be a sinner.

"It is true that I have sinned, my holy rebbe," she
sobbed, "but I have already repented; I have already
done whatever I could to cleanse myself of my sin."

"Be not sad, my daughter," said the tzaddik. "You are
no sinner. Quite the contrary. In heaven they have
recorded a meritorious deed, a great *zechus* to your
credit. Tell me please what has befallen you."

"My father and mother," began the lone young
woman, "used to live in a village not far from here. They
supported themselves through the dairy which they held
on lease from the squire who owned the village. When
they passed away — I was then seventeen years old — I
called on this *paritz* to ask him not to cancel the lease
which my parents had held for so long. But as soon as he
laid eyes on me the fire of desire burned within him. He
said something vulgar and even tried to touch me with
his hands. I pushed him away and turned to flee, but he
immediately changed his tone and spoke to me gently.
'Far be it from me to harm you,' he said. 'Look, I'll give
you a three-year lease on the dairy at half price. Just let
me kiss the braids of your beautiful hair.' And with that
he seized my long braids with both his hands, and kissed
them lustfully. When I came home I could find no peace,
and all that night I did not sleep a wink. In the morning I
picked up my scissors and cut off my locks. The next
day I left the village and the dairy and all, and went off to
settle here in Berditchev. For a few years I found work as
a maid in a few wealthy households, until I married. A
year has now passed since my husband died, and my
heart tells me that he died because of my sinfulness."

"And where are the locks you cut off?" asked the

tzaddik.

ראש
השנה

"Just one curl is all I kept as a memento of my long braids," said the young woman. "And whenever my heart is sore because of my ill luck, and my poverty, and my toil, I take out that curl. As I look at it I recall the sin of my youth, and quietly accept the just retribution of heaven."

A tear fell from the eyes of the tzaddik. He gave the young woman his blessing, and left the cottage.

When the Day of Judgment came every worshiper in *shul* could sense that Reb Levi Yitzchak was toiling with all his selfless might to help the prayers of the House of Israel ascend to the Throne of Glory, and to silence the strident voices of the prosecuting angels created by Israel's sins. The time came to blow the *shofar*, and though he had already immersed himself in the morning, the tzaddik left to immerse himself once more in the purifying waters of the *mikveh*. He was away for longer than ever before, for while there he was concentrating with devout intensity, creating such harmonies in the spiritual worlds that only tzaddikim can effect through their holy thoughts.

He rejoined the hushed congregation, and ascended the steps of the dais in readiness for the blowing of the *shofar*. He stood there without uttering a word — but his chassidim could hear the stifled sound of his groans and sighs.

Reb Levi Yitzchak suddenly raised his head, gazed aloft, and said: "Master of the Universe! If our sins are weighting Your scales towards a verdict of *Guilty*, please pick up the little curl of that unfortunate young woman. Put it on the other side of the balance, and I am sure that it will tip the scales in our favor!"

The hosts of heaven were thrown into turmoil; Satan's tongue was paralysed; the gates of heaven were flung wide open to admit the prayers of Israel. The tzaddik's face shone with exultation, and that year was filled to overflowing with God-given blessings.

✑§ No Worse than Moses

Happy is the People that knows the sound of
the shofar *(Psalms)*. The verse does not say
"that blows the sound," but "that knows the
sound" *(Traditional)*.

R eb Yaakov Yitzchok (the Chozeh) of Lublin once
invited all those who were going to blow the *shofar* in
his region to call on him before Rosh HaShanah in order
to receive his blessing. And Reb Simchah Bunem of
Pshischah, even though he had never blown a *shofar* in
his life, and did not even know how to, joined all those
who came.

When the Chozeh heard of his arrival he said: "The
Talmud teaches us that '*shofar*-blowing is a skill'
(חָכְמָה), and since Reb Simchah Bunem is a clever man
(חָכָם), it is he who will blow the *shofar* here."

When the guest entered the rebbe's study for
yechidus, the Chozeh first taught him all the kabbalistic
significations of the mitzvah. He then told him to take a
shofar in hand and to meditate as instructed in preparation for blowing the specified sounds.

"But never in my life have I been able to blow a
shofar!" protested Reb Simchah Bunem.

The rebbe expressed annoyance at this reply, so the
disciple went on: "It was the same with Moshe Rabbeinu. When he was first sent on his mission to the
Children of Israel, he asked: 'What shall I say to them?'
And then, even after the Almighty had answered his
question, he *still* protested: 'I am not a man of words.' "

"In that case," conceded the rebbe, "you may go in
peace."

✑§ Inadmissible Evidence

W henever Reb David of Lelov would travel to see his
rebbe, Reb Yaakov Yitzchak (the Chozeh) of
Lublin, he would take with him the boy whom he
brought up in his house, and who was later to be
renowned in ʌis own right as Reb Yitzchak of Vorki.

One Rosh HaShanah, when his congregation was רֹאשׁ
waiting for him to join them for the blowing of the הַשָּׁנָה
shofar, the Chozeh remained alone in his study for so
long that Reb David took the liberty of going there to
find out the cause of the delay. In answer to his query
the Chozeh explained that a dire verdict was threatening
the House of Israel in the Heavenly Court.

The moment of dread that followed was broken by a
question from the Chozeh, who had just noticed the boy
who had followed Reb David into his study.

"Who is this lad?" he asked.

"This is the orphan whom I am bringing up in my
home," answered Reb David.

The Chozeh turned to the child, and asked him what
subject he was now studying. The boy replied that he
was studying the Talmudic laws of testimony.

"And have you thrown any new light on this field?"
asked the Chozeh.

"I found it difficult to understand," said the boy,
"why the testimony of a relative is inadmissible in court,
whether in defense or in prosecution. In the case of
defense, then it is understandable that the court should
be apprehensive lest a witness lie in order to clear his
relative; such testimony is therefore outlawed to start
with. But why should the testimony of a relative be inadmissible if it is going to help prove the accused guilty?"

"And have you come up with an answer to your
question?" asked the Chozeh.

"Well, I have answered the question to my own
satisfaction at least," replied the boy. "You see, concerning witnesses the Torah says וְעָמְדוּ שְׁנֵי הָאֲנָשִׁים — and
the two people shall stand.' From this we see that
witnesses must be such as can be called 'people.' A
person who can offer evidence that will convict his
relative does not fall into the category of humanity, and
is therefore invalid as a witness."

When the Chozeh heard this he said: "With your
words, all the accusations that threatened us in the
Heavenly Court have now been nullified. For we are the
sons of the Almighty, and He is our Father. How, then,
will He be able to tolerate any incriminating evidence
against his sons and relatives?"

And with that the Chozeh rose, and joined his waiting congregation for the blowing of the *shofar*.

ᴥ§ More than Meets the Ear

Reb Chaim Avraham, the son of Reb Shneur Zalman of Liadi, found it difficult to walk in his old age. In time he was even unable to make the distance to the *beis midrash* of his nephew the rebbe, Reb Menachem Mendel of Lubavitch, though he dearly loved to hear him expounding the teachings of Chassidism, and was obliged to set up a *minyan* of ten worshipers in his own home.

One Rosh HaShanah, after his own little congregation had already heard the blowing of the *shofar*, the elderly chassid walked very slowly all the way to the synagogue of the rebbe, for he wanted to hear the *shofar* there again, the way *he* blew it.

Seeing with what difficulty he had managed to arrive, one of the rebbe's sons asked his great-uncle: "But why did you have to go to all that trouble?"

Reb Chaim Avraham was a humble man, and he answered simply: "The Psalmist does not say 'Happy is the People that *blows* the sound of the *shofar*'; he says 'Happy is the People that *knows* the sound of the *shofar*...' "

ᴥ§ A Still, Small Voice

> And the great *shofar* is blown, and a still, small voice is heard (*Prayers of the Days of Awe*).

Reb Menachem Mendel of Kotsk once honored Reb Yechiel Meir of Gostynin with the mitzvah of blowing the *shofar* in his synagogue. Despite all his strenuous efforts, however, the sounds that came forth from the ram's horn were pale indeed.

When the prayers were over the rebbe congratulated him for his work, and said that he had blown the *shofar* particularly well.

Then, paying more attention to the moral of his teaching than to the syntax of his paraphrase, he added: וּבְשׁוֹפָר גָּדוֹל יִתָּקַע — "If the *shofar* is blown by a *great* man, then even if קוֹל דְּמָמָה דַּקָה יִשָּׁמַע — even if only a **ראשׁ השׁנה** still, small voice is heard, nevertheless (continuing the quotation from the prayer book) מַלְאָכִים יֵחָפֵזוּן וְחִיל וּרְעָדָה יֹאחֵזוּן — the angels are still thrown into a flurry, and are seized with fear and trembling..."

◄§ Anger

Reb Yissachar Dov (who is known as the Sava Kaddisha, the "Holy Old Man") of Radoshitz took longer than usual one Rosh HaShanah to join his congregation for the blowing of the *shofar*. When he finally emerged from his study, before proceeding with the mitzvah, he addressed his chassidim as follows: "Let me tell you a story about my rebbe, the Chozeh of Lublin.

"One Rosh HaShanah the Chozeh spent a long time in his study. He was unable to leave it and join his chassidim for the blowing of the *shofar*, because he felt humble and heartbroken for not having to his credit one single *zechus* which would give him the strength to go ahead with the mitzvah. Finally he recalled that he had *one* meritorious point in his favor, after all: in the course of that year he had not spoken one angry word. On one occasion, to be sure, his attendant had forgotten to prepare a vessel with water next to his bed so that he would be able to wash his hands for *netilas yadayim* in the morning. He had then decided to scold the forgetful fellow for his negligence — until at the very moment he entered, the Chozeh recalled the warning of the Sages: כָּל הַכּוֹעֵס כְּאִילּוּ עוֹבֵד עֲבוֹדָה זָרָה — 'He who is angry, it is as if he worshiped idols.' He had then told himself: 'For the sake of the mitzvah of washing my hands in the morning, am I going to allow myself to become (God forbid!) an idolator?' He had therefore held his peace.

"And when the Chozeh reminded himself that he had this one *zechus* to his credit, he went ahead with the blowing of the *shofar*."

His story completed, Reb Yissachar Dov proceeded to lead his own congregation in the sevenfold reading of לַמְנַצֵּחַ — the forty-seventh *Psalm* on the majesty of the Creator, which serves as the solemn prologue to the blasts of the *shofar*.

Rosh HaShanah / ראש השנה **[49]**

◄§ A Plaint to the Creator

It was the custom of Reb Aryeh Leib of Shpola (who is
better known as "the Shpoler Zeide") to closet himself
in his study for some time before the blowing of the *shofar*. What he did there, no one knew. A certain in-
quisitive chassid from Reissin who was visiting Shpola
for the Days of Awe decided therefore to solve the
mystery once and for all. He crept up stealthily to a nook
near the rebbe's private room, and without being noticed
peered through a crack.

There he saw the Shpoler Zeide lying prone on the
floor, weeping bitterly, and saying: "Master of the
Universe! What do you want of Your People Israel?
Take my word for it, that if I did not see with my own
eyes how many mitzvos and good deeds they perform, I
would not believe that it was possible in this dark and
bitter exile to fulfill even one single mitzvah. And especially in this benighted world, where Satan himself
prances amongst them, fanning their Evil Inclination;
where all the things that provoke fleshly desires are
ranged before their very eyes, while the warnings of
retribution You have hidden between the covers of some
moralistic tome like *Reishis Chachmah*. You can be certain that if you had arranged things the *other* way
around — with the place of retribution right in front of
their eyes, and all the fleshly desires hidden away in
some learned old book — then not a single Jew would
ever do anything wrong!"

The chassid then watched from his hiding-place as the
tzaddik rose from the floor, dried his eyes with his hand,
and — roused for the occasion — walked to the synagogue, where he sighed repeatedly, and proceeded with
the blowing of the *shofar*.

◄§ But Can We Survive the Surgery?

Reb Yisrael of Ruzhin once walked into his *beis
midrash* and said to the chassidim who happened to
be there: "I will tell you a story.

"A villager once came to town for Rosh HaShanah.

Like many villagers in those days, he was so ignorant ראש
that he did not even know how to read the prayers. השנה
When he walked into the synagogue on the morning of
the holy day he gazed around in all directions without
opening his mouth. After a little while, when the other
worshipers reached *Shemoneh Esreh*, he observed that
some of them were weeping.

"Now this is strange,' he thought. 'There hasn't been
any fighting or anything. Why are they weeping?'

"He thought it out, and arrived at the conclusion that
they were no doubt weeping because they had to stay so
late in *shul*, when they were hungry. And since he too
was hungry, he soon found himself weeping together
with them all.

"After *Shemoneh Esreh* he had a new problem: why
did they not cry now? It then occurred to him that he had
noticed in the morning that his hostess had put a hard
lump of meat into the soup, and the longer it was left on
the fire, the easier would it be to chew. It followed,
therefore, that going home late was really no cause for
tears. But when the time came to hear the *shofar*, his
original question presented itself afresh, for everyone
was crying again! He soon found an explanation,
however, and told himself the following: 'True, it is that
the broth will be richer after all this time — *but we
haven't got the strength to wait so long!*' And with this
pathetic cry from the heart he again began to weep with
them all ... "

After Reb Yisrael had left the room, the chassidim said
to each other: "That was a parable about this long exile."

⊷§ A Shofar to Remember

On Rosh HaShanah of the year during which Reb
Yisrael of Ruzhin was to pass away, his son Reb
David Moshe (later known as the rebbe of Chortkov)
was unwell. He therefore spent the Days of Awe in bed,
and prayed at home, in his father's study. His father's
manner of worship was unusual that year, he observed;
in fact, he described it as being "quite beyond the laws of
nature."

After the prayers, the tzaddik of Ruzhin said to his

son: "Today I heard the blasts of the *shofar* of the Messiah."

And his son later said: "The *shofar* my father used ·was big and strange. Its sound was powerful, and the blasts were wondrously clear. But straight after Rosh HaShanah it disappeared, and was seen no more."

◄§ Where Ignorance is Bliss

The awesome moment had arrived. The rebbe was present — Reb Shlomo of Radomsk — but all eyes were focused on the pious and scholarly chasid whom he had singled out for the sought-after responsibility of blowing the *shofar* for the whole congregation. Despite all his efforts, however, he could not muster one solitary blast. A young man was called across to substitute for him, and all the sounds came out melodiously, without a single hitch.

After the prayers, seeing that the would-be blower looked somewhat crestfallen, Reb Shlomo called him across and said: "Here is a parable for you.

"In honor of the coronation of their new king, the people of a certain land fashioned him a magnificent gold crown. All that was now needed was to set it with precious gems, but no craftsman dared to undertake the delicate task, for fear lest he damage the priceless crown. At long last there arrived a master goldsmith who asked for one month in which to complete the work. For day after day and week after week he sat and studied the crown from all angles, contriving in his imagination how best to bedeck it. Two days before his time ran out he made a great effort and determined to overcome his apprehension — but the moment he actually took it into his trembling hands it slipped and fell. But how was the work to be done?

"He called in his apprentice — who did not know that this was the king's crown — and gave him precise instructions as to how to set the gems. He himself was still so seized by anxiety that he left the workshop and waited outside until the work was completed. And, indeed, the young lad carried out his task in a craftsmanlike manner, without a single hitch ..."

Reb Zvi of Portziva used to lead the congregation for the solemn *Musaf* prayer on Rosh HaShanah in the synagogue of Reb Yossele of Torchin, the son of the Chozeh of Lublin.

He was once asked by Reb Yitzchak Meir of Ger: "Perhaps you could repeat me some Torah teaching which you heard from the mouth of Reb Yossele?"

"I do not remember any *dvar* Torah," said Reb Zvi, "but I do recall a story. One Rosh HaShanah, just before the *shofar* was to be blown, Reb Yossele entered the *beis midrash* and said to his congregation of chassidim, some of whom were no doubt thinking at that auspicious moment of their requests to the Almighty for the coming year: 'I am not going to rebuke you with words of *musar;* nor am I going to teach you a *dvar* Torah; I am only going to tell you a story.

" 'In a certain city there lived a learned and wealthy wine-merchant who was honored one day by a visit from the local rabbi. Feeling deeply privileged, the host went out of his way to show his guest every due mark of respect. He quickly sent his servant down to the cellar, where he was to fill a bottle of wine from the middle barrel of the third row — for this was the choicest wine he owned. He himself continued to maintain scholarly conversation with his distinguished guest, but when he had waited a surprisingly long time for his servant to return, he begged to be excused, and hastened downstairs himself to find out what was amiss. He was stunned by what he saw there. Some of the barrels had been left uncovered; others were being drained of their precious contents because the taps had been left open; broken bottles jutted out of the puddles of wine on the floor; and the servant was nowhere to be seen. He returned to the house, sorely grieved by the serious damage which his servant had caused him, and began to look for him and call him by name. The servant finally answered — from a cozy nook over the fireplace, where he was sprawled at his leisure. And from up there he called out to his master: *Listen here! I want you to increase my salary by*

ROSH *so and so much; it isn't near high enough ...' "*
hashanah   Reb Yitzchak Meir of Ger thanked the storyteller
warmly.

"Now *that* is what I call a fine parable!" he exclaimed.

❧ Dust and Ashes

מוּסָף
Musaf,
the
additional
service

The source of man is dust, and his end is dust
(Musaf).

Reb Leib Sarah's, as is well known, spent all his days
ransoming captives and supporting the hidden tzaddikim of his generation. Accordingly, he was constantly traveling from town to town, borrowing large sums, collecting donations, and repaying his loans at the appointed times. He once came to a certain city and took up lodgings in an inn. There he summoned one of the servants and told him to call on a well-known local magnate, and tell him that Leib the son of Sarah required him to donate one hundred gold rubles.

The servant stepped back in dismay: everyone knew that individual to be a violent antagonist of the chassidim and their rebbes.

"How can I possibly approach a bold and wealthy man like that," he protested, "who lives ensconced in luxury in the inner chambers of a veritable palace, surrounded on all sides by servants and lackeys? How can a penniless pauper like myself dare to command him to contribute such a large sum to my rebbe?"

The tzaddik answered, and his words were words of fire: "Look down, and you will see that the place on which you stand is dust. This table here is dust, and so too are all the things we see here before us. The palace of that magnate is dust of the earth; his vessels of silver and gold are dust; his servants and lackeys and all his household are dust; and he himself is dust and ashes. *And you are afraid of dust?!* Go now, and have no fear."

These words put courage into the poor man's heart. His words in turn commanded obedience — and the magnate did as he was told.

Fire Trill

Reb Menachem Mendel of Kotsk was impatient of *chazzanim* who when leading their congregations in prayer would draw out the melodies of the poetic passages in an exhibition of their vocal virtuosity. The celebrated chassid who led the services in the rebbe's own *beis midrash* was Reb Zvi Hirsch of Portziva, the same who had led the prayers in the days of Reb Simchah Bunem of Pshischah. And from time to time one could hear the voice of Reb Menachem Mendel's *shammes* relaying a message to the *chazzan:* "Hirsch, speed it up a bit!"

One day, not long after the Days of Awe, this same *chazzan* lost all of his possessions in a fire that gutted his house. Naturally enough, he called on the Kotsker rebbe to tell him of his misfortune.

Said Reb Menachem Mendel: "It's all because on Rosh HaShanah, when you came to *Unesaneh Tokef,* the prayer which speaks of the varying fates of humanity, you trilled a little *too* fancily on the words מִי בָאֵשׁ — 'And who by fire ...' "

Why Stay Alive?

When Reb Chaim of Zanz came to visit his ailing relative-by-marriage Reb Eliezer of Dzikov, the son of Reb Naftali of Ropshitz, the patient appealed to him: "*Mechutan,* pray for me!"

"But why do you need this lowly world?" asked Reb Chaim. "Surely the World of Truth is far better!"

"Of course it is better," said Reb Eliezer, "but only for someone who has what to take with him."

"If only every one of our brethren had the same luggage of good deeds to take with him to the World Above as you have!" said Reb Chaim.

"But why do you not have pity on my sons," protested the sick man, "whom I am leaving without a livelihood?"

"So what would you do if you were alive?" asked Reb Chaim. "You would probably endeavor to find them rabbinical posts. Very well, then, I hereby promise that I will find them positions as rabbis just as if you were alive."

"My dear *mechutan!*" Reb Eliezer tried once more. "You know that when on the Days of Awe I sing the hymn אֵין קִצְבָה לִשְׁנוֹתֶיךָ — 'There is no limit to Your years' — all the hosts of heaven dance with joy. If I now die, the World Above will be deprived of that pleasure."

This was an argument for which Reb Chaim had no answer.

"In that case," he conceded. "I will have to intercede for you."

With that he went to immerse himself in the *mikveh*, and after a short while returned to tell the patient: "I have prayed for you."

Reb Eliezer regained his health, and lived on for another six years — until on the third of Cheshvan, in the year 1860, he set out with his blessed luggage to the World of Truth.

◂§ The Martyrdom of a Cat-Burglar

Near the resting place of the Shpoler Zeide, who passed away on the sixth of Tishrei in the year 1811, stands the tombstone of one of his contemporaries, a man who sanctified the Name of heaven in public. The grave is known by the local townsfolk as "the grave of the martyr, Yossele the thief."

But how does one call a martyr — a thief?

In 1929 there died in Jerusalem, at the age of ninety, a chassid by the name of Reb Raphael Wiltz (or Wolf) of Skoli, Galicia, who records in the memoirs which he left in manuscript that in 1881 he visited Shpola, in Russia. While there, he questioned a number of aged local residents about this curious grave, and the following is what he learned from them.

Reb Aryeh Leib of Shpola — known as the Shpoler Zeide — used to keep company with thieves, though no one knew what business he had with them. Whenever one of them was caught and had to serve a sentence, the tzaddik used to send him food and drink and to attend to all his needs. It was his custom to boast to the

Almighty about "my thieves," and people had even ראש
heard him say: "Master of the Universe! Just look at my השנה
thieves. Why, even the least worthy of them is full of
good points!"

One Rosh HaShanah when the prayers were over, he
told his congregation that during that day's *Shemoneh
Esreh* he had had to toil hard indeed. He had discovered
to his anguish that the accusing angels had erected a wall
between the prayers of the House of Israel and their
Father in heaven. He had turned and toiled in every possible way, seeking some opening through which he
might force his way through and gain entry to the other
side, so that he would be able to intercede on behalf of
his brethren — but the iron wall stood firm, locked and
bolted, defying any challenger.

"It was then that I recalled my thieves," the Shpoler
Zeide went on to explain his congregation, "for they are
able to break the strongest of locks. I quickly called
them, and straight away they shattered the locks and
broke down the wall. A new light shone forth, as the
Almighty rose from the Throne of Judgment and rested
on the Throne of Mercy. The angels of mercy brought in
the prayers of all Israel to the presence of Him Who
listens to prayer, and the supplications of His People
were accepted graciously. I thank the Almighty that
through my thieves I was able to bring about a salvation
for all of Israel for the forthcoming year."

Then he added: "*Nu*, what do you say about my
thieves? Just see what good points they have to their
credit!"

Now it once happened that the local thieves planned
to steal the whole fortune — silver, gold, gems — that was
to be found in the big church of Shpola. It stood in the
middle of the town, a solid stone edifice with a tall steeple. The only way to reach the interior was for one of
them to climb up the steeple, and to break his way inside
through a small window near the top. Now in Shpola
there lived a young burglar of slight and athletic build,
who could clamber up any stone wall with the greatest of
ease. He was known as Yossele Ganev ("Yossele the
thief"), and whenever his colleagues were confronted
with a professional problem involving a narrow passage

he would make his services available to the cause.

So it was that after they had all waited patiently for the end of the lunar month, the little band of burglars collected in the dead of the dark night behind the massive walls of the church, while Yossele climbed swiftly up to the top of the steeple, wriggled in through the little window, and found his agile way in the gloom down the steep interior staircase that took him all the way to the floor. Once there, he piled all the golden icons and other valuables into the tablecloths that he found there. While he was on his way up again to the little window, the night watchmen appeared on the scene outside the church. They raised a hue and cry, and with exemplary alacrity the waiting little band disappeared in all directions. And just at that moment, unaware of this sudden change of plan, Yossele stuck his head gleefully out of the window in order to give the signal to his cronies in robbers' slang that they should be ready to catch the loot — for he was afraid of being caught up in the bundles and ropes which he still had tied to himself. He called out again, but received no reply. The night watchmen, however, looked up and saw a man who appeared to be hanging near the top of the steeple, calling out in a language they could not understand. Overawed by this marvel, they surrounded the building, and decided to wake up the parish priest. All the local gentiles were soon on the scene, and when they opened the church they discovered to their horror that all their bejeweled objects of worship had — like Yossele — ascended on high. They kindled tall candles, and saw him stuck up there in the little window, trailing cumbersome bundles on all sides. They climbed up and seized him, and threw him into prison pending trial.

When the day came, and he was brought before the judges, Yossele argued that his intention was only to test whether the icon they worshiped was a thing of substance. He had therefore decided to visit it at night, undisturbed by anyone, and to pray to it that he be granted a more generous livelihood for the support of his wife and two children. If it helped, then he would know it was divine, and he would worship it all his life. When, however, he had prayed there a few times, and had

received no answer — a mouth that spoke not, eyes that ראש
saw not, ears that heard not — he had lost his patience, השנה
and had addressed it as follows: "Look, you're fooling
everyone around these parts into worshiping you
because they think you are divine. But I can see there's
nothing to you. Better that I take you and sell your gold;
that way at least I'll have a livelihood."

Yossele continued his explanation to the court: "So I
began to move him, and I saw that his hands and legs
made no move in self-defense. It was safe to assume, in
that case, that the smaller images would certainly be unable to raise any opposition. And so it was. I took them
all, together with their ornaments — and not one of them
said a single word in protest! You realize, therefore, your
honors, that I have done you a great favor, for now you
know that there is no point in worshiping things of nonsense."

The judges nevertheless sentenced Yossele to be
burned alive in front of the church in the presence of all
the populace.

After handing him the sentence in writing, the chief
justice said: "You still have a way of saving yourself
from this wretched death. Because you are so young, and
you showed such prowess in climbing to the top of the
steeple, we have decided that if you convert to our
religion we will let you live. Not only that: we will give
you all kinds of gifts, and make you rich."

The answer was bold and clear: "I, Yossele the thief,
have committed plenty of sins in my lifetime. But to
betray his faith — *that* Yossele the thief will never do,
even if he is tortured by all the means in the world. Tell
me: are you out of your minds? Who would do such a
thing — to exchange the living God for a dumb stone,
fashioned by the hands of mortal man, a thing which
wasn't even able to defend itself against me? True
enough, Yossele the thief is — Yossele the thief. But to
change his faith, that he will never do, whatever happens."

He was thrown back violently into his prison cell, and
when the day arrived an eager crowd assembled to watch
the spectacle. He was stood next to the fierce flames of a
burning barrel of tar, and the parish priest addressed him

in measured tones: "My son, you still have a chance to
save yourself from a horrible death — if you will convert
to the Religion of Love. And if not, you will be thrown
into this burning barrel. You will be boiled alive."

The answer rang loud and clear: "I, Yossele the thief,
am Yossele the thief, but to change my faith — never!"

They seized his shackled hands and plunged them into
the barrel.

"Your chance is not yet passed!" declaimed the priest.
"If you will change your religion, physicians will heal
your hands, and we will let you live long and happily!"

Yossele writhed in unspeakable agony. He was held
up only by the hands of the burly gentiles who surrounded him. But he cried out at the top of his voice:
"Yossele the thief will be burned in fire; he will suffer all
the tortures you can invent; *but he will not convert!*"

When it was all over, his mortal remains were handed
over to the Jewish community for burial, and the simple
gravestone in the old cemetery of Shpola records the date
of his martyrdom.

"You see," the Shpoler Zeide would say, "it is not in
vain that I speak in praise of my thieves!"

עשרת ימי תשובה

ten days
of penitence

◆§ The Penance

"For this commandment ... is not in heaven":
The Torah refers here to the mitzvah of
repentance *(Ramban)*.

When Reb Yechiel Michel of Zlotchov was a young
man he used to spend all day studying in the *beis
midrash* of his hometown.

It once happened that a simple wagon-driver who
lived nearby did not manage to come home on time one
Friday, and by the time he reached his home the Sabbath
had already begun. Deeply distressed, he told the local
rav of the misfortune which had occurred to him for the
first time in his life, and asked him to prescribe a
penance with which he could atone for his transgression.
Seeing how grieved he was over what had befallen him,
the *rav* gave him a lenient reply: if he would bring a
pound of candles to the synagogue in honor of *Shabbos*,
his sin would be atoned.

Hearing of this Reb Michel was shocked: for the
violation of *Shabbos* — a pound of candles?! But he mentioned the subject to no one.

On Friday the wagon-driver duly brought his pound
of tallow candles and put them where they belonged. But
after he left, before the holy day had even begun, a dog
broke into the *shul* and chewed them up. The wagon-
driver was upset by this, but when he told the *rav* that
his repentance had apparently not been accepted in
heaven, the *rav* reassured him that it was only a mishap
and nothing to worry about; he should simply bring a
fresh set of candles on the following Friday.

This time, however, after he had lit them on Friday
afternoon in honor of *Shabbos*, they melted so quickly
that by sunset nothing was left of them. Brokenhearted,
he once again called on the *rav*, who told him to try again
the following week. But as soon as *Shabbos* had started,
a sudden gust of wind blew them out.

More convinced than ever that his penitence was being rejected by heaven, he poured out his heart to the
rav, who said: "It seems to me that that young man who
sits and learns in *shul* is the one that is spoiling things
for you. I would suggest therefore that you make the
journey to the Baal Shem Tov and tell him the whole
story."

When the wagon-driver arrived at Mezhibuzh, which
was not far away, the Baal Shem Tov answered him as
follows: "The penance that your *rav* gave you was appropriate. Next Friday take a pound of candles to *shul*
once more, and I promise you that this time nothing will
go wrong. And here is a letter which I would ask you to
pass on to this young man called Reb Michel."

The wagon-driver came home with a happy heart,
delivered the letter to Reb Michel, and when Friday came
he did as instructed. And in fact this time nothing went
wrong: the candles burned brightly in honor of *Shabbos*.

Meanwhile, when Reb Michel opened his letter — it
was on a Tuesday or a Wednesday — he saw that the Baal
Shem Tov requested him to visit Mezhibuzh, so he hired
a wagon and set out without delay. The journey should
have taken him only a few hours, but the horses strayed
from the dirt track and wandered in all directions for
days on end, until by the time they reached Mezhibuzh
on Friday, there were only a few moments left before
sunset.

When Reb Yechiel Michel approached the Baal Shem
Tov, the tzaddik said: "Reb Michel, I have saved you
from violating the Sabbath ... And now learn your lesson: that if a Jew through a mishap comes to transgress
Shabbos, and he is earnestly grieved by it to the point
that his heart is broken within him, then one pound of
candles is quite enough penance for him."

◆§ A Certificate of Righteousness

It was a hot day, and Reb Zusya of Hanipoli was sitting
in the shade in his back yard. Along came some fellow
and asked him for a letter which would certify that he
was free from sin; otherwise he would not get his *kapote*
back. Reb Zusya, understandably enough, did not know

what he was talking about. The man explained that a עֲשֶׂרֶת group of chassidim had grabbed hold of him and had יְמֵי stripped him of his black coat. They claimed that he was תְּשׁוּבָה guilty of a certain sin, and informed him that they would return his *kapote* only if he would bring a piece of paper from Reb Zusya which testified that he was either innocent, or had duly repented.

"And how do I know that you are in fact innocent?" asked Reb Zusya.

"And what does it matter to you if you give me the piece of paper, and I'll have my *kapote* back?" retorted the unfortunate fellow.

But then, when he saw that no words of his were going to persuade the tzaddik to provide him with such a certificate, he shouted angrily: "Why, if I were to plead as hard as this *to the parish priest* he would have pity on me!"

Reb Zusya was overwrought by these words.

"Woe is me," he cried out bitterly, "that I caused a fellow Jew to speak like this!"

And he shuddered in such a frenzy of anguish that he fell into the nearby drainage canal. In the tumult that followed all the neighbors rushed along to help. They dragged him out, took him inside, changed his clothes, and laid him down to rest. But even in bed Reb Zusya continued to wail: "It was I who caused a fellow Jew to come out with those evil words!"

The unpleasant individual who had caused this whole misadventure slipped smartly away from the scene as soon as the excited neighbors arrived. He hid among the shrubs in a nearby garden, and while crouching there had time to consider with what self-sacrifice Reb Zusya had stuck by his principles. Perhaps, after all, it was time to repent ... He waited until he heard that all the helpful neighbors had gone home, then made his quiet way to Reb Zusya's bedroom, where he begged the tzaddik to direct him on how to go about repenting for his sins.

"Come now," said Reb Zusya, "what you have in mind is not repentance, but your *kapote* ..."

"No, rebbe, no!" insisted the other. "I am willing to forget the *kapote* altogether. Just teach me how to repent!"

Reb Zusya now saw that the man really meant what he said. He got down from his bed and sat on the floor, and answered quietly: "If that is the case, then let us both do *teshuvah* together."

And together they wept, the tzaddik and the stranger, until Reb Zusya had brought him to the kind of repentance that wells from the depths of one's heart.

◆§ One Pair of Tefillin

It was the custom in Berditchev that the *tefillin* of deceased townsmen would become the property of the local burial society, whose *gabbai* would sell them for the benefit of the *Chevrah Kaddisha*.

One day this functionary received a visit from Reb Levi Yitzchak, who asked to be shown all the *tefillin* on hand, for he wished to buy a pair for himself — and the tzaddik soon chose a particular pair. The *gabbai* gathered that he would not have come along to simply buy himself a nondescript secondhand pair of *tefillin*: there must be more to this purchase than met the eye. So he said: "Rebbe, I am willing to sell you all the pairs of *tefillin* you see here — except for this pair. This pair I am not willing to part with ..."

But it was only this pair that the tzaddik earnestly begged him to sell.

So finally the *gabbai* said: "Very well, I will agree to sell them to you — but only on condition that you tell me what is so special about them that makes you seek this particular pair."

"Very well," said the tzaddik. "As you no doubt know, for many years the brothers Reb Elimelech of Lyzhansk and Reb Zusya of Hanipoli wandered about among the townships and villages, with the aim of 'making *baalei teshuvah*' — firing people with a desire for repentance. Whenever they arrived at some place for the night, one of them would address the other as if he were a sinner turning to his rebbe, weeping over his imagined sins and requesting a suitable penance. And while so doing — within earshot of their host — he would list all the transgressions of which the host was in fact guilty. Overhearing this seeming confession of another, the host would recall that he too, as it were, had sinned in a like manner, and this recollection would cause him to repent.

"Arriving one night at the house of a Jew who lived in a certain village, Reb Zusya began to tearfully beg his brother to prescribe a penance for him for his negligence. Throughout his life, he had never had his *tefillin* checked to see whether the verses inscribed on the parchment scrolls inside them were still in valid condition. And now he had at last given his *tefillin* to a scribe for checking, and had found that there were no scrolls inside them whatever! If so, then he had lived all his life in an illusion, and clearly fell into the category of קָרְקַפְתָּא דְּלָא מָנַח תְּפִלִּין — 'a head that has never worn *tefillin*.'

"At this point Reb Elimelech took over, and explained his brother what a serious state of affairs this was. And as their host overheard this dialogue, he recalled that he 'too' had never given his *tefillin* to a scribe for checking. He ran off to fetch them, and when they were opened, he found that they were utterly empty! Alarmed by his discovery, he sobbed out his story to the two visitors, and begged them to direct him as to how to repent.

"Reb Elimelech now turned to Reb Zusya and said: 'Please write out a set of scrolls for the *tefillin* of our host. And as you do so, make it your solemn intention to draw down into their words the kind of light from Above that will be of the intensity appropriate to a man who has never fulfilled the mitzvah of *tefillin* in his life.'

"Reb Zusya took out parchment, quill and ink, and devoutly inscribed the passages required. Then he rolled up the tiny scrolls, placed them inside the black leather boxes of the *tefillin*, and returned them to their owner.

"But the divine light that those *tefillin* now irradiated was of an intensity that this man was unable to bear. Soon after this incident he moved here to Berditchev, and a short while later, died in our city.

"And these," concluded Reb Levi Yitzchak, "are the selfsame *tefillin* which thus found their way into the hands of our local burial society."

◆§ Soul of a Scoffer

Reb Zusya of Hanipoli recounted the following episode to Reb Shneur Zalman of Liadi.

"My brother Reb Elimelech was once sitting in the room next to the study of the Maggid of Mezritch, when he heard the Maggid calling him. When he entered the study, the Maggid said: 'Melech, do you hear what they're saying in the Academy on High? They are saying that *ahavas Yisrael* — the mitzvah of loving a fellow Jew — means loving an utter sinner just as one loves a perfect saint. It is within the power of a tzaddik to arouse the spiritual potential which lies concealed in every soul, and to give it the strength to return in repentance. A *minyan* of brethren of the *chevraya kaddisha* has the strength to arouse even an utterly wicked man to *teshuvah.*'

"In the morning, when my brother passed on the rebbe's words to the brethren of the holy fraternity, they said: 'Very well, then, it's time to get to work.'

"They discussed at length what the Maggid had taught them, illustrating the subject with stories and teachings of the Sages on the subject of penitents. A passerby soon joined them and listened in to their discussion. Then he burst out in a vulgar guffaw, and berated the men of the brotherhood for having gathered together in the *shul* to ponder on delusions of Torah and repentance. They were time-wasters and good-for-nothings, he claimed.

"Hearing this tirade, the men of the holy brotherhood began to pray earnestly and tearfully, and poured out their hearts in the ardent reading of *Psalms.* But though he scoffed at first, they began to explain to him in graphic terms what a precious thing each Jew's soul is in the eyes of the Creator. Their words finally gained access to his heart. The scoffer's soul was aroused, and before many days had elapsed he became a sincere penitent."

◆§ Letter-Perfect

Reb Shneur Zalman of Liadi once told his grandson, Reb Menachem Mendel of Lubavitch: "In the year

1768, on the *Shabbos* when the weekly Portion of *Ki Savo* was read, the Maggid of Mezritch delivered a mystical discourse on the verse וְשַׁבְתָּ עַד ה' אֱלֹקֶיךָ — 'You shall return unto the Lord your God.' The Maggid expounded this verse to mean that repentance should bring a man to such a level that the four-letter divine Name — which signifies the infinite essence of God, transcending creation — should be apprehended as being identical with the Name *Elokim* (the numerical value of whose letters equals the value of the word הַטֶּבַע, nature; hence God as He is manifested in the created universe). His disciples of the holy brotherhood found this exposition spiritually exhilarating. But Reb Zusya said simply: 'I cannot reach the level of repentance that our rebbe has described. I would rather divide *teshuvah* into five parts. For the word תְּשׁוּבָה is made up of the initial letters of five verses: תָּמִים תִּהְיֶה עִם ה' אֱלֹקֶיךָ — 'You shall be perfect with the Lord your God'; שִׁוִּיתִי ה' לְנֶגְדִּי תָמִיד — 'I have set the Lord always before me'; וְאָהַבְתָּ לְרֵעֲךָ כָּמוֹךָ — 'Love your neighbor as yourself'; בְּכָל דְּרָכֶיךָ דָעֵהוּ — 'Know Him in all your ways'; הַצְנֵעַ לֶכֶת עִם אֱלֹקֶיךָ — 'Walk humbly with your God.' "

❀   ❀   ❀

One day during the Ten Days of Penitence, a solemn host of chassidim were standing around Reb Zusya, watching him intently. He sat in a state of *dveikus*, his eyes and heart raised heavenwards, and his mind unfettered by thoughts of This World. A spark of *teshuvah* was kindled in the soul of one of the disciples, and his eyes streamed with tears. One spark ignited another, one glowing coal inflamed another: the souls of the brotherhood were on fire.

Seeing this, Reb Zusya raised his eyes aloft and said: "Master of the Universe! Without a doubt, now is the time for repentance. But You know the truth — that I don't have the strength to do it. What, then, *can* Zusya do? Zusya can raise up to You the initial letters of *teshuvah* — תָּמִים תִּהְיֶה; שִׁוִּיתִי ה'; וְאָהַבְתָּ לְרֵעֲךָ; בְּכָל דְּרָכֶיךָ; הַצְנֵעַ לֶכֶת. That's what Zusya will do for You."

◄§ Cleansed with Tears

Reb Elimelech and Reb Zusya had a third brother — a village tavernkeeper. Now would it not be interesting to find out what manner of man this was? Surely he was no common fellow! Fired by curiosity, the disciples of Reb Elimelech decided one day to make the journey to his village, in order to find out for themselves. There, sure enough, they found him — standing foursquare behind the counter of his tavern, selling vodka to the surly yokels of the province. There was certainly no hint here of any spiritual flights into the lofty Worlds Above. All they noticed was that from time to time he took out his little notebook and wrote a few words in it.

The bar was closed at nightfall, and they asked to sleep in the inn. Then, late at night, when the household was fast asleep, they listened in from the room adjoining his, and heard him turning pages and reading to himself, from time to time striking himself on the chest, and weeping bitterly all the while.

Overcome by inquisitiveness, they walked right into his room and asked: "How is it that a man should *strike* himself?"

Their host answered them simply that this was his regular custom. Every day, whenever it seemed to him that he had sinned in some way, or an unholy thought had crossed his mind, he noted this in his little notebook. Then, when night came, he would never go to sleep until he had repented with a *teshuvah* that came from the bottom of his heart. And he even had a sign by which he could know whether his repentance had been found acceptable in the eyes of Heaven. For when he saw that the ink in his notebook was blotted out by his tears, then he knew that in Heaven too his sins had been erased.

◄§ Asceticism of the Soul

It was a stern note indeed that the lean penitent showed Reb Elimelech of Lyzhansk. He had been ordered in writing by his dour spiritual mentor to undertake a formidable regimen of fasting and self-affliction, and he was weak and dispirited after having only just started. עֲשֶׂרֶת

"Do nothing more of what is written in that note," יְמֵי
ordered Reb Elimelech. "But you may rest assured that תְּשׁוּבָה
you will not leave here before you have repented
earnestly."

He then summoned his son, Reb Elazar of Lyzhansk,
and said: "Here, I am entrusting this visitor into your
hands. See that he eats well, and when he is strong and
healthy again, bring him back to me."

When Reb Elazar had carried out these instructions
faithfully, the robust visitor came back to Reb Elimelech,
who proceeded to explain to him the gravity of sin, the
blemish that he had brought upon his own soul by defying the commands of the King, and so on — until the man
wept so contritely that his soul almost left his body.

"My son," said the tzaddik, "Now say the first word
of the Confession: אָשַׁמְנוּ — 'We have transgressed!' "

But no sooner had the man pronounced the word than
he fainted from sheer mortification.

When he came to, the tzaddik said: "Now go and rest,
and when you are feeling perfectly well again come back
to me. But make sure: no fasting, and no self-affliction,
God forbid!"

A few days later when the man returned, Reb
Elimelech again described the serious nature of sin, and
then told him to say the next word of the Confession:
בָּגַדְנוּ — "We have acted perfidiously!"

Once again the poor man fainted under the intensity
of the experience — and so too again and again, until he
had finally completed the entire Confession. Reb
Elimelech then sent him on his way, a gladder and a
wiser man.

◦§ Pious Envy

"Would you believe that I envy you?" Reb Levi
Yitzchak of Berditchev asked the violent sinner
who stood before him.

"What is there in me that you could envy?" returned
the other.

"Why," said the tzaddik, "our Sages have taught that
'if a person repents out of a love of God, his intentional

transgressions are counted as meritorious deeds.' Now make a simple calculation. If a man with as many sins on his account as you have decides to repent wholeheartedly, and all the sins are converted into meritorious deeds, — how many mitzvos will you have! Far, far more than I've got, that's for sure!"

With this the tzaddik grasped him by his lapels and implored him so earnestly to repent that he made a firm decision to turn to the path of *teshuvah*.

◆§ Repentance for Mitzvos

Coming out of the *mikveh*, one of the disciples of Reb Dov Ber of Mezritch encountered a friend who addressed him in these works: "Brother, whatever will come of us, with all our sins?"

"It's not the sins that worry me," said the other. "For those, there's something called *teshuvah*. But whatever will be with our mitzvos? How well are we serving our King?"

◆§ Someone's Calling Us

One night, when Reb Menachem Mendel of Vitebsk was still in Safed (where he had settled in 1777, before he moved to Tiberias), he could not fall asleep.

"The air here is clear and pure," he said, "and voices can be heard from Heaven, appealing to us to repent. *That* is why it is hard for me to sleep here."

◆§ Mission Accomplished

Rend your hearts, and not your garments (*Yoel*).

The Maggid of Mezritch once dispatched his venerable disciple, Reb Menachem Mendel of Vitebsk, to Belorussia in order to arouse the people there to repentance through moral exhortation. Two years later he returned to Mezritch. Seeing him walking towards the Maggid's study, Reb Levi Yitzchak hastened ahead to bring the glad tidings to the rebbe.

"Mazel Tov!" he exclaimed. "Your elder disciple has עֲשֶׂרֶת arrived!"

עֲשֶׂרֶת יְמֵי תְּשׁוּבָה

Overhearing this, Reb Menachem Mendel protested: "But am I worthy of being a disciple of our rebbe? At most, perhaps I once handed the rebbe his *gartl* in readiness for the Afternoon Prayer — and our Sages do teach that waiting on a Torah scholar can be greater than actual study of the Torah."

When Reb Menachem Mendel then entered the rebbe's presence to receive his greeting, the Maggid asked him: "Well, what did you accomplish in Reissin?"

Thinking back over the chassidim whom he had found complacent and had left contrite, the disciple answered quietly: "I found whole hearts and torn *kapotes*, and I changed them to whole *kapotes* and torn hearts."

◄§ Priorities

The *kollel* of chassidim in Tiberias once owed a heavy debt to one of the other congregations in the town. During the Ten Days of Penitence an elder of that congregation called on Reb Avraham HaKohen of Kalisk to propose a certain plan which he had devised in an attempt to secure the payments that were owing.

"You are right," conceded the tzaddik, "but I must say that in my eyes you hardly appear to be a man. In a time like this, when every Jew should be preoccupied with how to make amends with his maker, is *this* what you have on your mind?"

◄§ A Sin-Offering

A wealthy landowner once called on Reb Shlomo Zalman of Vilipoli, a disciple of Reb Meir of Apta and Reb Naftali of Ropshitz.

"Tell us," asked the tzaddik, "what is your opinion about the אָשֵׁם שִׁפְחָה חֲרוּפָה — the sacrifice of a guilt-offering which the Torah imposes on a man who has violated a betrothed handmaiden? Does that sound to you like a fitting punishment — that a sinner like that should bring a guilt-offering that costs him two silver coins? Would a wealthy man like yourself, for example, shrink from going ahead and satisfying his lust because of a punishment as slight as this?"

The man remained silent, and the tzaddik went on: "Mind you, it was not at all as simple as some people might fancy. Imagine some villager coming up to Jerusalem in order to offer such a sacrifice. The poor ignoramus probably isn't familiar with the ins and outs of the law, so he first has to call on the Sanhedrin high court in order to be told exactly what sacrifice he is obliged to offer. As he approaches the Chamber of Hewn Stone where they hold their sessions, the guards at the door no doubt ask him what business brings him there. So he has to tell them just what happened back at home. Then he appears before the Sanhedrin and repeats his story. They rebuke him sternly, and send him off to the *Kohen Gadol.* The High Priest likewise makes sure that he grasps the seriousness of his sin, and directs him to the *kohen* who is on duty at that time. When he has paid his two silver coins, the *kohen* gives him a slip of paper which he has to present to the man in charge of the lambs. While they are arranging for him to receive his lamb for the sacrifice, these two *kohanim* utilize the opportunity of making their moralistic observations on the regrettable circumstance that brought him to them. They instruct him to take his lamb to the courtyard of the Temple.

"Feeling very sorry for himself, the poor fellow makes his way miserably toward the *kohen* who will actually perform the sacrifice — but at this point he has to make his confession. The *kohen* gives a signal to the Levites who are waiting there with their musical instruments. Within seconds the air is made heavy by a gloomy melody, whose somber strains cleave his innards and arouse in him pangs of conscience and intense remorse. He is overcome by the tears of a true penitent, until by the time the sacrifice is over he is like a man reborn, resurrected from the dead."

❁ ❁ ❁

The tzaddik's words were all too meaningful for the landowner who stood before him, listening intently. For

at that moment he himself should have offered that very עשרת
same guilt-offering ... Overcome by genuine remorse, he ימי
fainted on the spot. And some time after he came to, he תשובה
left the tzaddik's house a cleansed man.

◄§ Testament of a Tzaddik

I n the course of their business two Jews found their way
to the remotest inland provinces of Russia, where they
eventually settled. The years passed by, and their affairs
prospered — but they gradually disburdened themselves
of the yoke of the mitzvos and mimicked the ways of the
gentiles amongst whom they lived. After some time they
decided to return to their hometown in the Pale of Settle-
ment. They hired a wagon — for the railway engine had
not yet been invented — and stopped for the night at a
certain village in the province of Kursk. The gentile
whom they asked for a place to sleep received them
warmly and prepared them a samovar of hot tea. They
then said that they were hungry, and when he asked
them what they would like for supper they told him they
would appreciate a square meal — meat, vegetables, and
so on — and they would pay for everything.

"But my meat isn't kosher," their host pointed out.

"Don't let that bother you," they smirked.

"Very well," he said, "but you'll have to wait a while
until I heat the stove and cook everything."

A little later they were shocked to see their host at the
door, ax in hand, his face burning malevolently.

"Prepare to die," he said. "In a few minutes I'm going
to finish you off!"

"Why? What did we do wrong?" they wailed.

"Don't waste your words," he said. "They won't help
you anyway. You see, I rob folks that pass by with
money, and I'm just doing my job."

He stomped out, locking the door behind him, and
they heard him telling his son what they would do to
their prisoners at daybreak. In the background,
meanwhile, they could hear the rhythmic sharpening of
his ax.

There was no way out. As they recalled the events of
the past few years, they wept bitterly. Why had they left

their birthplace and chosen to wander in such distant provinces?

Their thoughts were interrupted by the entry of their host.

"Time's running out," he said. "If you want to confess or pray or something, I'll give you a special room. But don't spend too much time over all that, because very soon I'm going to do what I said."

As soon as they were led into the other room, they experienced a profound sense of regret for their past misdeeds, and a desire to repent. Piecing together whatever fragments they could recall of their daily prayers, they faced their Maker contritely and wept the tears of the humble.

After some time their host reappeared at the door — but he was not to be recognized.

"You are both free," he said with a smile. "I never intended to murder you, God forbid! I'm not *really* a murderer, you know ... Let me explain to you what it's all about.

"Many years ago a certain holy Jew passed through our village, and stayed in my house. He took sick, and died in this very room. Before his death he blessed me with long life and said: 'I have one request of you. Whenever Jewish travelers pass through your village, receive them cordially. But if any one of them wants to eat meat that is not kosher, threaten him harshly — even with murder. Only as an act, of course. Obviously, you are not to bring any harm upon them.'

"When the holy man passed away," the gentile continued, "his relatives took his body for burial in a town nearby. I locked this room straight after, and I never let anyone in it, unless it's a Jew who wants to pray.

"So now you know why I threatened to kill you!"

The two merchants were awestruck. They immediately began to investigate. Who could this tzaddik be, and where was his resting place? It transpired that the village was called Piena, and the tzaddik was none other than Reb Shneur Zalman of Liadi, the author of *Tanya*, who had fled with his family from the onslaught of Napoleon's armies in 1812. And from here he had been taken for burial to the town of Haditch, in the province of Poltava.

From Piena the two men took their wagon straight to Haditch, where they poured out their hearts at the resting place of the tzaddik, and at that very spot made the sober resolve to start their lives afresh.

◆§ A Novel Penance

"Whatever penance you prescribe, rebbe! Fasts, self-mortification, ascetic exercises, anything — so long as I can atone for my sins!" insisted a certain penitent who had just confessed his long list of transgressions in the hearing of Reb Mordechai of Lechovitch.

"And will you in fact undertake everything I instruct you to do, without turning left or right?" asked the tzaddik.

"Every single word!" exclaimed the penitent.

"In that case," said Reb Mordechai, "make sure that every morning you make your breakfast of fine white bread, roast chicken, and a casserole of meat and vegetables. Wash it down with a bottle of good wine — and do exactly the same in the evening. See to it that you sleep in a bed that has a cozy eiderdown, and don't even contemplate undertaking (God forbid!) anything resembling self-mortification. When you have done this for a whole year, come along here and we'll see then what to do next."

The penitent was wonderstruck. He had prepared himself to hear a forbidding list of fasts and ritual immersions and ascetic exercises such as rolling in the snow and who knows what else — and here the tzaddik had ordered him to wallow in the luxuries of This World! Was it possible that he would ever atone for his sins through *such* a penance? But there was no alternative: he had to obey the tzaddik.

Back at home, he discovered that whenever he sat down to his rich repast, he was tortured by the same thought: "Here I am, a sinner who has repeatedly rebelled against his Maker; I have dragged my soul from its heavenly source down into the mire of impurity. How, then, can I delight in the pleasures of This World and pamper myself with choice delicacies? What *I* deserve is to bite on a mouthful of gravel, to chew bitter herbs!"

At every meal he would go through this torment, shedding bitter tears and finding no peace. And though he had been a man of robust build, by the time the year was over he had shrunk to a wretched skeleton. Barely did he have the strength to make the long journey to Lechovitch.

The tzaddik took one look at him and said: "Enough!"

He then prescribed him a different lifestyle for him, and the man completed his days in joy and serenity.

⊷§ How to Marry Off Three Daughters

With three marriageable daughters in the house, the wife of Reb Avraham Mordechai of Pintchov final-ly persuaded her penniless husband to report his sorry situation to his rebbe, the Chozeh of Lublin.

"The best thing for you to do," advised the Chozeh, "is to head for Krasnik. There things will turn out well for you."

The chassid promptly filled a suitcase with books and clothes and his *tallis* and *tefillin,* and set out for Krasnik. The innkeeper there provided him with all his wants, as-suming that the guest with the large suitcase was no doubt a man of means. Reb Avraham Mordechai for his part spent all his time studying in his room.

As the weeks passed by, the innkeeper saw his tenant did not seem to be engaged in business of any kind, and now assumed that whatever chattels he owned would not be worth the amount that was owed until then.

"Tomorrow," he told his wife decisively, "I'll give this fellow his account. If he pays up — good for him; if not — then I'll take possession of his chattels and send him on his way."

That very evening, a *melamed* who had been hired to tutor the innkeeper's children called on Reb Avraham Mordechai furtively.

"There is something of a private nature that I would like to discuss with you," he said. "Could I ask you to undertake to keep the matter confidential?"

Then, having been given the promise, the *melamed* עשרת proceeded: "Some ten years ago our innkeeper went ימי away somewhere on business. When he came home he תשובה locked up the ten thousand rubles that he had earned in a drawer in his bedroom. In the middle of the night I woke up, and saw the key that he had forgotten on a table. The desire for money burned within me. I unlocked the drawer, and hid all the money in the yard. When the next day he discovered what had happened he made a great hubbub about the theft — but no suspicion fell on me, because they took me for a perfectly honest fellow.

"I regretted my action at once. I wanted to repent and return it all, but I was terrified of the consequences. The spirit of regret pounded constantly within me. I could find no peace. Over and over again I have decided: whatever happens, I will tell him my dreadful secret. But I am held back by shame and fear. In these ten years I have not touched the money, even though there were many times when my family barely had bread to eat. Now, however, when I saw by your face that you are a God-fearing man, I decided to tell you the whole story. I want to give you the money so that you can pass it on to the innkeeper. No one will suspect you, of course, because you were not even here at the time."

The *melamed* handed over the package, and went his way.

In the morning Reb Avraham Mordechai asked one of the attendants to tell the innkeeper that he would like to see him.

"I would like to have a word with you in private," he said, "but first I must ask you to promise me that you will not ask for any further information when I have finished."

That done, he proceeded: "Was a sum of money ever stolen from you?"

Though the incident had already slipped his mind, the innkeeper finally recollected it, and told his story. He was speechless with amazement at the sight of his money.

"How on earth ... ?" — but then he recalled that he had made a promise.

"Tell me, sir," he said, "what business brings you here?"

"To tell you the truth," answered the chassid, "I don't know either. All I know is that Reb Yaakov Yitzchak of Lublin told me to come here."

And he went on to tell him about his three daughters, and that his rebbe had told him that in this town things would work out for him. The innkeeper was quick to understand the intention of the Chozeh. He asked his guest how much he would need to marry off his daughters, and cheerfully gave him the full amount.

When Reb Avraham Mordechai returned at length to Lublin, the Chozeh said: "The strength of that *melamed's* desire for repentance didn't let me sleep."

◆§ One Hour of Repentance

Someone asked Reb Asher of Stolin: "But how can I repent? For I have committed one of the sins about which the holy books say that *teshuvah* is not effective."

"What has that to do with you?" answered the tzaddik. "You should go ahead and do what *you* are obliged to do. As to your concern as to whether you will be found worthy of being granted a share in the World to Come, our Sages have already taught: יָפָה שָׁעָה אַחַת בְּתְשׁוּבָה וּמַעֲשִׂים טוֹבִים בָּעוֹלָם הַזֶּה מִכָּל חַיֵּי עוֹלָם הַבָּא — 'One hour of repentance and good deeds in This World is better than all the life of the World to Come.' "

◆§ Repenting Properly

Whenever Reb Yossele of Tomashov (a disciple of Reb Chaim of Zanz) used to visit a certain town he stayed at the house of an old friend of his, a man of means. In the course of time this host married off his daughter to a scholarly young man who was a chassid of Reb Menachem Mendel of Kotsk. This was sufficient reason for Reb Yossele to stop his visits to his accustomed host, because he was one of those who did not approve of the teachings of the rebbe of Kotsk. The young son-in-law realized that it was his allegiance that caused the break, and went straight off to speak to Reb Yossele.

"The main objection that other tzaddikim have to my rebbe and his chassidim is the Kotsker custom of reciting the daily prayers after the prescribed time," he explained. "So let me ask you a question. The whole mitzvah of praying is of Rabbinic origin, is it not? And by suddenly stopping your accustomed visits you have shamed me publicly, which is a prohibition stated explicitly in the Torah, is it not? And the Sages teach us that הַמַּלְבִּין פְּנֵי חֲבֵרוֹ בָּרַבִּים ... אֵין לוֹ חֵלֶק לָעוֹלָם הַבָּא — 'He who publicly humiliates his fellowman has no share in the World to Come,' God forbid!"

Reb Yossele was deeply affected by these words, and said: "I really regret my action, and will repent over it."

"And can teshuvah that takes one moment be called teshuvah?" the young man retorted.

"Of course," replied Reb Yossele. "The Talmud teaches explicitly: 'If a man marries a woman on condition that he be righteous, and it transpires that he is a sinner, the marriage is still valid — for in his heart he may have had a thought of repentance.' From this we see that a thought of repentance is already considered a thing of substance."

On his next visit to Kotsk, the young man repeated this exchange to Reb Menachem Mendel. The tzaddik answered: "If Reb Yossele had given me that argument, I would have told him that the case he cited was irrelevant to the subject under discussion. For in that case, we are speaking of a bridegroom; and a bridegroom (as we learn in the Jerusalem Talmud) is one of three who are forgiven for all their sins. For a bridegroom, then, a mere thought of repentance counts as enough — but for any other man a mere thought is not enough: he has to repent properly!"

◆§ Credit Account

A man came to Reb Yisrael of Ruzhin and said: "I am a sinner, and want to repent."

"So why don't you?" asked the tzaddik.

"Because I don't know how to," said the other.

"So how did you know how to sin?" asked the tzaddik.

"First I acted," said the man, "and only later I found out that I had sinned."

"So do the same thing now," said the tzaddik. "Repent now, and the accounting will come later ... "

↝§ The Man with the Long List

A penitent with a most unsavory past handed Reb Mordechai of Chernobyl a *kvitl* on which he had listed all his sins — including the gravest of the grave — and asked the tzaddik to guide him as to how to go about cleansing himself.

"I am an old man," said the Maggid of Chernobyl, "and no longer have the strength to undertake the rehabilitation of a man with such a list. I would advise you to call on Reb Yisrael of Ruzhin. He is still a young man; he will receive you well, and help you."

Reb Yisrael read his list and prescribed a course of action. In the first place, he was to be punctilious about not saying any prayer or even the simplest blessing by heart: every word was to be read carefully from a *Siddur*. Secondly, whenever the tzaddik conducted a *tish*, this man was to watch him attentively the whole time, taking care not to be distracted.

The son of the tzaddik — Reb David Moshe of Chortkov — later said that he knew this penitent. In fact, in the course of time he grew to be a man of considerable spiritual stature.

"But you should not be surprised," he would add, "at the seemingly easy directives for repentance that my father prescribed him. The point is that when he fulfilled these instructions faithfully, then as a matter of course he knew exactly what he had to do. And in fact he did go on to repent earnestly and systematically on each separate item."

↝§ Silence Implies Dissent

One of the chassidim of Reb Shmuel of Zichlin was trying hard to convince his friend that the divine in-

spiration of *ruach hakodesh* rested on his rebbe to such a עֲשֶׂרֶת
degree that he was able to read on any man's forehead יְמֵי
everything that he had done since his youth. תְּשׁוּבָה

"Very well, then," said his friend. "I have sinned in various matters that no one knows of. Let us make the journey to Zichlin and see if he senses that I have these sins on my account."

But when they entered the rebbe's presence to receive his greeting, he said not a word.

"So where's your rebbe's *ruach hakodesh*?" the skeptic taunted the chassid.

"You're still here in town," replied the chassid. "When you go in to take your leave of the rebbe, he will no doubt tell you everything."

His friend, however, did not feel inclined to spend any more time in Zichlin, and decided to go straight home, without staying for the customary leavetaking. Since, however, the sun was about to set and it was time for the *Minchah* prayer, they stepped into the *beis midrash* of the tzaddik in order to worship with the congregation that had assembled there.

Now it was the custom of Reb Shmuel Abba to expound a passage of *Midrash Rabbah* to his chassidim every day after *Minchah*. In the course of his teaching, he would find ways of making the text peculiarly relevant to the spiritual lives of his listeners — sometimes, indeed, to the inner life of *one* of them — though no one else ever knew whom he was discreetly addressing.

That day's text was from the comment of the *Midrash* on the opening words of Deuteronomy, in the course of which the Sages cite a verse from *Psalms:* אֵלֶּה עָשִׂיתָ
וְהֶחֱרַשְׁתִּי דִּמִּיתָ הֱיוֹת אֶהְיֶה כָמוֹךָ אוֹכִיחֲךָ וְאֶעֶרְכָה לְעֵינֶיךָ
— "These [sins] you have done; and if I keep silence, you would think that I was quite like yourself; but I will reprove you, and set the matter before your eyes."

Reb Shmuel Abba began to expound: "There are people who come to visit a rebbe. Though they are full of sins and blemishes, thay have the effrontery to conclude that since the rebbe does not tell them explicitly that they have sinned, he certainly knows nothing and senses nothing. Nothing could be further from the truth. The tzaddik sees and knows, and if he says nothing it is ten days of penitence because he does not want to put them to shame. However, if the sinner does not take his situation seriously and decide to do *teshuvah*, and persists in assuming that the tzaddik is a simple fellow who knows nothing, then — in order to guide him back to the right path — the tzaddik is compelled to tell him explicitly that he has committed these and these sins. And this is what the verse in *Psalms* means: 'These sins you have done; and if I keep silence, you would think that I was quite like yourself' — a plain, ordinary man like yourself. Therefore, 'I will reprove you, and set the matter before your eyes.' "

And the tzaddik proceeded to explain his meaning in detail: "There are people who do so and so" — and he enumerated various sins, explaining as he went along what spiritual damage was caused by each, and what means of spiritual restitution were appropriate for each kind of transgression. And the sins that he enumerated, sure enough, were exactly the ones of which this skeptic was guilty. The *beis midrash* was packed with chassidim — but only one man present knew exactly to whom the message was beamed ...

The heart of that man melted. Humbled and contrite, he turned to his friend; he wanted to visit the rebbe in order to be told how he should cleanse himself, but he was overcome by shame — even by fear. His friend offered him words of encouragement.

"Right where you find the greatness of our rebbe," he said, "there you discover his humility. He is a man who is always found approachable by those who truthfully seek to do *teshuvah*. Besides, as you know, our Sages teach us that מָקוֹם שֶׁבַּעֲלֵי תְּשׁוּבָה עוֹמְדִים שָׁם צַדִּיקִים גְּמוּרִים אֵינָן עוֹמְדִין שָׁם — 'In a place where penitents stand, even tzaddikim cannot stand.' "

When the former skeptic later entered the rebbe's study, Reb Shmuel Abba could tell that this man's regret was sincere. He made not the merest mention of what was on his visitor's mind: on the contrary, he greeted him warmly and affectionately, and gave him his blessing that the Almighty should help him to return in earnest. And indeed, his blessing was richly fulfilled.

עשרת
ימי
תשובה **◄§ Benefit of the Doubt**

When he was still a newly-married young man
supported by his father-in-law, Rabbi Yosef Shaul
Natanson once passed through Premishlan on his way to
visit his father in Birzan. Though this outstanding
Talmudic scholar was no chassid, he decided to utilize
the opportunity of his being in Premishlan to call on Reb
Meir, for he had heard from reliable informants that this
tzaddik had an uncanny ability to read men's thoughts.

He found the tzaddik sitting at his table, but with no
book before him. Being himself a scholar of renowned
assiduity, the visitor's first thought was: "How is it possible that a man who sits idly — instead of engaging in
the study of the Torah — should be divinely inspired
with *ruach hakodesh?*"

As he approached the tzaddik to greet him with
Shalom Aleichem, Reb Meir said: "Young man, are you
not the author of *Mifresei HaYam?*"

And without waiting for an answer, he went on: "I
would like you to give me an explanation of a well-
known quotation from the Talmud. We are taught: אִם
רָאִיתָ תַּלְמִיד חָכָם שֶׁעָבַר עֲבֵרָה אַל תְּהַרְהֵר אַחֲרָיו שֶׁמָּא עָשָׂה
תְּשׁוּבָה — 'If you see a Torah sage who has committed a
sin do not harbor doubts about him, for he may have
repented.' On this statement the Sages query: שֶׁמָּא עָשָׂה
תְּשׁוּבָה — תְּשׁוּבָה סַלְקָא דַעְתָּךְ? אֶלָּא וַדַּאי עָשָׂה תְּשׁוּבָה — 'Do you
mean to say *he may have repented?!* Say, rather, *he has
certainly repented.'*

"Now this is a remarkable quotation. If the sages term
this person a *talmid chacham*, a Torah sage, then he must
certainly be a God-fearing man. How then is it conceivable that he should commit a sin — publicly,
moreover — so that we need to be given an assurance that
he has since repented?"

Rabbi Yosef Shaul had no answer, so the tzaddik continued, referring to himself (as was his wont) in the third
person: "So Meir will give you a good answer. In fact, a
true *talmid chacham* does not commit a sin. What *could*
happen is that you could find him at some time not

engaged in the study of the Torah. And since he might
then appear to you as a transgressor, the Sages warn
you: 'Do not harbor doubts about him, for he was certainly repenting at that time.' You see, when the Chozeh
of Lublin would open his *Gemara* for study, he would
first say: 'Master of the Universe! It could be that I am
one of those whom the Psalmist addresses as wicked. I
therefore undertake to do *teshuvah*.' Now for the
Chozeh of Lublin, one moment's thought on repentance
sufficed. I, however, needed longer than that to concentrate my thoughts, and to accept the yoke of heaven
upon myself before I begin to study.

"This, then, is what the Sages mean: 'If you see a
talmid chacham who has committed a sin' — that is, who
is at the moment not engaged in the study of the Torah —
'do not harbor doubts about him, for he may have been
repenting *at that time*.' "

Rabbi Yosef Shaul later related that he had then asked
the tzaddik to advise him as to whether he should accept
a rabbinical post that he had been offered in a small
township.

"No, young man," said the tzaddik, "for a greater rabbinical position is waiting for you."

Sure enough, soon after this encounter Rabbi Yosef
Shaul was inducted as the *rav* of Lvov.

◆§ A Visit to Paris

No one knew what lay behind it all: Reb Shmuel of
Lubavitch simply said that he had to make the
journey to Paris. He was attended on the way by his two
gabbaim, and was accompanied as well by two wealthy
chassidim, Reb Monye Monissohn and Reb Yeshayahu
Berlin.

When they arrived there and Reb Yeshayahu asked
the rebbe where they were going to lodge, he answered:
"In the Alexander Hotel."

Now this was one of the most prestigious hotels in the
city, frequented by visiting ministers of state and
members of the nobility.

The rebbe went on: "Since you're something of a

batlan and do not speak French, I will speak to the people there."

At the desk the rebbe asked for a good suite, and when he was offered one for 200 francs a day, he asked for a better one — in fact, a suite on the same floor as the gaming rooms. He was warned that the one remaining three-room suite there was even more expensive, but he took it all the same, while his two wealthy chassidim took rooms in a different hotel, because of the prohibitive cost.

A few hours later Reb Shmuel went to the betting parlor. There he took a seat next to a young man who was playing cards, and refreshing himself from time to time with a sip of wine.

The rebbe rested his hand on the cardplayer's shoulder and said: "Young man! It is forbidden to drink non-kosher wine."

A few moments later he added: "Non-kosher wine dulls the spiritual sensitivity of the mind and the heart. Behave like a Jew!"

Then, saying *Shalom*, he left the room in great agitation. Reb Yeshayahu Berlin later reported that he had never seen the rebbe in such a state.

Some hours later the young man came around to enquire after the person who had spoken to him earlier. He was shown into the rebbe's room, where he stayed for a long time. And the very next day the rebbe set out for Lubavitch in northern Russia.

On his return the rebbe said: "A soul as pure as this has not descended to This World for quite some generations — except that it fell into the depths of impurity."

In the course of time that young man became a *baal teshuvah* with all his being, and eventually became the head of a God-fearing family of good name.

◆§ Too Good to be True

In a townlet near Ushamir in the Ukraine there lived a Jew who was manager of the estates belonging to the local *paritz*. This manager was an evil man — evil in the eyes of heaven and evil in the eyes of man — and the Jews of the township suffered bitterly at his hands.

Now one day Ushamir was visited by Reb Mordechai

ten days of penitence Dov of Hornisteipl, and great numbers of chassidim from all the surrounding regions converged on the town in order to greet him — and among them, of course, came the embittered townsfolk of that little place. When their turn came to speak to the rebbe they told him of their woes, and asked his advice as to what they should do.

"I'll visit your township (God willing) myself," he said, "and once there we'll see what to do."

When he paid his promised visit hundreds of people accompanied him, some by wagon, some on foot. As the rebbe and this whole retinue passed by the house of the manager, someone pointed it out to the rebbe. He motioned the wagon-driver to stop, turned to face the house, and gazed upon it at length. Meanwhile, since the rebbe's carriage stopped, all the other carriages halted too, as did the hundreds who had followed on foot. And as that vast crowd stood there watching the rebbe, they were quite certain that he was gazing so intently on the house that at any moment the hated man inside would be miraculously turned into a heap of bones.

When the man inside looked through the window and saw the silent multitude outside his house he went out to the balcony and surveyed the strange sight. For some time the rebbe looked him straight in the eye. Then he stepped down from his carriage, and with measured steps walked into the house. The master of the house meanwhile went downstairs, and met the rebbe inside. There, facing one another in a room alone, sat the two, and for five whole minutes exchanged not a word. Then the rebbe left the house, accompanied by the other, stepped up to his seat in his carriage, and went off to his lodgings.

After spending *Shabbos* in the township and reciting *Havdalah* to mark the departure of the Day of Rest, the rebbe was sitting in his room, with large crowds of people at his door waiting to see him. Suddenly the man whom everyone dreaded appeared at the door, and asked to be admitted to the rebbe's presence. The tzaddik was asked, and gave the order that he should be allowed in at once. What they spoke about while alone there for two hours no one knows. But the man who came out of the room at the end of the two hours was a different man.

The first thing he did was to hand out money for the עֲשֶׂרֶת
purchase of refreshments for a chassidic celebration. He יְמֵי
danced with all those present and hurried home, where תְּשׁוּבָה
he shattered his *trefah* kitchenware. He replaced it all
with new utensils, and from then on conducted his
household conscientiously according to the dietary laws
for the preparation of kosher food. And, as he became a
penitent in all the areas of his life, he went out of his way
from that day on to deal kindly and charitably with his
fellows.

Just half a year later he died. He was buried with every
mark of respect, and was mourned with genuine regret
by all the townsfolk.

Some time later the tzaddik of Hornisteipl visited
Ushamir once again. And again, among those who
flocked there to see him were of course the citizens of
that little township. But this time, as they took their
turns for a private audience with the tzaddik, he asked
each one of them in turn: "Well, what do you have to
say about my *baal teshuvah?*"

And in this way, each one of them praised at length
the acts of charity which had distinguished the last
months of this man's life. This exchange was repeated so
many times that the townsfolk finally understood the
rebbe's intention: the more said to his credit in This
World, the better would it be for his soul in the World
Above.

The last townsman to enter was an individual who had
not yet forgotten all the suffering that he had undergone
in former years at the hands of the estate manager. When
the rebbe asked his question, therefore, he enumerated
bitterly all the acts of undeserved malice and spite that
were still fresh in his memory.

The rebbe interrupted his tirade with an original
paraphrase of a Talmudic teaching. There is a statement
in Tractate *Sanhedrin* that if *all* the judges of the high
court are unanimous in saying "guilty," then the accused
is to be returned innocent. With this at the back of his
mind, Reb Mordechai Dov said: "It seems that if *all* say
'innocent', that is likewise not desirable ... "

And from then on he never spoke of that man again.

⊷§ A Measure of Remorse

"Rebbe," said an old man to Reb Yissachar Dov of Belz, "I have reached a ripe old age, and thank God am lacking nothing. Only one thing: that you should promise me that I will be granted forgiveness for the sins of my youth."

"If you regret them utterly," answered the rebbe, "then that secures their forgiveness."

"And what in your eyes is the required measure of remorse?" asked the old man.

"Let me tell you a story," said the tzaddik. "A prosperous merchant once made haste to arrive at the big fair in Leipzig a little earlier than all the other merchants, and the wagonloads of goods that he brought with him were very much in demand. The day he arrived it began to rain, so that for a number of days no other merchant dealing in the same line was able to bring his merchandise to the fair. All the potential customers therefore milled around his stand. Seeing how intense was the demand, he decided to keep them all waiting for a few days so that the price would rise. And indeed, from day to day the rain fell harder and day by day the price rose higher. Then in the middle of the night the rain stopped. Before dawn the marketplace was clattering with all the wagons that were trundling in from the provinces on all sides — and the price of his goods plummeted instantly.

"Now, then," concluded the tzaddik. "if you find that your remorse over the sins of your youth is as intense as the regret of that merchant when he realized how much his greed had cost him, then you may be sure that your regret is sufficient to secure you forgiveness."

⊷§ Reason to Fear

A sick man cried out to Reb Hillel of Radoshitz: "Rebbe, I am afraid of death!"

Replied the tzaddik: "If you will be anxious instead about your life, and repent, then you will not be anxious about death."

◆§ *Top Priority*

A chassid of Reb Yehudah Aryeh Leib of Ger once
called on him during the Ten Days of Penitence to
ask his advice on some business transaction. According
to custom he made a note of the matter on a *kvitl* which
he handed to the rebbe, and added that the answer was
urgently needed that same day.

"The matter that is urgently needed today," said the
rebbe, "is to do *teshuvah*."

יום הכפורים

yom kippur

◆§ Double-Entry Bookkeeping

A venerable and prosperous chassid of Reb Elimelech כַּפָּרוֹת
of Lyzhansk once came to visit him on the evening *Kapporos*
before the eve of the Day of Atonement, and asked to be
allowed to watch how the tzaddik performed the expiation ceremony of *kapporos*. For on that evening many
people take a rooster or hen and circle it three times over
their heads, saying meanwhile certain Biblical verses on
the subject of atonement and reciting a sentence which
begins with the words: זֶה חֲלִיפָתִי זֶה תְּמוּרָתִי זֶה כַּפָּרָתִי —
"This is my exchange, this is my substitute, this is my
expiation."

"For decades now I have been coming here to
Lyzhansk for the Days of Awe," said the chassid, "and I
have never once seen this. I really do desire most deeply
to see how you, rebbe, do *kapparos*."

"And how do *you* do it?" asked the tzaddik.

"Rebbe, are you making fun of me?" returned the
chassid. "What is there worth seeing in my *kapparos*?"

"Tell me all the same," said the rebbe, "how you do
it."

"Look, I'm a plain ordinary fellow," said the chassid.
"I simply pick up a *Siddur* and start reading aloud what
it says there."

"Very well," said the tzaddik, "that's exactly what I
do too. The only difference between us is that you no
doubt follow the custom of buying a white rooster, while
I take a rooster that is white or black or whatever."

"But can't I watch?" the chassid persisted.

"Here, listen to some sound advice," said the rebbe.
"Go along to such and such a village, find the home of
such and such a Jew who lives there, and there you will
see a nice way to do *kapparos*."

The chassid lost no time, had his horse harnessed, and
set out immediately to the nearby village. He asked for
the whereabouts of the man he was directed to, and was
directed to a house on the outskirts of the village. By the

time he arrived it was an hour before midnight. The
house in which he now found himself was a tavern for
the local gentiles, who were lolling around on all sides
noisily swilling vodka and puffing clouds of smoke into
the gloom. The visitor sat quietly and waited to see what
would eventuate. As soon as the tavernkeeper caught
sight of him he came across and asked him what he
wanted there.

"I'm simply a bypasser," said the chassid, "and I
would like to spend the night here."

The householder hedged a little, and stammered a few
excuses: he did not really have much room, and there
were other houses in the village that were more spacious,
and so on. But the visitor asked him earnestly to be allowed simply to sit in a corner until dawn, when he
would be on his way. To this the host finally agreed.

When midnight drew near the tavernkeeper began to
clear the tavern of its unruly patrons; some were simply
cajoled into leaving, while others were persuaded only by
sterner means. Then, having flung open the shutters to
admit a breath of fresh air, he called out: "Yente-Beile!
Bring me the notebook that's sitting on the chest of
drawers in the other room!"

And when his wife had brought it, he sat down and
read out to himself in an undertone the whole list of sins
which he had recorded there in the course of the past
year: "On such and such a morning I read *Shema Yisrael*
after the prescribed time; on such and such a day ... " —
and so on. By the time he came to the end of his list he
was sighing and sobbing.

"*Ribbono shel Olam* — Master of the Universe!" he
exclaimed. "Didn't I do *teshuvah* last year, and promise
to be good and pious and not to repeat any of my
weaknesses? And now look what's come of me! Can't
You see I'm full of sins of all kinds?"

A few minutes later he called out again: "Yente-Beile
mine! Bring me the other notebook — the one on the top
shelf!"

And he started reading the other list that he had built
up in the course of the year: "On such and such a day I
went out to the forest to bring home firewood and a gang
of gentiles attacked me and broke my bones; on such and

such a day my little daughter passed away ... " and so on יוֹם
with all the woes and misfortunes that he had suffered הַכִּפּוּרִים
throughout the year.

"Look here, *Ribbono shel Olam*," he wept again,
"didn't I ask You clearly last year to give me a year of
blessing and life and peace? And didn't I trust you, and
believe You that that was what was going to be? And
now look what's come of all that!"

After a little while his tears dried up, and he said:
"When all's said and done, this *is* the eve of Yom Kippur, and now's the time when everyone has to bury the
hatchet. Let's call it quits, *Ribbono shel Olam*. You don't
owe me anything, and I don't owe You anything.
Okay?"

Then he took a piece of string, tied the two dog-eared
notebooks together into one bundle, whirled them three
times over his head, and said with gusto: זֶה חֲלִיפָתִי
זֶה תְּמוּרָתִי זֶה כַּפָּרָתִי — "*This* is my exchange, *this* is my
substitute, *this* is my expiation ... " — and tossed his
notebooks out the window.

The chassid, overwhelmed, quietly took his leave and
headed straight for the home of Reb Elimelech.

"Tell me what you saw over there," said the tzaddik.

And when he had heard the whole story, he remarked:
"Now you can better understand what the Psalmist
meant when he said: כִּי עֲוֹנֹתַי עָבְרוּ רֹאשִׁי — 'For my ini-
quities have passed over my head'; and yet, *at the same
time,* וְאַנְחָתִי מִמְּךָ לֹא נִסְתָּרָה — 'My sighing is not hidden
from You.' "

◦§ The Uses of Money

On the night before Yom Kippur eve, Reb Yerachmiel
Moshe of Koznitz — a greatgrandson of the Maggid
of Koznitz — once told his sons: "Go and ask your
mother if she needs money for *kapparos*."

Now on the surface that question innocently asked
whether the good woman needed money to buy poultry
for the ceremony of *kapparos*. But her husband's question punned with the Yiddish idiom: *Es teig af kapparos*
— "It's good for *kapparos*" — which signifies that the
object in question is absolutely needless. When his sons

came back, therefore, with the answer that their mother "needed money for *kapparos*," he commented: "It's a good thing when people know that money is needed *af kapparos* ... "

◦§ A Sound to Rend the Skies

If you walk into any old-fashioned *shul* on the morning of Yom Kippur Eve, you will see people on all sides busily collecting charity in little bowls for all kinds of worthy causes. Now the congregants of the township where the Baal Shem Tov lived — Mezhibuzh — decided that in the public interest this custom had to be abolished: it caused too much clatter and disorder.

Word of this reached the Baal Shem Tov, who did not allow the proposed regulation to be enacted. He explained that one year all the forces of impurity in the universe — the *kelippos* — banded together on the eve of Yom Kippur in order to make an impenetrable barrier that would not allow the prayers of Israel to ascend. However, as soon as people in the World Below started rattling their little bowls in solicitation of charity, and congregants around the globe created a clatter with the coins they threw in energetically, the *kelippos* were torn asunder by that very noise.

◦§ Nothing is by Chance

Yom Kippur would not begin until the close of the following day — but the journey to the town where the Baal Shem Tov lived was so long that a certain chassid decided to set out early. Just to be sure, he traveled all day and all night, and by daybreak on Yom Kippur Eve he was only a matter of miles away from his longed-for destination, Mezhibuzh.

"Now that I am so near the end of my journey, thank God," he said to himself, "and my poor old horse must be exhausted after such a long stretch, this is a good time for me to take a break and recite my morning prayers. The old nag can munch some grass and take it easy meanwhile."

But he was so sleepy after his prayers that he thought: יוֹם
"Why shouldn't I take a nap here for an hour or two? הַכִּפּוּרִים
The horse can rest too, and then we'll gallop along
energetically and still get to town before midday."

With that he sprawled out fatigued on his wagon. He
was overtaken by a deep slumber, and slept soundly until dusk. When he awoke and realized that the holy day
had already set in, he was most perturbed. What a bitter
disappointment! What effort and trouble had he gone to
in order to make his exhausting journey so that he could
spend this day of days in the presence of the Baal Shem
Tov! And here he was, only a few miles out of
Mezhibuzh, stranded out in the fields, alone, without as
much as a *minyan* with which to pray. All that night and
throughout the next day he wept, torn by anguish.

Night came, and Yom Kippur was over. He bridled his
horse and drove off quickly to Mezhibuzh, where he was
greeted by the Baal Shem Tov. A smile lit up on the face
of the tzaddik as he said: "Know, my good man, that
with your prayer you had to raise up to the heavens the
prayers of the people out in the fields, who throughout
this day did not join any congregation in prayer. And
that is why Divine Providence so arranged things that
you should spend Yom Kippur out there in the fields."

◆§ Don't Worry about Me

One year Reb Levi Yitzchak of Berditchev asked the
local synagogue wardens to announce that on the
following day, the eve of Yom Kippur, he would be
available throughout the day to receive *kvitlach*. Any
townsman who so desired was welcome to write down on
a slip of paper the subject of the prayer which he wished
the tzaddik to offer up on his behalf. There was only one
condition — that for each person who sought his intercession in heaven he was to be given a *pidyon* of two
copper coins, which would then find its way to a
charitable cause.

From early morning when he took his seat almost all
the townsfolk came along. Half of his table was covered
with little notes, and half with copper coins.

As sunset drew near and the whole congregation was

already assembled in the synagogue for the *Kol Nidrei* prayer, the elders saw that the tzaddik alone was absent, so they sent the beadle to call him. Reb Levi Yitzchak told the *shammes* that there were still a few people who were due to bring their *kvitlach*. While the *shammes* stood by and waited a woman came along with a note, and placed two copper coins on the table. The tzaddik told her that he would not accept her *kvitl*, for he saw that it bore two names, and she owed him another two coins.

"Holy rabbi!" she cried, "I've spent all day in search of a loan, and I managed to borrow two copper coins. That's all I have. Whatever else can I do?"

But the tzaddik was firm: less than that he would not accept.

"I know what!" exclaimed the woman. "Let's not worry about me: the two coins will be for my only son."

The tzaddik thereupon took her note and walked briskly off to the synagogue, where he was being waited for by so many worshipers, each of them about to begin a day of requests for himself.

And as he walked along he thought of the Children of Israel, who are God's beloved sons and cried out aloud: "I am going to follow the example of that wonderful mother, who isn't going to worry about herself — *so long as her child is saved!*"

◈§ It's the Thought that Counts

> The words [of prayer] are reckoned according to the intention of the heart (*Talmud, Tractate Berachos*).

Aged and weak, Reb Avraham Yehoshua Heschel of Apta lay in bed. By his side sat Reb Menachem Mendel of Rimanov, and near them sat Reb Naftali of Ropshitz, still a young man.

"Rabbi of Ropshitz!" said the bedridden tzaddik, who is commonly called the Ohev Yisrael ("the lover of his fellow Jew"). "What do you say to the language of the *Shemoneh Esreh* prayer on the eve of Yom Kippur this year?"

The rabbi of Ropshitz smiled.

Now the *shammes* who attended Reb Menachem Mendel of Rimanov was no simpleton. He approached Reb Naftali and asked him to explain what lay behind this little exchange. He did not quite dare to ask his own rebbe, nor would he be so bold as to ask the tzaddik of Apta.

Reb Naftali obliged, and explained that on the eve of that Day of Judgment a grievous decree had hovered over the House of Israel, threatening the lives of women, especially those that were with child. A simple villager was making his fervent requests at the afternoon *Minchah* prayer just before the fast-day began. As he was stumbling his unlettered way through the *Shemoneh Esreh* prayer he came to the words: וּבָרֵךְ שְׁנָתֵנוּ כַּשָּׁנִים הַטּוֹבוֹת — "Bless our year like the good years." In his ignorance the good man had transposed a few letters here and there: וּבָרֵךְ נְשׁוֹתֵינוּ כַּנָּשִׁים הַטּוֹבוֹת — "Bless our wives like the good women ... ." And on he went, until he arrived at the conclusion of that paragraph, which reads: בָּרוּךְ אַתָּה ה' מְבָרֵךְ הַשָּׁנִים — "Blessed art Thou, O Lord, Who blesses the years." Here too, with his urgent plea still foremost in his mind, he had earnestly read: מְבָרֵךְ הַנָּשִׁים — "Who blesses the womenfolk ... ."

His innocent prayer, surging forth from the deepest recesses of his heart, had risen to the highest heavens — and the decree was annulled.

And that was why the tzaddikim had exchanged a smile.

❈   ❈   ❈

Of all people, it was a tailor from Brody whom Reb Shalom of Belz summoned one Yom Kippur night to expound to him the meaning of a phrase from the Book of *Jeremiah* which is quoted in that day's prayers. The words in question were: אִם עֲוֹנֵינוּ עָנוּ בָנוּ — and the verse means: "O Lord, if our sins testify against us, act [benevolently] for the sake of Your Name."

"Rebbe, you amaze me," said the tailor. "Why, the meaning is perfectly clear."

And, untrammeled by mere considerations of grammar and spelling, he went straight ahead to explain the

yom verse: אִם עָוִינוּ — "Even though we have sinned," אָנוּ בָנוּ
kippur — "we are Your sons!"

So impressed was Reb Shalom with this novel interpretation that he repeated it over and over with delight.

◄§ A Stitch in Time

In his youth, Reb Mordechai of Neshchiz was one of the brotherhood of the disciples of Reb Dov Ber, the Maggid of Mezritch.

A message-boy in the household of the Maggid once came along to him and asked him for a donation. Reb Mordechai instructed his chassidim to lay him out on the table and to give him a sound slapping. When this was over, the youth returned to his place of work vexed and distressed. He was met there by Reb Moshe Leib of Sasov, who inquired as to the reason for his low spirits. He was shocked at the answer.

"How could a thing like this happen amongst us?" he cried.

But when word of the incident reached the Maggid, Reb Moshe Leib observed that his rebbe did not express any objection at all.

Years passed, and the Maggid passed away. Long after, that same messenger was stricken by paralysis that numbed his arms and his legs. His mother brought him to the tzaddik of Neshchiz who by now was renowned as a wonder-worker. Going out to see him lying prostrate in the wagon, Reb Mordechai recognized him at once, and said: "You were already chastised in your youth. You don't have to suffer any more. Stand up on your feet: you are healthy."

And so it was. The messenger stood up on his feet, and was as robust as ever.

◄§ A Mother's Tears

Is Ephraim not My beloved son, is he not a precious child? (*Book of Jeremiah*)

In keeping with honored custom, the sons and daughters of Reb Yaakov Yisrael of Kremenets would

always call on their saintly father during the late after- יום
noon of Yom Kippur Eve to receive his blessing. It so הכפורים
happened that one of his daughters once saw that she
would not have time to find him still at home, so she
quickly made her way to the synagogue, and waited for
him at the door. When the tzaddik arrived he found her
standing quietly there with a little child in her arms.
They were both crying.

The tzaddik addressed himself to his grandson: "Why
are you crying?"

"I see that my mother is crying," he replied, "so I'm
crying too."

The tzaddik entered the synagogue at once, went up to
the dais before the Holy Ark, and with tears in his eyes
told the congregation what the little boy had said. Then
he added: "If that young child cried after having seen his
mother weep only once, then surely, do we not all have
good cause to weep? For in our hearts of hearts we know
full well that the Divine Presence is weeping over the
state of Her children, as it is written: בְּמִסְתָּרִים תִּבְכֶּה נַפְשִׁי
— 'In hidden places My soul weeps.' And we know too
what our Sages teach us on this verse: 'A heavenly voice
murmurs like a dove and says, Woe to the sons through
whose sins I have destroyed My House and set fire to
My Sanctuary, and have exiled them amongst the nations of the world!'

"Then surely," concluded the tzaddik of Kremenets,
"do we do not all have good cause to weep?"

Hearing these words the entire congregation was
moved to tears. Indeed, the Chozeh of Lublin testified
that their resolve to repent was so earnest that it caused a
tumult in the very heavens.

◄§ A Time to Weep, and a Time to Laugh

In preparation for the Day of Judgment, Reb Shalom
Ber of Lubavitch would customarily remain awake
throughout the preceding night, and would recite the
Shacharis prayers at dawn. By noon he had completed
his festive meal — for Yom Kippur Eve bears the festive
name of *Yom-Tov* — and then he would recite *Psalms*

yom until one, and proceed with the afternoon's *Minchah* **kippur** service.

One morning, soon after the *Shacharis* prayers, a chassid from a nearby village called on the rebbe, and in a cheerful and confident voice wished him a good *Yom-Tov*.

The rebbe, who at that moment was soberly engrossed in his books, replied: "True enough, now is in fact *Yom-Tov*, a time of מוֹעֲדִים לְשִׂמְחָה — 'festivals for joy,' as we read in our prayers. But after all today is *Erev* Yom Kippur. At a time like this we should be arousing the deepest stirrings of repentance, regretting the follies of the past, and making firm resolves for the future."

"Rebbe," replied the villager, "we are soldiers. The Almighty has told us that Yom Kippur Eve is a *Yom-Tov* and has commanded us to be happy. After midday we are told to say the *Minchah* prayer, to read the confession and to repent. As for now, rebbe, would you give me some *lekach*, please?"

Well pleased with his answer, the tzaddik handed the villager a slice of the sweet cake that congregants traditionally give each other after the morning prayers on Yom Kippur Eve. "Here is your sweet *lekach*," he said, "and may the Almighty grant you a sweet year!"

ᵉᶳ More Eloquent than Words

כָּל נִדְרֵי
Kol Nidrei

One Yom Kippur Eve — so recounted Reb Tzvi Elimelech of Dinov — the Baal Shem Tov arrived at his *beis midrash* for the *Kol Nidrei* prayer in visible distress. After *Kol Nidrei* he rested a little while, and the worshipers around him saw that his melancholy vanished, and a new spirit animated him. In fact, he prayed the remainder of the evening service with joy and melody.

When after Yom Kippur his elder disciples asked him the meaning of this change in mood, he told them that in a certain village there had lived a leaseholder who was very much liked by his estate-owner. When the poor man and his wife passed away, this gentile squire felt compassion for the little orphan they had left alone. He took the child into his home and his heart, and brought

him up as his own. Needless to say he knew nothing of יום
Jewish law and faith, but the squire told him that he was הכפורים
born to Jewish parents, and now that he had adopted
him he would one day inherit all his possessions. He told
him further of the few meager chattels that his parents
had left behind them. He showed them to the child —
mere oddments, a few *Chumashim*, and the *Korban
Minchah* edition of the prayer book from which the
child's mother used to pray daily — fond mementos of
his unfortunate parents.

One morning, in the days before Rosh HaShanah
when people rise piously at dawn to recite the penitential
Selichos prayers, the child observed small groups of Jews
from the neighboring villages huddled in wagons which
trundled their way along the highway that led to town.

"Where are you going?" asked the curious little boy.

"Why," they said, "the Days of Awe are just around
the corner. On Rosh HaShanah the verdict is inscribed,
and on the fast of Yom Kippur it is sealed. So we're on
our way to yonder big town to pray with all our brothers
there. For God always has an ear for the prayers of the
many!"

From that moment the spirit of God stirred his soul,
for he had long known that he was of Jewish stock.
When he lay down to sleep that night his parents appeared to him in a dream.

"Come back to your faith," they urged him. "You are
a Jew!"

Night after night, throughout the Ten Days of
Penitence, he dreamed this dream. When he told his
benefactor of it he made nothing of it — but that did not
stop the dream from recurring. Indeed, one fearful night
he even dreamed that his parents threatened to punish
him if he did not return to the faith of his fathers. By the
time Yom Kippur Eve came, he again saw wagonloads of
Jews making their earnest way to town.

"And why are going there today?" he asked.

"We are getting ourselves ready for the Holy Day,"
they said, "for it is a day of forgiveness."

He darted home, took his mother's *Siddur* out of his
little bundle of belongings, and ran all the way to town.
He arrived at *shul* breathless, just in time for *Kol Nidrei*.

All around him stood the worshipers robed austerely in white, with their prayer books in their hands, and weeping quietly as they prayed. He too wept bitter tears, but the poor child did not know how to recite the prayers. With each anguished sob the seven heavens resounded. And the Baal Shem Tov, a witness from afar, shared the child's distress, and sought desperately to intercede in heaven that this wordless prayer be accepted, so that he be helped to remain constant in his resolve to follow the faith of his fathers.

Then the boy cried out: "Master of the Universe! I don't know what to pray or how to pray. So here you are, Master of the Universe: I'm giving you my whole *Siddur!*"

With this he bowed his head over the prayer book that lay open on the lectern before him, and wept honest tears. His prayer from that unread *Siddur* soared ever upward, and came to repose before the Throne of Mercy.

And that was when the melancholy of the Baal Shem Tov had vanished, and a new spirit animated him, and he prayed with a melody in his heart.

⋅⋅§ *Humiliation vs. Humility*

During the time when Reb Shmelke Horovitz was the Rabbi of Nikolsburg, there lived in the town a wealthy and prominent burgher who was a *misnaged*, an outspoken antagonist of the local chassidim. Once on the eve of Yom Kippur he decided to pay a visit to the tzaddik. He brought him a bottle of strong, old wine — ostensibly as a gift, but in fact as a ruse by which he hoped that the tzaddik would arrive at the synagogue tipsy, and make a fool of himself. To his glee, the tzaddik drank one glass after another as his guest eagerly filled them. Nevertheless when the sun was about to set, the tzaddik entered the synagogue in solemnity and awe, looking as always like the High Priest standing ready to perform his divine service in the Holy of Holies.

It was his custom year after year to spend the entire night and day of Yom Kippur in the synagogue. After the *Maariv* service in the evening he would recite the Book of *Psalms* aloud, leading the entire congregation who would repeat it after him verse by verse. This time too he did the same, until he reached the verse: בְּזֹאת יָדַעְתִּי כִּי חָפַצְתָּ בִּי כִּי לֹא יָרִיעַ אֹיְבִי עָלָי. The plain meaning of this verse is as follows: *By this I know that You favor me, because my enemy does not triumph over me.* But when Reb Shmelke reached it he repeated it several times over, and paraphrased it in Yiddish in such a way as to interpret it thus: "By this I know that You favor me, if You will bring no harm (רָעָה) upon my enemy on my account." Then he added: "And even though there may be enemies who desire to humiliate me, please forgive them! Let them not be punished because of me."

The congregants were electrified by this mystifying plea and together broke into tears. But one man present understood it full well. He made his way to the front of the synagogue, threw himself at the feet of the tzaddik, and confessed publicly to his unseemly stratagem.

The tzaddik responded quietly: "Do not imagine that I accepted the post of rabbi of Nikolsburg for the sake of honor. No, my son. If you were to humiliate Shmelke, what a great favor would you be doing him! From how many transgressions would you have cleansed him if you had brought him to shame and scorn! And what a pity indeed that this was withheld from me!"

Hearing a reaction of this nature the poor penitent wept even more bitterly. He begged to be forgiven and thereafter held Reb Shmelke in esteem and affection all the days of his life.

◆§ A Toast to the Creator

The synagogue was hushed, the worshipers were expectant — but Reb Levi Yitzchak of Berditchev, who stood before them at the lectern, robed in white, as they waited for him to thrill the air with the haunting strains of *Kol Nidrei*, remained silent. Dusk thickened into night, but still the tzaddik stood silent. Struck by wonder, restrained by awe, no man ventured to approach him and to remind him that it was time to begin.

Suddenly the door flew open. A simple fellow bustled his way inside, found a spot to stand and pray at the back wall — and the tzaddik began *Kol Nidrei*.

The curiosity of the congregants ran high. As soon as
the prayers were over they surrounded the stranger and
showered him with questions from all sides: "Who are
you?" "What brings you here?" — and so on.

"I'm just an ordinary tailor," protested the little man,
"and I live in a village."

"Come now," they insisted. "Do we seem to you like
the kind of folks who can be satisfied with some lame excuse like that? Didn't we see with our own eyes that our
rebbe held up the prayers until you arrived?"

But they could not extract another word out of him.

"We're not going to let you out of here," they warned
him, "until you reveal to us your true identity."

The deadlock was finally broken by the question of
one of the locals: "Perhaps you'd like to tell us why you
came to *shul* so late, and how you spent your day?"

"Okay," said the tailor, "I'll confess the whole truth.
This morning, Yom Kippur Eve, at breakfast, I poured
myself a wee bit too much of the bitter drop. After that
my head was heavy, so I lay down a bit to rest. But when
I finally woke up I saw that I wouldn't have time to eat a
square meal before the fast and travel to town here as
well. So I decided to forget about the meal, and just
poured myself a tiny glass of vodka — just enough to say
LeChaim. But I didn't have anyone around to say
LeChaim to! So what did I do? I decided to say *LeChaim*
to the Almighty. So I said: 'LeChaim, Master of the
Universe! Let's talk brass tacks. In the course of this last
year — begging Your pardon, Master of the Universe —
You haven't quite behaved Yourself. Look how many
women you left widowed, look how many children have
been orphaned! How many fathers have You taken from
their children, and how many children have You taken
from their parents! And not only that. If we investigate a
little bit more, we'll even discover that You're guilty of
talebearing. Because how did my local squire ever find
out about that spot of monkey business with the remnants of cloth, if You hadn't helped him smell a rat? ...
Nevertheless, Master of the Universe, we're willing to
forgive You for everything — provided that You forgive
us too.' Then I drank down the vodka, and set out to
town to pray in your synagogue here."

His listeners heard his story, and let him go his way. And after the Day of Judgment the tzaddik of Berditchev told them that the *LeChaim* of that tailor had burst its way through all the heavens; it was only right that they should all wait for him for *Kol Nidrei*.

◆§ Your Own Words

One Yom Kippur night, when in the course of the prayers Reb Levi Yitzchak of Berditchev came to the verse: וַיֹּאמֶר ה' סָלַחְתִּי כִּדְבָרֶיךָ ("And God said, 'I have forgiven according to your words' "), he interrupted the service and turned to address the congregation.

"Gentlemen," he said. "Do not our Sages teach us that 'He who cites a quotation in the name of him who first said it brings redemption to the world' (כָּל הָאוֹמֵר דָּבָר בְּשֵׁם אוֹמְרוֹ מֵבִיא גְאוּלָה לָעוֹלָם)? Very well, then, let us together say something in the name of its author: '**And God said, I have forgiven according to your words**'!"

◆§ The Price of a Dog

The sun had already set, but still the Chozeh of Lublin did not start intoning *Kol Nidrei*. The congregants were puzzled enough by his silence, but were puzzled still more when he turned around to face those standing near him and said: "Call me the man from Pelov, if he is here with us."

A man from Pelov immediately stepped forward, and the rebbe asked him: "Would you happen to know how much the local squire paid for the dog that he bought this year?"

"I was in the house of the *paritz* at the very time that he bought it," said the man. "He paid one thousand gold rubles."

The tzaddik turned around again, and with a joyful voice began to sing *Kol Nidrei*. And the man from Pelov was as nonplussed as everyone else.

On *Motzaei* Yom Kippur, when the Day of Judgment was over, the Chozeh explained what had happened. At the height of the trial of the House of Israel, the prosecuting angels had raised a furor in the Heavenly

Court. They were pointing an accusing finger which could not be ignored, for not long before a penniless Jew had done the rounds of the doors of his wealthy brethren, asking them to help him marry off his daughter. And if the truth must be stated, they had not responded with their accustomed generosity. Sorely tried, the poor Jew had then knocked on the door of this gentile *paritz*, who immediately handed him three hundred silver rubles!

"I therefore challenge this Court," the Prosecuting Angel had concluded sarcastically, "to prove the existence of the House of Israel's supposedly *'unfailing and — er — compassionate* generosity' which we are always hearing so much about ... "

And at that crucial moment, when the threat of a dire verdict hovered darkly over the heads of the community of Israel, the Chozeh had stepped forward. As soon as his voice was heard in the Heavenly Court, he silenced the Prosecutor with a counter-argument: "Does the Court suppose that the wealthy squire gave that amount because he felt compassion for the suffering Jew? Not at all! He did it simply because money is of absolutely no value in his eyes — as witness the fact that on a mere dog he squandered one thousand gold rubles!"

The verdict was quashed.

⋖§ Knowing What to Request

Standing obscurely near the back door of the synagogue amongst all the poor craftsmen of his town was Reb Shabsai the bookbinder. That Yom Kippur, after the silent *Shemoneh Esreh* of the Evening Service, a petty argument broke out among the congregants, some of whom disapproved of the way in which the *chazzan* had been leading the prayers. Reb Shabsai took no notice of their rumblings, and continued to take his time concentrating over his prayers.

When he was finished, one of the humble fold nearby approached him and said: "Shabsai, I see you've taken a long time over *Shemoneh Esreh*, and at the same time secured yourself a prosperous New Year. Because while our friends here were having their little argument, each of them stressed his point by slapping his *Machzor* energetically. Some tried to signal the *chazzan* to give up and stop singing altogether. Others tried to urge him by the same sign that he should sing more loudly. The upshot of it all is that the covers of plenty of prayer books must be falling off by now — and you're going to be blessed with enough work to keep you busy right through your prosperous New Year!"

"No," replied Reb Shabsai quietly, "I succeeded in having myself inscribed for a better year than *that*. For this year a son will be born to us who will light up the world."

And within the year his wife gave birth to the child who was to become renowned as Reb Yisrael, the Maggid of Koznitz.

⊷§ One Word from Your Mouth

It was to be the last Yom Kippur spent by Reb Yisrael, the Maggid of Koznitz, in This World and, as always, he began to lead the congregation in the evening prayers. He soon came to the verse: וַיֹּאמֶר ה' סָלַחְתִּי כִּדְבָרֶיךָ — "And God said, 'I have forgiven according to your words.'"

At this point he stopped short and said: "Master of the Universe! Who can express the extent of Your might? (For there is no might save Yours!) As Joseph Albo wrote in his wisdom: אִלּוּ יְדַעְתִּיו, הֱיִיתִיו — 'Were I to know Him, I would *be* Him.' And the extent of my physical weakness likewise no man knows — but You alone. For as you see, it has been my custom year after year to lead the congregation in prayer every day, and this year I had to break with that custom. And You, Master of the Universe, know that the reason is simply my failing health. You also know that this year during Elul, the month of penitence, when I did lead the worshipers in their prayers and petitions, I did not do it for my sake but only for the sake of Your people, Israel. I therefore have one question for You. Why is it easy for me to undertake to bear the yoke of Your children, and despite the weakness of my constitution to toil in prayer for their sake, while You, Master of the Universe, Who are mighty and powerful, find it difficult just to utter the two words סָלַחְתִּי כִּדְבָרֶיךָ — 'I have forgiven according to your words'?"

Then he went on: "Perhaps You are thinking that there aren't any tzaddikim in the world, and that is why You do not say those two words? — But look: in Rimanov You have Reb Mendele of Fristik, who equals all the righteous men of the entire generation! Or perhaps Your reason for not saying those two words is that today You no longer have the sacred oracle of the Urim and Tummim? — But in Lublin You've got the Chozeh, Reb Yaakov Yitzchak the Seer, who radiates light like the gems of that sacred breastplate that hung over the heart of Aharon the High Priest! Or perhaps You will argue that what the world is lacking is *baalei teshuvah*, genuine penitents? — Then here I am, though weak in body, ready to repent for the entire House of Israel! Now please, *Ribbono shel Olam*, I beg of You: say סָלַחְתִּי — 'I have forgiven'!"

And he repeated his request three times.

Soon after, he called on his choirboys to harmonize a sweet and happy melody. Then, in a voice loud and clear, he himself called out the awesome words: וַיֹּאמֶר ה' סָלַחְתִּי כִּדְבָרֶיךָ — "And God said, 'I have forgiven according to your words.'"

❀   ❀   ❀

When certain men who were present repeated this incident to Reb Yisrael of Ruzhin, he said: "I believe with perfect faith that the Maggid of Koznitz heard those words from the mouth of the Almighty Himself, just as Moshe Rabbeinu did; and if not, *he would not have continued with the evening service.*"

And on the same Yom Kippur night, after the evening prayers, the Chozeh of Lublin was heard to say: "God grant that when this Day passes we will hear glad tidings from Koznitz, for there is an ailing man there who from his sickbed hurled echoes throughout all the heavens."

◅§ *What the Doctor Prescribed*

I t was 1812, and in the course of Napoleon's bold march on Moscow a vast contingent of French soldiers tramp-

ing through Poland encamped at Pshischah, the hometown of Reb Simchah Bunem. Now before he was appointed rebbe, this tzaddik practiced as an apothecary.
So it was that in the middle of the *Kol Nidrei* service,
while he was standing before the whole congregation, a
squad of soldiers knocked on the synagogue door,
flourishing a medical prescription which the regimental
doctor required at once for a certain officer. Observing
that he was engrossed in the silent *Shemoneh Esreh*
prayer they waited until he was ready to listen to them.
He read the prescription, assured them that after the
service he would call on the commanding officer himself,
and they left.

Returning to his home after the service, he was
amazed to be met there by the regimental doctor and his
children. They were all sitting on the floor in tears, and
begging him to save their lives by not going to visit the
commanding officer. It transpired that he had written
out the prescription with the malicious intent of disturb-
ing the tzaddik during prayer. The Almighty had caused
him to err while writing it, and he now realized that in
his confusion he had prescribed a lethal dose. In time of
war a false step like this could cost him his life.

Word of this little drama soon got around, and in no
time all the townspeople of Psischah were crowding
around Reb Simchah Bunem's home. Indeed, so many
people heard the doctor's words that his confession of
the truth was a veritable sanctification of the Divine
Name.

At first Reb Simchah Bunem was adamant in his
refusal to forgive the mischiefmaker. The desperate fellow even threw himself on the floor at the feet of the
townsfolk, pleading with them that they should intercede with their *rav* on his behalf. But only when he
promised never again to do harm to any Jew did the tzaddik finally forgive him.

◄§ A Name that Rings a Bell

It was the custom of Reb Yisrael of Ruzhin to speak of
Reb Levi Yitzchak of Berditchev every year on the
night of Yom Kippur. He explained this by saying that

yom kippur since that tzaddik was the arch advocate of the People of Israel in the Heavenly Court, the mere mention of his name serves to moderate the sternness of the verdict on the Day of Judgment.

The son of Reb Yisrael of Ruzhin, Reb Avraham Yaakov of Sadigora, went further: "The mere mention of even the *town* of Berditchev is enough to activate the merit of Rav Levi Yitzchak on Israel's behalf. This can be proved by an analogy from the *mishnah* in Tractate *Yoma* which describes the procedure followed in the Temple on the morning of the Day of Atonement. There we find that when the sentry standing on a high vantage point in the *Beis HaMikdash* was asked at dawn whether there was enough daylight to begin the day's offerings, he was not asked the question directly. Instead, he was asked whether the rays of the sun had already reached — 'until [those who are in] Hebron.' Explaining this circumlocution, *Rashi* quotes the Jerusalem Talmud: that the burial place of the Patriarchs was thus mentioned — 'in order to recall the merit of the Patriarchs.'"

◆§ *A Life for a Life*

צוֹם הֶעָשׂוֹר
The fast of the tenth day

Among those who visited Reb Yisrael of Ruzhin every year at the Days of Awe was a chassid by the name of Reb Asher. The tzaddik showed him visible marks of respect, and said of him that he was the possessor of a lofty soul. This chassid was however a man of very frail health, and since he suffered from a serious lung condition the tzaddik used to order him every year to break his fast on Yom Kippur. He would take him into his private study between *Shacharis* and the *Musaf* service, and there see to it that Reb Asher took some light refreshment that his rebbe had prepared for him.

On Yom Kippur in the year 1849, however, Reb Yisrael became so deeply engrossed in the *Shacharis* service that he did not leave the synagogue at all for the brief break which he usually took, and even forgot about Reb Asher altogether. The chassid persevered in his fast to the end of the day, and completed it in a state of exhaustion. On the following day he passed away.

When word of this reached the tzaddik he was deeply

grieved, and said — "A life for a life." And his chassidim יום
understood that he was referring to himself. הכפורים

On the following Yom Kippur, in the year 1850, Reb
Yisrael suffered an agonizing thirst. He turned to the
worshipers in his synagogue and said: "I am thirsty!"

But of all the prominent rabbis who were assembled, it
did not occur to a solitary one of them that if the tzaddik
said this, he must have felt that his life depended on it,
that it was a question of setting aside the prohibition on
drinking in order to save a life. So it was that they all
held their peace. And since none of them took the in-
itiative to urge him to break his fast he suffered so intensely that he developed a heart ailment. No treatment
availed, and three weeks later, on the third of
MarCheshvan, he returned his soul to his Maker.

⋅§ A Drink to Your Health

R eb David Moshe of Chortkov once told the following
story to illustrate the degree to which Reb Uri of
Strelisk loved his fellow Jew in fulfillment of the mitzvah of *ahavas Yisrael.*

One Yom Kippur, in the middle of the night, Reb Uri
observed his attendant waking up, running across the
room, drinking thirstily, and going back to sleep. Seeing
how thirsty he appeared to be, Reb Uri understood that
this must have been a question of life and death. If
therefore he were to remind him that it was Yom Kippur,
the *meshares* might endanger his life by refraining from
drinking.

A little later the attendant again jumped up and ran as
in a frenzy, and again drank a whole cupful. This time
too the tzaddik neither attempted to persuade him to
refrain, nor did he even mention that it was Yom Kippur.
For could it not be that the man still stood in danger of
his life?

When the same story repeated itself again, however,
Reb Uri was certain that the thirsty man was no longer in
danger. He called him across and told him calmly: "You
know, it's Yom Kippur today."

The attendant sprang back in shock, and was dis-

yom tressed that through his forgetfulness he was guilty of
kippur having drunk on the fast-day.

❈ ❈ ❈

"So intensely did the fire of *ahavas Yisrael* burn in
Reb Uri's heart," concluded Reb David Moshe, "that
with all the awe that Yom Kippur commanded in him, he
was utterly incapable of causing anguish and the risk of
danger to a fellow Jew by reminding him that this was
indeed the Day of Atonement."

ᴥ§ The Joy of the Obedient

So dangerously ill was Reb Menachem Mendel of
Vizhnitz that when Yom Kippur approached, his doctors forbade him to fast. Fearful that he might ignore this
instruction — which the Torah of course would oblige
him to heed — his chassidim turned to Reb Yehoshua of
Belz: perhaps *he* could persuade their rebbe to eat.

Reb Yehoshua thereupon wrote the ailing tzaddik a
letter which ran as follows: "When my late father, Reb
Sar Shalom of Belz, was dangerously ill one Yom Kippur, I recall how anxious we were lest he refuse to eat.
Being the saintly man he was, though, he tackled this
task with the same alacrity that he brought to the performance of any regular mitzvah. Immediately after the
evening prayers he asked that food be brought to him,
for he was under doctor's orders to eat at that hour. He
then said, as he was accustomed to say before he performed many other mitzvos: הֲרֵינִי מוּכָן וּמְזוּמָן לְקַיֵּים
מִצְוַת בּוֹרְאִי ... — 'I am herewith ready and willing to
fulfill the commandment of my Creator as laid down by
the Sages.' He then ate with a joy that could be equalled
only by the joy he experienced on *Seder* night in the performance of the mitzvah of eating *matzah,* or on Sukkos
when he pronounced the blessing over the *lulav.*"

ᴥ§ Thoughts during Prayer

The *chazzan* who was to lead the *Shacharis* prayers on
the morning of Yom Kippur arrived very late at the
synagogue of Reb Sar Shalom of Belz. He had stayed

back at his inn to make a cup of tea for another lodger יום
who was seriously ill, and by the time he arrived the הכפורים
service was well under way.

A few minutes later, when it was his turn to step
forward and to intone the passage beginning: הַמֶּלֶךְ, in
which the King of Kings is addressed in all His awe, he
shuddered. For at that moment there came to mind the
retort which the Roman general Vespasian made to Rabbi Yochanan ben Zakkai when the latter addressed him
as king: — "If I *am* a king, why did you not come to address me as such *until now?*"

When the *Shacharis* service was over, Reb Sar Shalom
of Belz approached the *chazzan* and asked: "What was it
that came over you today during the morning prayers?"

The poor fellow was terrified. Clearly his rebbe's
question was intended to rebuke him on two counts:
firstly, for desecration of the holy day by preparing the
hot drink for the sick stranger, and secondly, for coming
to *shul* so late. He therefore launched forth at once on an
explanation which would excuse his conduct.

He barely started when the tzaddik cut him short:
"Ah! For I *felt* that some deed of unusual merit had come
your way today. Do not our Sages say: — 'Whoever
saves the life of one fellow Jew, it is as if he preserved the
entire world'? Be assured, my good man, that your
prayers have been accepted On High. Your reward will
be rich!"

◆§ A Money-Back Remedy

A minor commotion drew everyone's attention just
before the concluding *Ne'ilah* service of Yom Kippur
in the synagogue of Reb Chaim of Zanz. A local magnate
— a notorious skinflint — had just about fainted of thirst.
There were those present who even took the liberty of a
jibe at his expense: "Throughout the year he was too
mean to give a beggar a drop of water to drink: let him
feel the taste of thirst himself!"

But when those around him saw that his life might be
in jeopardy they quickly approached the rabbis to ask
for instructions. They were duly told to give him spoonful after spoonful of water at intervals, less than a

yom
kippur mouthful at a time. But with each spoonful his thirst only grew stronger. At this point Reb Beirish the *dayyan*, who was the head of the local rabbinical court, was no longer willing to rely on his own opinion. He approached the tzaddik, interrupted him in the midst of his divine service, told him the whole story, and asked him what to do.

Reb Chaim's answer was simple: "Tell him that for every cup of water he drinks today he is to give a hundred coins tomorrow for charity. If he is agreeable to that, let him drink as much as he wants."

The message was relayed, and the skinflint's thirst vanished as if by a miracle.

◆§ A Reason to Rejoice

עַל חֵטְא
The
confession Arriving at a certain town once before Rosh HaShanah, the Baal Shem Tov asked the local people who led the congregation in prayer during the Days of Awe, and was told that the *rav* of the town acted as *sheliach tzibur* himself.

"And how does he conduct himself during the prayers?" the tzaddik asked them.

In the course of their reply they told him that on the Day of Atonement their *rav* had the unusual custom of singing the lengthy confession to jolly melodies.

The Baal Shem Tov at once called for this man. On asking him the meaning of his custom he was answered as follows: "If the lowliest of a king's servants, whose task it is to rake away the filth from the gutters of the royal courtyard, *loves his king*, then as he works he sings with joy out of the sheer pleasure he derives from making him happy!"

"If this is what you have in mind while you are at prayer," said the tzaddik, "would that my lot be at one with yours!"

◆§ An Infinity of Forgiveness

Reb Yisrael of Ruzhin was visiting Odessa on the orders of his doctors who had advised him to bathe in the sea. While there he heard that in the city there lived a

grandson of the celebrated Rabbi Yaakov Emden by the
name of Meir, who had jettisoned the ways of his
fathers, and was living in poverty. Reb Yisrael invited
him to join him on his return to Ruzhin, where all his
needs would be attended to. The tzaddik was as good as
his word. Not only did he attend to all of Meir's material
needs, but in addition he guided him along the path of
repentance.

He nevertheless found him one day looking very
despondent. He asked for the reason, and added: "If it's
because of your transgressions, then repentance is effective."

"I have sinned so much," explained the unfortunate
fellow, "and I have sinned again even after repenting, so
that I am no longer certain if my *teshuvah* will ever again
be acceptable. How then should I not be dejected?"

"They say that in your time you had a reputation as an
ilui in Talmudic scholarship," said the tzaddik, "so let
me answer you in the language of scholars.

"In the prayers of the Day of Atonement we say:
'For You are the Forgiver (סָלְחָן) of Israel and the Par-
doner (מָחְלָן) for the Tribes of Yeshurun' (i.e., of Israel).
Now why this noun form — סָלְחָן and מָחְלָן — instead of
the verbal form we would normally expect: סוֹלֵחַ and
מוֹחֵל?

"This we can understand by considering a similar construction elsewhere. In the Torah we read: 'If you see
the donkey of a person that hates you lying (רֹבֵץ) under
its load, and would refrain from unloading it, you shall
surely unload it with him.' In discussing the manner in
which this obligation applies, the Talmud notes that the
word used in the Torah is רֹבֵץ, rather than רַבְצָן. The latter word Rashi explains as referring to an animal which
habitually lies down under its load. From this we see that
the letter ן *nun,* at the end of the word indicates an *ongoing* status. And so too in our case. The words סָלְחָן and
מָחְלָן indicate that even if a man slips back and sins again
after repenting — and even if this repeats itself many
times over — the Almighty nevertheless forgives him
each time afresh."

⋖§ A Soul Sings

When the minstrel played, the hand of God came upon him (*II Kings*).

It was Reb Moshe Teitelbaum who gave the following description of Reb Shmelke of Nikolsburg at prayer on *Shabbos* and festivals.

During the Days of Awe in particular, and especially during the *Avodah* — the graphic description given in the Yom Kippur prayers of the service of the *Kohen Gadol* in the Temple — as he said the words אֶחָת, אַחַת, וְאַחַת and so on, Reb Shmelke used to pause between one word and the next. While so doing the most wondrous melodies would pour forth from his mouth, melodies which had never been heard before by his ear nor by the ear of any man. Nor did he himself know what melodies these were or whence they came, for his thoughts during those hours were roaming freely in the world Above, where they found a place to leave. And all the while those around him stood transfixed by the enchantment of his song.

⋖§ Divine Service

The *Kohen Gadol* entered the Holy of Holies to take out the spoon and the ashpan of the incense (*Talmud, Tractate Yoma*).

Whenever Reb Elazar of Ternigrad used to visit Reb Yaakov Yitzchak, the Chozeh of Lublin, his host would always make a point of personally attending to his needs in some way, in fulfillment of the mitzvah of waiting on a Torah scholar. Once, after serving his guest coffee, he returned the cup to its place. The guest thereupon asked why he should trouble himself even for this detail.

The Chozeh replied: "When the *Kohen Gadol* took out the empty incense spoon and the ashpan from the Holy of Holies on Yom Kippur, this too was part of the divine service of the *Avodah*."

◄§ Cause No Anguish

In order not to cause anguish to Israel
(*Talmud, Tractate Yoma*).

A few days before Yom Kippur, Reb Nasan David of
Shidlovitz caught such a severe chill that his doctors forbade him to immerse himself in the *mikveh*.
When the eve of the holy day arrived, the tzaddik mentioned to those around him that he intended to ignore the
advice of his doctors, since — "Those undertaking a mission for the sake of a mitzvah do not come to harm."

He was challenged by one of his learned chassidim:
"Rebbe, is there not an explicit statement in the Mishnah
on this subject? On his way out of the Holy of Holies
after burning the incense, the *Kohen Gadol* did not pray
at length, 'in order not to cause anguish to Israel,' since
the waiting congregation were anxious lest he come to
harm in that awesome place. In the same way, even
though you yourself, Rebbe, are certain that the immersion will not affect your health, yet we chassidim are
fearful. It follows that you are obligated to refrain from
going to the *mikveh* 'in order not to cause anguish to
Israel.' "

The *rebbe* however had a reply: "Reb Shlomo of
Radomsk used to interpret that passage otherwise:
"What was the *content* of the short prayer which the
Kohen Gadol offered? — It was "Do not cause anguish to
Israel." Since Israel stand in fear of the Day of Judg-
ment, and of exile, and of all kinds of other tribulations,
the High Priest used to plead with the Almighty — 'that
He should not cause anguish to Israel.' "

◄§ Praying with Others

It once happened that Reb Avraham, the Maggid of
Trisk, passed through Volodovka, which was then the
hometown of Reb Tzadok HaKohen, later of Lublin. On
Shabbos, he addressed the gathering at his *tish* on the
subject of tzaddikim who say their daily prayers at times
other than those prescribed by law. Whatever time a

yom tzaddik devotes to prayer, he said, is a propitious time, at
kippur which his prayer is found acceptable.

In support of this statement he cited the comment of
the Midrash on a verse in *Lamentations:* "Even when I
cry and call for help, he stops up my prayer." In praising
worship with a congregation as opposed to individual
prayer, the Midrash says: "If one prays together with
tzaddikim, to what may this be likened? — To a group of
men who fashion a crown for their king. Along comes a
pauper and adds his contribution. What then does the
king say? 'Just because this man is a pauper, shall I
therefore not accept the crown?' And he takes it at once
and places it on his head. Likewise, if ten righteous men
join in prayer and one sinful man stands among them,
what then does the Almighty say? 'Because of this one
sinful man, shall I therefore not accept their prayer?'"

When this teaching was reported to "the kohen," as
Reb Tzadok was known, he raised an objection: the
Midrash says כָּל הַמִתְפַּלֵל עִם הַצִבּוּר — "If one prays together with a *congregation;*" it does not say עִם הַצַדִיקִים
— "with *tzaddikim.*"

Word of this found its way back to the Maggid, who
replied that this wording was the result of a printer's error. The copy used had given an abbreviation, as is common in Rabbinic works. Seeing the letters עם הצ', the
printer had expanded it to עִם הַצִבּוּר ("with a congregation"), whereas in fact the text should have read
עִם הַצַדִיקִים ("with tzaddikim").

Chassidim busily researched old printed editions of
the Midrash, and found that the Maggid of Trisk was
right. And for some time thereafter Reb Tzadok was
grieved at having levelled his criticism.

Many years later, when he was living in Lublin, the
Maggid of Trisk spent some days in the city. This was
the opportunity that Reb Tzadok had been waiting for.
He decided to pay the Maggid a visit and to make
amends.

When he arrived the Maggid said: "I envy you, who
are constantly engaged in the study of Torah and the
service of the Creator, whereas I am always wandering
from place to place."

Replied Reb Tzadok: "Not so. Your own service is

loftier than mine. In fact the High Priest used to perform יום
his divine service in the *Beis HaMikdash* on only one day הכפורים
in the year."

⋖§ *Straight from the Heart (i)*

Open the gate for us at the time that the gate is נְעִילָה
locked (*Neilah* Service).

Ne'ilah,
the

After the passing of the Baal Shem Tov, one of his *concluding*
elder disciples by the name of Reb David of Mikliev *service*
adopted Reb Pinchas of Korets as his spiritual mentor.
His custom was that every time he made the journey to
Korets he would take one of his own disciples with him
as a traveling companion.

Once on the eve of Yom Kippur, Reb David drank
mead in preparation for the fast, and the young disciple
who had accompanied him to Korets did likewise — except that the sweet beverage put him into such a stupor
that he slept from the beginning of the fast, right
through the night and the day. By the time he awoke it
was close to sunset: the congregation was already beginning to recite *Ne'ilah*, the concluding service of the holy
day. He realized that he had lost the precious hours
without having said even a word of prayer, and from the
depths of his heart cried out aloud in his anguish. No one
could pacify him. Just imagine: a man goes to all the
trouble of making the arduous journey in order that he
should be able to worship in the company of tzaddikim.
And in the end what does he do? He flounders in sleep,
and doesn't even simply recite the prayers like the most
unpretentious Jew in town. And on he wailed, contrite
and brokenhearted, while the congregation went ahead
and finished their prayers.

When *Havdalah* had been recited to mark the passing
of Yom Kippur, Reb Pinchas of Korets asked Reb
David: "Who was that young man who cried out so
violently during the *Ne'ilah* service?"

So Reb David told him that this was the young man
whom he had brought with him.

"This young man," said the tzaddik, "illumined my
eyes. Let me explain. The prosecuting angels were lining
up a fearful verdict for the whole House of Israel. Their

case grew more eloquent at *Ne'ilah* time when the worshipers were already weary after a long day in the synagogue. There was nothing I could do about the state of affairs in the Heavenly Court, because for that the congregation had to be spiritually wide-awake and praying energetically. I was deeply distressed. Then suddenly the outcry of this young man made all the heavens resound. The more vigorously he cried, the more was the voice of the prosecution dimmed. In the end, thanks to his prayers straight from the heart, I was able (thank God!) to have the verdict annulled altogether.

"Give that young man my thanks!"

◆§ Straight from the Heart (ii)

So earnest were his supplications, so desperately did he plead, that the disciples of the Baal Shem Tov realized that the balance of judgment On High at this critical moment — the *Ne'ilah* service — did not augur well for the House of Israel. They redoubled the intensity of their prayer. Seeing this, the congregants around them and in the women's gallery were likewise electrified. Their hearts were shaken within them, and they too wept as they prayed.

This scene was being watched all along by a shepherd boy from a nearby village, who had come to town in order to spend the Days of Awe in the synagogue of the Baal Shem Tov. Since he was quite illiterate, he simply stood and observed the face of the *chazzan* as he led that fervent congregation. He sensed the terror in the air, and saw people weeping on all sides around him. He too was moved to give vent to his feelings. Now of all the sounds that he knew from the farmyard, the one that most appealed to him was the cock's crow. So filled his lungs and burst forth at the top of his voice: "Cock-a-doodle-do! God, have mercy on us!"

The men were shocked by this outburst, and the women were alarmed. Indeed some of the congregants were so outraged that they tried to silence him, and would even have forced him to leave. But he had an answer: "*I'm* Jewish, too!"

A few moments later they could all hear the Baal Shem

Tov and his disciples making haste to complete the service before the holy day came to an end. The face of the tzaddik was radiant. With a melodious voice he sang repetition of the *Shemoneh Esreh* of *Ne'ilah*, and with visible elation led his chassidim in the reading of the verses which declare the unity to the Creator: שְׁמַע יִשְׂרָאֵל — "Hear O Israel"; בָּרוּךְ שֵׁם — "Blessed be His Name"; ה' הוּא הָאֱלֹקִים — "The Lord is God." And he rounded off the day's prayers by singing a medley of joyous melodies.

That night, as the tzaddik sat at his table, he told the chassidim who surrounded him that a dire threat had hung over a certain community. When he had sought to intercede on their behalf, the Heavenly Court had turned its accusations against *him:* had he not urged his followers to settle in villages and at the crossroads of country highways, where they stood in danger of learning from the evil example of the gentiles among whom they lived? And as the Heavenly Court began to investigate the lifestyle of those Jewish villages, the Baal Shem Tov saw what a dread sentence would soon be meted out to them.

But right at that very moment the heavens rang forth with a strange outcry: "Cock-a-doodle-do! God, have mercy on us!"

So pleased was the Heavenly Court with this prayer that the accusations against the threatened community and against the Baal Shem Tov were silenced forthwith.

◆§ Straight from the Heart (iii)

Torrents of rain beat down on his face, but the tempest did not prevent Reb Leib Sarah's from reaching a village, only several hours before the beginning of Yom Kippur. He was some distance from his intended destination, but he was relieved to learn that in this village too there would be a *minyan* with which to pray — eight local villagers would be joined by two men who lived in the nearby forest. He immersed himself in the purifying waters of a river in preparation for the holy day, ate the meal which precedes the fast, and hastened to be the first in the little wooden synagogue. There he

yom kippur settled down to recite the various private devotions with which he was accustomed to inaugurate the Day of Atonement.

One by one the eight local villagers arrived in time to hear the words of *Kol Nedrei* — but there was no *minyan*, for it transpired that the two Jewish foresters had been arrested on some malicious lie.

"Perhaps we could find just *one* more Jew living around these parts?" asked Reb Leib.

"No," the villagers all assured him. "there's only us."

"Perhaps," he persisted, "there lives here some Jew who converted out of the faith of his fathers?"

The villagers were shocked to hear such an odd question from the stranger. They looked upon him quizzically.

"The doors of repentance are not locked even in the face of an apostate," Reb Leib continued. "I have heard from my teachers that even when one pokes about in the ashes one can light upon a spark of fire ... "

One of the villagers now spoke up.

"There is one apostate here," he ventured. "He is our *paritz*, the squire who owns this whole village. But this *meshummad* has now been sunk in sin these forty years. You see, the gentile daughter of the previous squire fell in love with him. So her father promised him that if he converted and married the girl, he would make him his sole heir. He didn't withstand the temptation, so he did exactly that."

"Did his gentile wife bear him any sons or daughters?" asked Reb Leib.

"No," they all chorused. "She died some years ago, and he was left childless."

"Show me his mansion," said Reb Leib.

He removed his *tallis* in a flash, and ran as fast as he could in the direction of the mansion, with his white skullcap on his head and his white *kittel* billowing in the wind. He knocked on the heavy door, opened it without waiting for a response, and found himself confronting the squire. For a few long, long moments they stood in silence face to face, the tzaddik and the apostate. The latter's first thought was to summon one of his henchmen to seize the uninvited intruder and hurl him into the

dungeon in the back yard. But the luminous countenance יום
and the penetrating eyes of the tzaddik softened his הכפורים
heart.

"My name is Leib Sarah's," began the visitor. "It was
my privilege to know Reb Yisrael, the Baal Shem Tov,
who was admired even by numerous noblemen. From his
mouth I once heard the every Jew should utter the short
prayer that was first said by King David: 'Save me, O
Lord, from blood-guilt.' (מִדָּמִים) But דָּמִים means not only
blood, but also money. So my Teacher expounded the
verse as follows: '*Save me*, so that I should never regard
money as my *Lord* ... '

"Now my mother, whose name was Sarah, was a holy
woman. One day the son of one of the local gentry took
it into his head to marry her, and promised her wealth
and status if she would agree. But she sanctified the
name of Israel. In order to save herself from that villain
she quickly got married to an old Jewish pauper who was
a schoolteacher. You did not have the good fortune to
withstand the test, and for silver and gold you were willing to apostatize. Realize, though, that there is nothing
that can stand in the way of repentance. Moreover, there
are those who in one hour earn their portion in the
World to Come. *Now is that hour!* Today is the eve of
Yom Kippur. The sun will soon set. The Jews who live in
your village are short of one man to make up a *minyan*.
Come along now with me, and be the tenth man. For the
Torah tells us: 'The tenth shall be holy unto God.' "

The squire paled at the words spoken by this man
with the singular face and who was clothed in white.
And meanwhile, down the road, the eight local villagers
waited in *shul*, huddled together in frozen dread. Who
could tell what calamity this odd stranger was about to
bring down upon their heads?

The door burst open, and in rushed Reb Leib, followed closely by the *paritz*. The latter's gaze was downcast, and his eyelashes were heavy with tears. At a sign
from Reb Leib, one of the villagers handed the apostate a
tallis. He enveloped himself in it, covering his head and
face entirely. Reb Leib now stepped forward to the Holy
Ark, and took out two Scrolls of the Torah. One he gave
to the oldest villager present, and the other — to the

paritz. Between them at the *bimah* stood Reb Leib, and he began to solemnly chant the traditional tune: עַל דַּעַת הַמָּקוֹם וְעַל דַּעַת הַקָּהָל... — "By the sanction of the Almighty, and by the sanction of the congregation, ... we declare it permissible to pray together with those who have sinned ... "

A deep sigh broke forth from the depths of the broken man's heart. No man there could stand unmoved, and they all wept with him. Throughout all the prayers of the evening, and from dawn of the next day right until nightfall, the *paritz* stood in prayer, humbled and contrite. And as his sobs shook his whole body as he recited the confession the other nine men shuddered with him.

At the climax of the *Ne'ilah* service, when the congregation were about to utter together the words *Shema Yisrael*, the *paritz* leaned forward until his head was deep inside the Holy Ark, embraced the Torah Scrolls that stood there, and in a mighty voice that petrified those present cried out: "Hear, O Israel, the Lord our God, the Lord is One!" He then stood up straight, and began to declare with all his might: ה' הוּא הָאֱלֹקִים — "The Lord is God!" With each repetition his voice grew louder. Finally, as he cried it out for the seventh time, his soul flew from his body.

That same night they brought the remains of the *paritz* to burial in the nearby town. Reb Leib himself took part in the purification and preparation of the body for burial, and for the rest of his life observed the *yahrzeit* of this penitent every Yom Kippur by saying *kaddish* for the elevation of his soul.

◄§ Sensitizing One's Chassid

The Patriarch (Avraham) who knew You from his childhood (*Neilah* service)

In the days when Reb Nata of Chelm was a young man, a disciple of Reb Elimelech of Lyzhansk, he was employed as a tutor in the household of a villager. Both sons of his employer where slow in grasping and did not derive very much benefit from their studies, but Reb Nata nevertheless taught them conscientiously all day

and part of the evening as well, as the Torah prescribes. יום
When the family was asleep, he would retire to his room הכפורים
and there serve his Maker with a rapturous love of
which no man guessed.

When on *Shabbos* and festivals he sat with the family
at their table, he made as if to eat, but in fact hid the food
he took in a handkerchief which he held in his hand.
Then on Friday nights when the family went to sleep, he
would recite the evening prayers joyfully in his room,
make *Kiddush* over the two loaves he had prepared, take
out those morsels of food about which he had no qualms,
and eat his modest meal in purity. The same sequence
was repeated at the midday *Shabbos* meal.

It once happened that the lady of the house woke up
in the middle of the night, and was alarmed to hear an
unexpected sound. She tiptoed from her room, and came
to the room of the tutor. From the other side of the closed
door she heard a man singing the Friday evening prayers
with such bewitching sweetness that her soul almost fled
from her body out of sheer ecstasy.

The next day she made it her business to scrutinize his
every move. For the first time she noticed what was unusual about his eating habits and his lifestyle in general.
By now she gathered that this tutor was no ordinary fellow, but a holy man. After careful observation her husband likewise concluded that this man was most
probably a hidden tzaddik. They talked it over, and then
called on him together.

"From us you will never again be able to keep any
secrets," they said, "for by now we are familiar with
your holy way of life. We have come to you now with a
request — that from today on you lead your life according to your heart's desire. You will lack nothing, for
it will be our privilege to wait on you and provide you
with whatever you need. As to your employment, we can
see that our sons are not going to grow up to be Torah
scholars. We will be happy if they will be able to study
the weekly portion of *Chumash* with Rashi's commentary, and be able to read ethical works so that they will
live their lives as upstanding Jews. So when you have
time you can teach them some Torah and *Musar*, and we
hope that in the meantime they will learn from you the

love and awe of the Creator. But beyond that, there is no
need for you to take off more time from your own divine
service."

Reb Nata was agreeable to their offer, and as time
went on the local villagers who knew him came to regard
him as a holy man. His reputation soon spread to the
neighboring town of Vladova, and several young men
from there came to hear expositions of Torah from his
lips. Whenever they arrived the householder would
provide them with meals, and would wait on them personally. In the meantime the Almighty prospered his affairs, and he grew very wealthy indeed.

Eventually the heads of the community of Vladova
called on his celebrated guest and invited him to settle in
their town. His fame spread far and wide during the
several years he lived there, until one day the elders of
the community of Chelm in East Poland invited him to
be their *rav*. It was to this town that people flocked from
all sides as he became renowned as a rebbe.

Years passed, and the village householder who had
once received him so warmly gradually came down in the
world until he was quite penniless. One day he sat down
with his wife to consider what to do. They had already
sold all their possessions, and the house was bare. Recalling happier days, the good woman said to her husband:
"Listen here; I have an idea. You've heard no doubt by
now that Reb Nata, who used to be a tutor here, has
become known as a tzaddik who helps people out of
their troubles and works wonders. Go off and call on
him. For sure he'll remember all the kindness we showed
him in the good old days, and will intercede on our
behalf so that we'll be helped by merciful heaven."

And off the husband went to Chelm. What an encouraging picture it was to enjoy in anticipation! He
would barely step on the threshold, and the tzaddik,
remembering all his favors, would run across eagerly to
greet him.

He arrived, and found himself to be one of many who
stood and waited until the tzaddik opened the door of his
study. When this finally happened and each chassid approached the door in order to exchange greetings of
Shalom, he took his turn along with all the others, and

received exactly the same indiscriminating *Shalom* as did יום everyone else. At first he was deeply disappointed. After הכפורים a moment's reflection, however, he decided to give the rebbe the benefit of the doubt. After all, was it not the eve of *Shabbos?* The rebbe obviously could not have the time now to show that he recognized him. But when night fell and the holy day was ushered in, and the tzaddik sat at his leisure at the head of his *tish,* the one-time host again waited in vain for some sign that he was remembered, that his presence was appreciated. So it was too at the *Shabbos* midday meal, and so again at the Third Meal at dusk.

His *Shabbos* in Chelm was over. He called on the tzaddik briefly to pay his respects before leaving, and according to custom handed him a *kvitl* on which he had noted his requests. The rebbe wished him well — exactly as he did to all the others who were now leaving town.

This was too much for the poor fellow.

"Rebbe," he said, "I have one question that bothers me, and I would very much like you to answer it."

"Ask, my son, ask," said the tzaddik.

"Every day throughout the year," began the visitor, "we make mention of the merits of the Patriarchs in the course of our prayers. So, too, during the season when we are preparing for the Days of Awe we again say in the penitential prayers of *Selichos:* 'Remember the covenant You made with Avraham and the binding of Yitzchak on the altar.' Again on Rosh HaShanah and in the Ten Days of Penitence and on Yom Kippur we ask the Almighty to help us by virtue of the merits of the Patriarchs. Finally comes *Ne'ilah,* the hour at which our verdict is to be sealed. In fact it is for this reason that we add a special *Shemoneh Esreh* to the regular number of daily prayer services. Surely for this occasion we should have had something new to add. So what do we say right at the outset? אָב יְדָעֲךָ מִנּוֹעַר — 'The Patriarch (Avraham) who knew You from his childhood.' Now have we not been making mention of the merits of our Patriarchs constantly? What then is added by *this* phrase?"

"You no doubt have an answer ready for your own question," replied the tzaddik. "Tell me, my son, what *you* have to say on this."

"Very well," said the chassid. "When it comes to the climax of the Day of Judgment we are afraid that some voice in the Heavenly Court might challenge us and say: 'What's all this talk about the merit of the Patriarchs? Supposing the Patriarchs had never existed, wouldn't everyone still know of the greatness of the Almighty, Who creates and gives continuing existence to whatever is in heaven and earth?' And that is why we introduce a new note into our mention of the Patriarchs, when we say אָב יְדָעֲךָ מִנּוֹעַר. True, we concede: even without them the Almighty is the Creator of everything. But in the period of the Patriarchs there was no one in the world to *recognize* His greatness, and it was Avraham who first made His name known in the world.

"Same with me," the chassid concluded. "Without me too, rebbe, you would be a holy man. But who knew of you and who ever heard of you? Was it not I who made your name known in the world? Why then, rebbe, do you not see to my wants when I am naked and in need?"

The rebbe was well pleased with this argument.

"Go in peace, my son," he said with a smile, "and from this day on the Almighty will prosper you in all your affairs."

And so it was. Within a short time the chassid regained his wealth, and lived on to a happy old age.

Reb Nata was fond of telling his chassidim of this man's background, and would always speak highly of his little speech.

As for the chassidim, they used to comment: "Not in vain did our rebbe at first withhold his warm welcome from that chassid. For he wanted to bring him to a frame of mind in which he could hit upon such an insightful comment on those words in the *Ne'ilah* service."

᪥ Thinking along Different Lines

Reb Menachem Mendel of Lubavitch, the author of *Tzemach Tzedek*, was once telling his son Reb Zalman (later rebbe in Liadi) of the greatness of his own grandfather, Reb Shneur Zalman of Liadi.

Then he went on to speak of the latter's son, Reb Dov Ber of Lubavitch, who was always having to contend

with his father's policy of withholding for a time the יום
delivery of the chassidic discourses in which he would הכפורים
reveal the secrets of the Torah; the aim of this was to in-
tensify his son's thirst to hear them. The son was
therefore obliged to contrive to outwit his father, as it
were, by utilizing the good offices of various elder chassidim who would make it their business to persuade the
rebbe to share his insights with them

Speaking of Reb Dov Ber, then, Reb Menachem
Mendel continued: "And do you think you know what
kind of a man *your* grandfather was? It was said of his
colleague Reb Avraham 'the Malach,' the son of the
Maggid of Mezritch, that when in the course of his
morning devotions he reached *Birkas Yotzer*, which
speaks of the eternally ongoing wonder of creation, he
was so inflamed by ecstatic fervor that if someone had
touched him with a match it would have ignited. And of
your grandfather I can tell you that if he were to cut his
finger, it would not bleed blood, but chassidic teachings.

"Listen to a story about him. It once happened that his
father, the author of *Tanya*, called him to his room at the
conclusion of Yom Kippur. He went there, and I followed him stealthily. When he entered my grandfather's
room and wanted to close the door I tried to hold it ajar
without being seen. But at that moment your grandfather turned around and caught sight of me. I signalled
him a silent plea: I so much wanted to hear what my
grandfather told him. And he obliged. And that is how I
came to hear my grandfather speaking to him.

" 'Bishe,' he said, calling him by the familiar
diminutive form of his name, 'the Prosecution in the
Heavenly Court had some very stern things to say about
you today. There were those who spoke in favor, and
those who spoke against. Fortunately for you, it was an
auspicious hour for prayers to be accepted. Besides, I
helped you too.'

"Now don't you believe for a moment," Reb
Menachem Mendel concluded his conversation with his
son, "that your grandfather batted an eyelid when he
heard from his father about the danger which had just
hovered over his head. He was thinking along altogether
different lines. He was thinking: *'If only I could now get*

*hold of some chassid who would be able to exploit this
rare moment to persuade my father to sate our thirsting
souls with a chassidic discourse!' "*

⋅ঙ Losing No Time

O ne Yom Kippur, Reb Chanoch Henich of Alisk (the
son-in-law of Reb Shalom of Belz) took longer than
usual over completing the midday *Musaf* service. A little
later, before beginning the afternoon *Minchah* prayers,
he told the congregation the time at which he intended to
finish the concluding service of *Ne'ilah*. The time came
— but he was still only halfway through the *Ne'ilah*
service.

The congregants looked up at the clock on the synagogue wall. It had stopped at precisely the moment the
tzaddik had announced that he was going to finish, and
did not resume until he completed the service.

In the words of the Book of *Job*: "You shall decree a
thing, and it shall be established unto you."

⋅ঙ What You Prayed For

מוֹצָאֵי
יוֹם
הַכִּפּוּרִים
*The close
of
Yom
Kippur*

A fter the Day of Judgment had drawn to a close, Reb
Levi Yitzchak of Berditchev turned to one of his
chassidim and said: "Here, let me tell you what you
prayed for today. First you asked the Almighty to give
you a thousand rubles in cash, in order that you should
be enabled to devote yourself to the study of the Torah
uninterrupted by worries. Then you thought it over, and
concluded that if your request were to be granted you
would no doubt open a shop, so that once again you
would have the bother of a business on your head. And
that's why you asked to be given the same amount in two
instalments, each of five hundred. Just before the *Ne'ilah*
service, you thought that this request would be an
impertinence on your part, so you asked the Almighty to
divide up his gift into four equal payments, two hundred
and fifty rubles at three-monthly intervals, so that you
should be able to serve your Maker in tranquility.

"But not once did it occur to you that perhaps the
Almighty does not *want* your divine service and your

Torah study; perhaps he prefers your bother and exertion ... " יום הכפורים

⋖§ A Question of Precedence

In the days when Reb Levi Yitzchak of Berditchev was a young married man and a devoted disciple of Reb Dov Ber, the Maggid of Mezritch, a letter from his father-in-law reached him in Mezritch on the eve of Yom Kippur. He did not open it. He put it aside, thinking: "I'll read it when Yom Kippur has passed."

The next night, when he arrived at his lodgings after *Ne'ilah*, he began to read: "I support you financially, and provide you with whatever you need. So now I ask you: Is *this* the recompense you give me? Is *this* fair — to forget everything, and journey away to Mezritch, and to spend there months upon months? Is *this* the kind of Torah you learn there, that teaches you to repay evil for kindness?"

Reb Levi Yitzchak put the letter down and said to himself: "My father-in-law is right. But hasn't the Almighty bestowed favors on me even more generously than my father-in-law? I think it's only right that I thank Him first."

⋖§ What Tears can Accomplish

When the Day of Judgment came to an end, it was the custom of certain individuals to call on Reb Yaakov Yitzchak, the Chozeh ("Seer") of Lublin, to ask him how their verdict had been sealed in the Heavenly Court. To some of these people he would give an answer.

Once Reb Simchah Bunem — later to be renowned as the rebbe of Pshischah — came in to ask such a question, and the Chozeh answered: "This year you will lose all your money."

And so it was. That year his wife and all his children were seriously ill, and his entire fortune of fifteen hundred rubles — quite a sum in those days — had to be spent on doctors and medicaments. Off he went to Warsaw in the hope that the Almighty would send some means of livelihood his way, and took up lodgings in a luxurious hotel, exactly as he had done in more prosperous times. Weeks passed during which he ate and drank there, though without a penny in his pocket. As time went on he was distressed at the possibility of a *Chillul HaShem* — for would it not be a desecration of the Divine Name if a person known to be a Torah scholar did not pay his debts?

He broke into tears at the thought — but was interrupted by a waiter at his door: "Goose today, sir? Or perhaps something else for a change?"

This question only added salt to his wounds.

His eyes were still red when a messenger called on him from Tamar'l, a pious lady who owned extensive business interests, and was celebrated for her philanthropy. A note from her offered him employment as a cashier in one of her regional offices, at a salary of six rubles a week.

"From this it is clear," said Reb Simchah Bunem to the messenger, "that the Almighty has already helped me, and has reopened for me the gates of success. Since that is the case, then I am once again the Reb Simchah Bunem that I once was. If so, I don't want to be a clerk on weekly wages: I want to be a partner in the business."

When Tamar'l received his answer she was so incensed by his presumptuousness that she did not even send a reply. But so certain was Reb Simchah Bunem in his faith that the Almighty had no doubt sent his salvation already, that he for his part found the peace of mind to settle down at once to his accustomed routine of divine service and Torah study. And indeed, a few days later Tamar'l not only sent him a message that she was agreeable to his proposal, but in addition forwarded him sufficient money to cover his debts. Sure enough, that year the business made enormous profits.

It was time to revisit Lublin. Reb Simchah Bunem had barely opened the door when the Chozeh said: "What I told you was true — it was in fact decreed for you as I told you. But then we didn't take into account what tears can accomplish."

סוכות
sukkos

◆§ To Build a Sukkah

עֶרֶב סוכּוֹת / The eve of Sukkos

If you were on the poor side, finding boards out of which to build the walls of your *sukkah* was always a problem. Year after year, therefore, Reb Mordechai of Lechovitch used to prepare a stock of them, and lend them out to the poor folk of the town during the few days between Yom Kippur and the festival of Sukkos.

One year, on a Friday, the very eve of Sukkos, a threadbare cobbler, lame in one leg, made his way up to the door of the tzaddik. Could he borrow just a few planks for his *sukkah?* The tzaddik answered that there were none left.

Looking out of his window, he then saw the ragged fellow limping from house to house, still in search of a few boards. He felt so sorry for him that he burst into tears.

"Master of the Universe!" he cried. "Just look how Your Children cherish the mitzvah of living in a *sukkah!* See with what self-sacrifice they are determined to fulfill it! It's raining outside. The alleys are full of mud and mire. Yet there he tramps, that ragged cobbler, lame in one leg, and wearing torn shoes — looking for boards for a *sukkah!* Look down, then, Master of the Universe, from Your holy dwelling-place in heaven. Bless Your People, Israel; וּפְרוֹס עֲלֵיהֶם סוּכַּת שְׁלֹמֶךְ — and spread out over them Your *Sukkah,* Your Tabernacle of Peace."

The tzaddik then climbed up to the roof of his house, and searched about until he found a few boards. These he handed to his attendant with the instruction that he should run after the cobbler with them, and since it was the eve of *Shabbos,* when time would be even shorter than usual, he should help him to build his *sukkah* as well.

◆§ The Nerve to Enter

On one of the days between Yom Kippur and Sukkos, the sons and disciples of Reb Chaim of Zanz were perplexed to find the tzaddik sitting at his table —

sukkos dressed in his festive clothes and his fur-brimmed *shtreimel*, according to his custom during these days — and sighing. Where was the joy of the festive season? Fearing that he was not feeling well, they asked him what was the matter. But in reply, he asked them to summon to him a group of his wealthy chassidim who were lodging at a certain inn.

When they stood before him, Reb Chaim said: "Rosh HaShanah has passed; Yom Kippur has passed; but I haven't yet repented! How will I have the nerve to enter the *sukkah*?"

The chassidim were distressed to hear words such as these.

The tzaddik continued: "I need the sum of several thousand reinish for charity, but I haven't got it. If you lend me that amount, then I will be able to do *teshuvah* as I ought to do, and in a few weeks, God willing, I will return it all."

Without any hesitation, the chassidim of course promptly brought him what he asked for, and once again the tzaddik's countenance beamed with the joy of the festive season.

On the evening that the festival began, he returned from the synagogue cloaked in his *tallis*, as was his custom, walked straight towards his spacious *sukkah*, paused a moment at the door, and entered.

Standing near his chair at the head of the table, he said: "Rosh HaShanah has passed; Yom Kippur has passed; but I haven't yet repented! How do I have the nerve to enter the *sukkah*? But the Psalmist has written: אֲנִי בְּצֶדֶק אֶחֱזֶה פָנֶיךָ — 'With righteousness (*tzedek*) will I behold Your countenance!'" (For the Hebrew word for "righteousness" also brings to mind the related word *tzedakah*, meaning "charity".)

◆§ One Saving Grace

For the sake of Your *tzedakah*, save us! (*Hoshana* prayers).

The lengths to which Reb Chaim of Zanz went in distributing charity amazed all those around him. His own household was conducted with frugal austerity —

but as for others, in their thousands and tens of thou- סוכות
sands, whoever was bitter at heart and cramped in spirit
received with an open hand. His generosity reached its
peak every Sukkos eve, in accordance with the teaching
which is to be found in the writings of Rabbi Yitzchak
Luria, the Arizal. He started by distributing every single
coin that was at hand. He then proceeded to exert himself
to secure loans from all sides, sometimes by pawning
various objects.

One year, on the eve of Sukkos, one of his sons said:
"Father, I have never seen it written that there is a mitzvah obliging one to give charity even after he hasn't got a
solitary copper coin left in his pocket!"

Reb Chaim was displeased with this comment.

"I am amazed that a son should be thus able to take his
own father's life!" he said. "You can see for yourself
that your father hasn't got even an inkling of Torah
study, and not even a trace of the awe of God, and all he
has is just one tiny speck of charity. And now you want
to stop him from doing that too?"

⋗ Fadeless Beauty

A nother year, again on the eve of Sukkos, Reb Chaim נוי סוּכָּה
of Zanz told his sons that he needed several thou- *Decorating*
sand rubles. As soon as they brought him the amount *the*
that they had quickly borrowed from various wealthy *sukkah*
householders, he distributed it all to the needy.

As he entered his *sukkah* that evening he said: "People are accustomed to decorate their *sukkah* with all
kinds of pretty ornaments. But the beauty of my *sukkah*
is different: *tzedakah*, charity — *that* is what makes my
sukkah beautiful!"

⋗ Depends who Your Great-Uncle was

For man is a tree of the field (*Deuteronomy*).

A n epidemic raged through Nadvorna as Sukkos was
approaching, and the physicians warned the townsfolk to take all possible hygienic precautions for fear of
contagion. The local judge, an unusually evil man, was
told that Reb Mordechai of Nadvorna had just built

sukkos himself a *sukkah*. He at once dispatched a messenger with a court order to demolish it forthwith, because it supposedly contravened the municipal health regulations. Reb Mordechai ignored the message.

Within minutes a squad of police arrived at his doorstep to warn him of the consequences of his defiance. He replied: "I built my *sukkah* in order that it should stand, not in order that it should be demolished."

This time the judge sent the tzaddik a summons. When this too was ignored, the judge decided to descend on his victim himself. He ordered the tzaddik in harsh terms to dismantle the *sukkah* immediately, and warned him of the severe punishment which any further disobedience would earn him. These threats and warnings did not shake the tzaddik's equanimity in the slightest. He simply answered coolly in the same words that he had told the policemen — that he had built his *sukkah* in order that it should stand, not in order that it should be demolished.

The judge was incensed.

But the tzaddik merely added: "I would like you to know that Reb Meir of Premishlan was my great-uncle."

At this the judge flew into a rage: "Who cares *who* your great-uncle was? Just demolish that thing, and that's all!"

Reb Mordechai now repeated what he had just told the judge, then asked him calmly to wait a moment; he wanted to tell him an interesting story.

The judge obliged, and Reb Mordechai began: "Once there lived a priest who had ten sons, all of them as robust and strong as cedars. He owned a beautiful big park, full of trees that delighted God and man alike. One day he decided that he would add grace to this grove by planting a little flower garden next to it. So he uprooted a few of his trees, and in their place he planted fragrant flowers. But no sooner had he finished this work than his sons fell ill, one after the other. First the oldest weakened and died, then the second — and so on, until the very youngest fell ill. The priest was at his wit's end. He summoned the most expert doctors, and even consulted sorcerers — but to no avail. At this point several people advised him to make the journey to visit Reb Meir

of Premishlan. Who knows? Perhaps salvation might **סוכּות**
come through him, for he was reputed to be a holy man.
By now there was no alternative open to him, and he was
desperately eager to save the life of his last surviving
son. So with a heavy heart he travelled to Premishlan.

"Arriving there he told the holy man of all the trials
that had befallen him — and now even his last son was
mortally ill, and no physician could cure him. Heaven
alone could help him now.

" 'You had a beautiful garden full of goodly trees,'
Reb Meir told him, 'but because you wanted a flower
garden as well, you chopped down the trees of God. And
that is why He has now chopped down *your* trees, *for
man is a tree of the field.* But since you have already
come here, and your time has not yet run out completely,
I promise you now that your youngest son will be helped
from Above, and will soon be cured.'

"The holy man then prayed that the Almighty heal the
priest's son, in order that His Name be sanctified
wherever people would hear of his story. This prayer
was accepted, and the son grew up to be a man.

"I want you to know," Reb Meir concluded his story
to the judge, "that *you are the son of that priest* ... Tell
me, now, is *this* the way you repay the kindness that my
great-uncle showed you by saving your life?"

The judge fell at his feet, and wept.

"True, true, I know it all!" he sobbed. "Forgive me
now, rabbi, for what I've done to you. You can build
even *ten* of those things — but only promise that you will
forgive me!"

The promise was given, and the judge went his way in
peace.

◄§ Inside Information

The brother-in-law of the Baal Shem Tov, Reb **לֵישֵׁב**
Gershon of Kitov, lived in Brody. In the same town **בַּסֻּכָּה**
lived Rabbi Chaim Tzanser (not to be confused with Reb *To dwell*
Chaim of Zanz), an eminent scholar who is remembered *in the*
as one of the earliest *misnagdim* to express their an- *sukkah*
tagonism to "the Sect," as the chassidic movement was
nicknamed in its infancy.

One year it rained on the first night of Sukkos, so that Rabbi Chaim was distressed that he would be unable to fulfill in a leisurely manner the mitzvah whose special time was that very night. In the meantime a visitor came in and told him that no rain was falling in Reb Gershon's *sukkah.* Rabbi Chaim immediately sent his son to check if this report was true. Sure enough, after only a few minutes the son returned and confirmed the story: Reb Gershon was sitting in his *sukkah,* and not a solitary drop of rain was to be felt.

Rabbi Chaim was not a man to be quickly impressed. He stayed at home in his own *sukkah,* and spent the evening exchanging jests with his son about the weird wonders and miracles that the so-called tzaddikim of "the Sect" occupied themselves with, in defiance of the spirit of the Torah.

The next morning Rabbi Chaim and Reb Gershon met on their way to immerse themselves in the local *mikveh,* in preparation for fulfilling the mitzvah of the *lulav.*

"Rabbi," said Reb Gershon to Rabbi Chaim, "since when is one permitted to sit in one's *sukkah* and speak *lashon hara,* slander?"

Rabbi Chaim was astonished. "But how on earth did you find out about *that?* My son and I sat alone, and no one else was with us at the time. I must therefore conclude that an angel from heaven came along and told you. And if that is so, then how is it possible that an angel should speak *lashon hara? ...*"

Reb Gershon had an answer.

"Our Sages," he said, "teach us: 'Whoever fulfills one mitzvah acquires one angel to speak up in his defense, and whoever does one transgression acquires for himself one prosecuting angel.' Very well, then, that very prosecuting angel who was created by your slanderous talk, he's the one who came and told me about it ..."

◆§ No Tricks

The rain was thundering down in torrents and drenching all the streets of Brody. Of all nights, it was the first night of Sukkos, and the learned Rabbi Yitzchak Halevi, head of the local rabbinical court, had

postponed his festive evening meal until midnight. סוכות
While he stood at his window, waiting for the rain to
stop, he saw a man walking down the street with *challos*
and a bottle of wine under his arm. He sent his attendant
to call the man inside, and when he entered asked him
where he had come from and where he had eaten his
festive meal. The stranger answered that he had eaten in
the *sukkah* of Reb Gershon of Kitov, because it wasn't
raining in there. The rabbi thereupon told his attendant
to take some *challos* and a bottle of wine, and to accompany him to Reb Gershon's *sukkah*.

Reb Gershon was taken aback to see the local *rav* at
his *sukkah* door.

"Why did you have to go to the trouble of coming to
my *sukkah?*" he asked. "After all, rabbi, you too could
have arranged things through the exercise of practical
Kabbalah so that it shouldn't rain in your *sukkah*
either."

The rabbi promptly told his *shammes* to pick up their
loaves and wine.

"Off we go," he said. "I have no inclination to make
use of tricks of this sort."

◆§ Living in One's Plate

In the days before Reb Yissachar Dov (the Sava
Kaddisha) of Radoshitz became known as a rebbe, he
was so poor that he often fasted because he simply had
no bread to eat. One year he had eaten nothing for a few
days before Yom Kippur, and even after the fast was
over he had nothing better than meager rations of bread
and water. Nor could he afford to prepare anything at all
for the oncoming festival of Sukkos.

After the evening service on the first night of the
festival he remained in the synagogue, for he knew that
at home there was nothing to eat. But he did not know
that on the eve of the festival his wife had sold some
modest item of jewelry that she had found among her
possessions, and with the proceeds had bought braided
challos and candles and potatoes.

When he decided that most people had by now
finished eating in their *sukkah* and had probably

sukkos returned to their houses, he left the synagogue and went home. Entering his *sukkah*, he was overjoyed to see candles and *challos* on the table. He washed his hands, recited *Kiddush*, and sat down to eat. By this stage he was well-nigh starving, so he ate the potatoes which his wife served him with a ravenous appetite.

While he was eating a thought flashed through his mind.

"Berl," he said to himself, "you're not sitting in the *sukkah:* you're sitting in your plate!"

And he stopped eating.

⋖§ Choose Life!

A tailor who had a request to make of Reb Chaim of Zanz wrote out his story on a *kvitl* which he handed to the tzaddik. The story ran as follow.

Many years earlier, whenever Reb Chaim's late father Reb Aryeh Leibush slept in his *sukkah*, this tailor — who was then a youth — slept there too, so that the *rav* should not be out there alone. One exceptionally cold night the youth refused to sleep in the *sukkah*, no matter how earnestly the *rav* implored him to agree. This went on until the *rav* promised him that if he would oblige, he would give him half of his own portion of the World to Come. The lad quickly obliged.

Some fifty years later the tailor fell ill. As he lay on his sickbed, the *rav* appeared to him and said: "You should know that the time has come for you to leave This World. Choose now between two alternatives: either you waive your right to the half-portion in the World to Come which I promised you — in which case you will regain your health; or you may come with me to eternal life and receive your portion."

The tailor chose to continue living in This World, and said that he was prepared to forgo his claim on the promised share in the World to Come — so long as he could continue living in This World.

When he regained his health, however, he regretted having chosen as he had. He therefore came now to the son of the departed tzaddik, Reb Chaim of Zanz, with the request that he annul his waiver.

Reb Chaim only smiled, and replied not a word.

סוכות

✺§ A Potsherd

Man is likened to a broken earthenware vessel
(Prayers of the Days of Awe).

The chassidim stood around in silent wonderment:
why did their rebbe, Reb Avraham of Trisk, pause so
long at the door of his *sukkah* on this first night of the
festival, without entering?

Finally the rebbe spoke: "As I approached the *sukkah*
it occurred to me that only a few days ago, in the prayers
of the Days of Awe, I said the words מָשׁוּל כְּחֶרֶס הַנִּשְׁבָּר
— man resembles a broken earthenware vessel. And we
are forbidden to treat a *sukkah* disrespectfully by bringing into it vessels made of such cheap material. Then I
recalled that in connection with another law we learn
that כְּלִי חֶרֶס אֵין לָהֶם תַּקָנָה אֶלָא שְׁבִירָה — there is nothing
that can be done to set aright an earthenware vessel that
has ceased being kosher: the only thing to do is to break
it. Let us therefore approach our Maker with broken and
contrite hearts, for as the Psalmist says: — 'You, God,
will not spurn a broken and contrite heart.' *Then* we will
be able to enter the *sukkah.*"

✺§ Fellow Feeling

It once happened that Reb Avraham Yaakov of
Sadigora sat down to eat in his *sukkah* and forgot to
pronounce the blessing — which praises Him "Who
commanded us to dwell in the *sukkah.*" He realized his
omission a moment late, when the bite of bread over
which he had recited the blessing of *HaMotzi* was
already in his mouth. He intended therefore to
pronounce the *berachah* over the next mouthful of
bread, from the other *challah* on the table — but then he
forgot again. This he realized when the fish course was
served, and at this point he shared his distress with those
who sat at his table.

On this occasion he told the company at his table that
it once happened that Reb Avraham Yehoshua Heschel
of Apta forgot on the *Seder* night of Passover to recite
the blessing — praising Him "Who commanded us con-

cerning the eating of *matzah.*" When he realized his mistake, he quoted the Mishnah which says שְׁגָגַת תַּלְמוּד עוֹלָה זָדוֹן. Now in its plain sense this quotation means that an unwitting error in observance caused by insufficient study is accounted as wanton transgression. The tzaddik of Apta however interpreted the word עוֹלָה — is accounted, on the non-literal level of *derush* in its variant meaning "is elevated": the שְׁגָגַת תַּלְמוּד — the unwitting error — of a tzaddik occurs for the sake of others, so that he should be thereby enabled to עוֹלָה זָדוֹן — elevate and rectify the transgressions of his fellows. For if he is to be enabled to achieve this he must *himself* first be obliged to do it for himself, since we have a rule, "Whoever is not obliged to perform a certain mitzvah himself is not able to fulfill it on behalf of others."

And that explains why the Almighty causes an unwitting transgression to come the way of a tzaddik — so that he will be able thereafter to elevate the transgressions of his fellow Jews.

◆§ An Old Meyuchas

He was a simple fellow, Yosef Mordechai — an odd-job man in the household of Reb Shmuel (the Maharash) of Lubavitch, and of his father before him, Reb Menachem Mendel (the Tzemach Tzedek) of Lubavitch. One day he blustered into the rebbe's *sukkah* a few minutes after having lost his temper on one of the kitchen staff, and was still simmering.

Reb Shmuel reprimanded him affectionately: "Yosef Mordechai! It's true that as a *meyuchas* you have the right to preferential treatment — but a person has to conduct himself properly when he's in the presence of the *sechach.* You see, the *sechach* up there that covers the *sukkah* doesn't like anger."

Now why did the rebbe call him a *meyuchas*? — There's a story behind that.

The previous rebbe, Reb Menachem Mendel, once told this attendant that he should sleep in the *sukkah.* In fact there were two *sukkos* — one inside the house, under a ceiling which could be opened and closed, and one in the yard.

"But rebbe," protested Yosef Mordechai, "it's cold out סוכות there."

"Amalek is cold," said the rebbe; "a Jew has warmth. Go and sleep in the *sukkah*, and you'll be blessed with long life."

And that is why Reb Shmuel now called him a *meyuchas*.

In fact Yosef Mordechai lived to one hundred and three, and old-timers from Lubavitch will tell you how they saw him dancing like a lively lad on the roof of the big study hall, when he was ninety-eight.

✦§ By Way of Recompense

The following story was retold several times by Reb Yechezkel of Shiniva, the son of Reb Chaim of Zanz.

In a village there once lived a poor man who was quite unlettered, but God-fearing. The eve of the festival arrived, and he still had no branches with which to cover his *sukkah*, nor could he afford to buy any. So he went out with his wife all the way to the forest that they may cut branches themselves. The shadows were lengthening, and they were afraid that if they would continue pulling down branches with their hands they would soon be desecrating the festival which would begin at sunset. They therefore decided in their simplicity that the best thing to do would be to bite off twigs and leaves from the trees with their teeth. And this they did, despite the scratches and weals that they suffered on their lips and faces.

Echoes of their self-sacrifice pealed throughout the heavens. Indeed, the Heavenly Court decided that Avraham Avinu, the first of the *Ushpizin*, would call on this poor man in this humble *sukkah*, and would be seen by him.

Sure enough, that same evening, the poor man looked up and saw a stranger standing in his *sukkah*. Assuming that this was some unfortunate pauper in search of a place to eat, he said: "I'm sorry, sir, but I myself am a very poor man, and there isn't a mouthful of food here to eat. But I've got an idea. Why don't you go over the road to that house over there? He's a rich man, and I'm sure you'll be served a square meal in honor of *Yom-Tov.*"

"But I didn't come to eat of your bread," said the stranger, "nor to take anything from you. I am your Father Avraham. I have come to visit you in your *sukkah* and to be seen by you here, by way of recompense for the self-sacrifice and suffering with which you fulfilled the mitzvah of the *sukkah.*"

With that, the stranger vanished.

⊷§ Inextinguishable Love

In the course of the midday festive meal, Reb Shmuel Abba of Zichlin was in the middle of delivering a learned discourse on the secret teachings of the Torah. Suddenly the *sukkah* was drenched by a furious cloudburst. The *tzaddik* did not interrupt his train of thought. On the contrary, he became more and more inflamed by the sheer ecstasy of the holy words, until the *sukkah* was almost covered with water.

He rose quickly from his chair and cried out the words from the *Song of Songs* which testify to the steadfastness of Israel's love to her Maker: מַיִם רַבִּים לֹא יוּכְלוּ לְכַבּוֹת אֶת הָאַהֲבָה — "Turbulent waters will not be able to extinguish the love!"

At once the rain ceased, and as the clouds dispersed, the sun shone again on the *sukkah* of the tzaddik.

⊷§ The Trials of Being a Tzaddik

אוּשְׁפִּיזִין
Ushpizin,
the souls of
our holy
forebears
who visit
their children
in the
sukkah

Night and day they knocked on his door in their hundreds and thousands — chassidim of all ages, people seeking spiritual guidance, people who begged him to intercede for them and give them strength in their trials and tribulations. So much did this distract Reb Pinchas of Korets from his *own* service of his Maker that he prayed one day that he should be disliked. That would solve everything: people would no longer disturb him, and he would be quite free of all bothersome contacts.

And indeed from that day on he secluded himself for lone communion with the Creator. He lived austerely,

and was never seen in company except for when he at- סוכות
tended synagogue for communal prayer.

The festival of Sukkos drew near, and he was obliged
to hire a gentile to build his *sukkah*. No fellow Jew
would help him, for he was disliked by them all. The *goy*
did not have the tools that were needed, so the *rebbitzin*
had to call on the neighbors to borrow from them.
That too was difficult to arrange, because her husband
was so disliked.

Came the first night of the festival, and when Reb
Pinchas asked various folk to be his guests in honor of
Yom-Tov, not a single one would accept his invitation —
for the same reason.

He walked home alone. Entering his *sukkah*, he began
to chant the traditional invitation to the first of the
Ushpizin. He looked up, and saw the Patriarch Avraham
standing just outside the door of the *sukkah* — though
not entering.

Reb Pinchas turned to him in anguish: "Why do you
not enter my *sukkah*? What is my sin?"

And Avraham Avinu replied: "It is not my custom to
enter a place where there are no guests."

From that day on Reb Pinchas prayed to the Almighty
that he be restored to his former lot, and that he should
once again find favor in the eyes of men.

◄§ With Our Own Eyes

There are two customs regarding the order of the
Ushpizin. Either, following a chronological sequence,
Joseph is fourth — immediately after his father, Yaakov,
and before Moshe and Aharon. Or, based on Kabbalistic
teachings, Joseph follows Moshe and Aharon as the
sixth guest.

Reb Yitzchak Aizik of Komarna once decided that he
would like to reverse the usual order in which he invited
the *Ushpizin* to the *sukkah* on their respective nights.
This year he would like to adopt the other custom and
invite Joseph before Moshe Rabbeinu. But he first sent
his son Reb Eliezer to Reb Yitzchak Aizik of Zhidachov
to ask for his opinion on the matter.

Replied the latter: "I am surprised that your father

sukkos should propose this change. For last year we saw with our own eyes how Moshe Rabbeinu entered our *sukkah* before Yosef HaTzaddik."

✺§ Why Not?

Reb Avraham Mordechai of Ger once arrived late at the *sukkah* of his father, Reb Yitzchak Meir (author of *Chiddushei HaRim*). In reply to the question as to how he was delayed, the young man said that his little son — later to become famous as Reb Yehudah Aryeh Leib of Ger, the author of *Sfas Emes* — had cried; he insisted that he be shown the *Ushpizin* in the *sukkah*.

Said the grandfather: "So why didn't you oblige?"

✺§ As if We had Eaten

No matter how eager all the housewives of Zichlin were to welcome the festival by preparing fish in its honor, there was absolutely no fish to be bought. Even Reb Shmuel Abba himself was distressed by this, because he regarded it as somehow disrespectful to the *Ushpizin* who would be visiting the *sukkah* in the evening.

On the first night of the festival the tzaddik was sitting at the head of his table with a large gathering of chassidim around him. As soon as he had tasted the *challah* over which he had recited the blessing he launched on an involved discourse which was compounded of all the learned sources which touch on the mitzvah of eating fish in honor of *Shabbos* and *Yom-Tov*. He drew on the Talmud, the Midrash, the *Zohar* and other kabbalistic works — explaining the mystical *tikkunim* which restore harmony to the universe through the eating of fish on *Shabbos* and *Yom-Tov* with the appropriate intentions. The chassidim listened intently, amazed by the sheer breadth and depth of his treatment.

When the discourse finally came to an end, the tzaddik took a drop of vodka, as is the custom after the fish course, and exclaimed : "Thanks be to the Almighty, by Whose grace we were now able to effect the same harmonious *tikkunim* in the universe as if we had actually eaten fish!"

◄§ The Yardstick of Heaven

R eb Michel of Zlotchov had one treasured possession
in his house — the *tefillin* which he had inherited
from his saintly father, Reb Yitzchak (or Reb Itzikl) of
Drohovitch. These he cherished more than all else in the
world. In fact there was a time that certain chassidim offered him an enormous sum — about fifty reinish — for
these *tefillin*, and though he lived all his life in abject
poverty he would not even listen to them. His wife
nagged him constantly. If he would sell them, they
would at least have a little money for basic necessities.
After all, he did have another pair of *tefillin* which he
could use every morning for his prayers. But Reb Michel
did not budge.

אֶתְרֹג
Esrog,
the citron
one of the
Four Species
over which
a blessing is
pronounced
on Sukkos

Along came the festival of Sukkos, and in the whole of
Zlotchov there was not a solitary *esrog* to be had. The
community waited anxiously for one to be brought from
this town, from that — but in vain. How would they be
able to recite the blessing over the Four Species without
an *esrog*? Finally, on the very eve of the festival, a
stranger arrived at Zlotchov with a prize *esrog* for sale.
Its price: exactly fifty reinish. Reb Michel thought for a
moment, sold his *tefillin* for fifty reinish, and bought the
esrog. He brought it home lovingly, taking care that the
little *pitom* at the tip remain intact, for otherwise the
beautiful fruit could not be used for this mitzvah for
which one had to wait a whole year.

His wife gathered at once that this purchase had cost
her husband a considerable sum. She began to crossexamine him energetically: where had he got hold of all
that money? Reb Michel tried desperately to evade her
questions, but in vain. She was so persistent that in the
end the truth came out — he had sold the *tefillin*.

"Are you serious?" she fumed. "How many times
have I begged you to sell those *tefillin* for the basic
necessities of the house? And did you sell them? Never!
And now, for an *esrog*, you went and sold them?"

And so furious was she that she snatched the *esrog*
from the table, bit off the *pitom*, and spat it out on to the
floor.

Reb Michel breathed not a word in complaint, nor showed the slightest cloud of annoyance. He only said: "Master of the Universe! If that's what you please, that my *esrog* should become unfit for a blessing, then that's fine by me too: I accept your verdict lovingly."

✿ ✿ ✿

His father appeared to Reb Michel later in a dream and told him that his second accomplishment — his self-restraint — had made its mark in heaven more eloquently than his first, his purchase of the *esrog* at a crushing price.

⟜§ A Blessing over a Horse

Reb Yitzchak of Neshchiz recounted that his father, Reb Mordechai of Neshchiz, was a merchant before he accepted a rabbinical post, and every time he returned home from a business trip he would set aside a modest portion of his profits toward the price of an *esrog* when the time came.

Once, when he had patiently saved six silver rubles in this way, he set out for Brody to buy an *esrog*, for at that time he lived in those parts. On the way he was surprised to hear the sighs and sobs of a water-carrier. It transpired that the poor fellow's livelihood had just been cut off: his old horse had just died, and his wagon was useless without it. The tzaddik left him for a few moments, and with his six silver rubles bought him a new horse.

After having handed it over he said to himself: "So what's the difference? Buying an *esrog* is a mitzvah commanded by the Almighty, and so is this a mitzvah commanded by the Almighty."

In fact he found his situation amusing, and joked to himself: "Everyone will pronounce their blessing over an *esrog*; I'll pronounce *my* blessing over a horse ..."

As it happened, though, someone later brought him a fine *esrog* in time for the festival, so that in fact he made his *berachah* not only over the horse, but over an *esrog* as well.

סוכות

~§ Rewards are to be Earned

All of Berditchev was in a quandary. Sukkos was just
around the corner, and there was not a solitary *esrog*
in the whole town. At length Reb Levi Yitzchak told a
group of his chassidim to wait at the nearby crossroads
in the hope that they would encounter some passerby
who owned an *esrog*. Sure enough a wagon soon
trundled by, and the man inside it had an unusually
beautiful *esrog* with him. He was on his way home. The
trouble was that his home was in some far-off town, and
he was only bypassing Berditchev. They brought the
stranger to their rebbe, who immediately entreated him
to spend the festival with them, and by lending his *esrog*
enable the whole community, including the tzaddik
himself, to carry out the mitzvah of pronouncing a blessing over the Four Species. The stranger would not agree.
He was on his way home to spend *Yom-Tov* with his
family. How could he suddenly upset their festive joy
and his own? The tzaddik promised him the blessings of
wealth and children, but even this did not help. He had
wealth and children, thank God, and was in need of
nothing.

Then the tzaddik said: "If you will oblige, I hereby
promise you that you will share my lot in the World to
Come!"

The stranger immediately changed his mind, and
stayed on in Berditchev for the duration of the festival.
The tzaddik was overjoyed, and so was the whole community — and so was the stranger.

Now at this point a secret order was issued by the
tzaddik to all the townsfolk of Berditchev: no one was to
allow this guest to eat in their *sukkah*. Not a soul could
guess what the reason could be, but — it was an order
from the rebbe.

On the first night of the festival that unsuspecting fellow returned from the synagogue to the room which he
had rented in someone's house. There, indoors, he found
everything prepared — wine for *Kiddush*, two loaves,
candles, and a festive meal. He was dumbfounded. Could
it be that the householder, such an upstanding and

sukkos observant Jew, did not have a *sukkah?* He went out to the yard, and duly found a *sukkah* set up exactly as the Law requires. Inside it he could see his host and all his family sitting happily around the table. He asked to be admitted, but was refused. Why so? There was no answer. Somewhat downcast, he proceeded to call on the neighboring families, each of which he found sitting happily in its *sukkah.* He begged to be admitted — but in each case the response was the same baffling refusal.

It finally came out that behind all of this there was an order from the tzaddik. He ran off to his house in consternation, and asked: "What's this all about? How have I sinned to deserve this?"

Reb Levi Yitzchak replied: "If you will waive your claim to that promise I made you about the World to Come, then I'll straight away give the order that you should be admitted to a *sukkah* ..."

The stranger was shocked — but held his peace. What was there to do now? On the one hand there was this promise of the tzaddik that he would share his lot in the World to Come. On the other hand, there was a mitzvah waiting to be fulfilled — to eat in a *sukkah.* The *sukkah* won the day. Unthinkable, that's what it was — that a Jew like himself, who all his days had observed the mitzvah of the *sukkah,* this year shouldn't? All the House of Israel were sitting in their *sukkos* on this night — and he would be eating like a *goy, indoors,* God forbid?

He told the tzaddik that he released him forthwith from his promise about the World to Come, and (at the tzaddik's request) even gave him his hand in confirmation. Then off he went and quietly ate his festive meal in someone's *sukkah.*

As soon as the festival came to an end, Reb Levi Yitzchak called for him.

"Now," he said, "I hereby return my promise to you. I wanted you to learn, my son, that I didn't want you to pick up your portion in the World to Come cheaply, through an easy bit of bargaining. I wanted you to *earn* it, through your deeds. That is why I so arranged matters that you should be put to the test with regard to the mitzvah of the *sukkah.* Now that you have withstood the test, and demonstrated the self-sacrifice of *mesirus nefesh* for the sake of fulfilling that mitzvah, you truly סוכות deserve to share my portion in the World to Come!''

⋅⋅§ Think Positive

I t was the same old problem all over again. Berditchev was utterly without an *esrog*, and when one was finally secured, it was of course handed over to the safekeeping of Reb Levi Yitzchak, and the whole town had to come to his home to take turns at pronouncing the blessing over it.

Now the good-hearted simple fellow who was the rebbe's attendant started thinking. No doubt after the tzaddik had himself pronounced the *berachah* first, then all the elder chassidim and scholarly folk in town would be next in line after him. After them it would no doubt be the turn of all the well-to-do householders. And by the time it came to his own hands, it would no doubt be perilously close to sunset, after which it would be too late to perform the mitzvah altogether. The Evil Inclination egged him on: ''Why should *I* lose out? Am I not as much a Jew as the rest of them? Just because it's my good fortune to be the *shammes* of the tzaddik, should I therefore have to suffer?''

He had a solution! Early in the morning, very early, when the tzaddik was still occupied immersing himself in the *mikveh*, and taking his time over all the mystical thoughts that he was always busy with, he, the *shammes*, would take hold of the *esrog* — quietly, secretly — and use it to pronounce the *berachah* first!

At the crack of dawn on the morning of the first day of Sukkos the tzaddik went off to the *mikveh*. Taking his cue, the *shammes* picked his way stealthily to where the *esrog* was kept. But at this point Satan himself intervened. For so anxious was the *shammes* lest he be found out, that his hands trembled. The *esrog* fell to the floor, the *pitom* at its tip snapped off — and the *esrog* was invalid!

The unfortunate fellow was so alarmed that he almost fainted. What on earth could he do? Not only would his shameful deed be discovered — that he had planned to

use the *esrog* before the tzaddik — but now the tzaddik
would have no *esrog* at all. And he himself, the *shammes*, was the only one to blame! There was no way out.
He would have to tell the whole sorry story to the rebbe,
come what may.

Wretched and disconsolate he sat and waited — until
at length the tzaddik came home in lively anticipation of
the mitzvah. And as the honest *shammes* sobbed out his
disjointed account of the calamity his innards trembled
within him. Surely the holy man would now call down
upon him all the well-deserved wrath of heaven ... To
his amazement, however, the tzaddik showed no trace of
anger or irritation. Instead, he took up the despoiled *esrog* in both hands, and in the voice of joyful ecstasy
which was his whenever he spoke up in Israel's defense,
he exclaimed: "Master of the Universe! Just look down
and see how Your Children cherish Your mitzvos! So
much so, in fact, that even an unlettered fellow like my
shammes here is willing to risk getting himself into trouble by invalidating the *esrog*, all because he is so keen to
perform the mitzvah with alacrity, to be one of those
who are eager to be the first to obey Your commands ..."

◆§ A Penetrating Glance

One year it was very difficult to acquire the fresh
myrtle twigs that are needed on Sukkos for the
blessing over the Four Species; all the twigs of *hadassim*
that were imported into Poland were dry. Reb Shmuel
Abba of Zichlin bought a number of bunches in the hope
of finding a few suitable twigs amongst them, but was
disappointed at not finding even one.

The chassidim who converged on Zichlin for Yom
Kippur of course heard about this. One of them, a
wealthy chassid by the name of Reb Yitzchak Zifkovitz
from Azarkov, recalled that the squire who lived in a village near his hometown had found myrtles growing in
his garden. He therefore spoke to the rebbe as soon as the
fast was over, and undertook to supply him with the
hadassim that he so keenly wanted.

Once home, Reb Yitzchak called on the squire per-

sonally to ask him to sell some myrtle branches. Unfor- סוכות
tunately, though, there was nothing left to sell: people
had come from all the surrounding district, leaving
nothing. Reb Yitzchak's distress was visible.

"Seeing that you are so obviously disappointed," said
the squire, "I have an idea for you. The squire who lives
in that village over there also has myrtles growing in his
garden, but it seems that the word hasn't yet got around.
Let me send my man there to bring some for you."

The twigs he brought were so fresh and unblemished
that Reb Yitzchak was happy to pay a good price for
them. Early next morning he dispatched them by special
messenger to his rebbe.

On his arrival at Zichlin with the precious bundle in
hand, excitement ran high. Every elder chassid there
wanted to be the first to bring the glad tidings to the
tzaddik. The rebbe was indeed happy to hear the news,
and eagerly awaited the twigs themselves. Finally the
messenger brought them proudly into the rebbe's study.
The rebbe took one glance at them and said: "I won't
pronounce a blessing over these twigs, for I can see the
shape of a cross on them."

And he gave the order that they be removed from his
house at once.

The messenger was dumbfounded. So much bother,
so much exertion — only to have the rebbe decline to use
them for the mitzvah? But then what was there to do? He
took his leave of the rebbe, and set off on his doleful
journey home. Reb Yitzchak, understandably enough,
was equally vexed, and decided to investigate exactly
where these *hadassim* had been taken from.

On one of the Intermediate Days of the festival,
therefore, he travelled to the village where that squire
lived, and posed his question carefully: since he had
been fortunate in acquiring here the world's most
beautiful myrtle twigs, he earnestly desired to see with
his own eyes the spot in which they grew. The squire
willingly obliged, for Reb Yitzchak's name was known
to him, and took him to that spot. Now all was clear: the
myrtles grew among the gravestones, each topped by a
crucifix, in the squire's family cemetery.

Reb Yitzchak realized now what kind of vision his

rebbe was blessed with. As the Psalmist says: — "The secret of God is with those that fear Him."

⇜§ Not Mine

A chassid once journeyed to Warsaw to buy an *esrog* for Reb Avraham of Chechanov. It was a bad year for *esrogim*, but there was one specimen there that he rather fancied. When he asked the price, the dealer told him that this particular *esrog* was being kept for Reb Leibl Eger of Lublin. The chassid was persistent, and under the pressure of his entreaties the dealer finally agreed to sell it to him. The chassid was delighted — as, too, was his rebbe when he saw it, for it was indeed a particularly fine *esrog*.

The first day of Sukkos arrived, but when the tzaddik took it in hand in readiness for pronouncing the blessing over it, he began to consider it pensively from all angles. After quite some time had elapsed, he sent for the chassid who had brought it.

"Tell me, please," said the tzaddik, "exactly how you came to buy this *esrog*."

The chassid of course told him the whole story.

"If so," said the tzaddik, "this *esrog* is not mine."

He was as good as his word, and did not recite the *berachah* over it.

⇜§ Duress

Time was running out, and Reb Chaim Meir Yechiel of Moglenitz still did not have an *esrog*. Finally, when Sukkos was very near, his chassidim got wind of a rumor that a certain wealthy individual in Preissin owned an exceptionally handsome *esrog*. A delegation of chassidim promptly set out, and begged him to sell it to them for their rebbe — but to no avail.

At length he said: "If the rebbe promises that my wife will give birth to a son, I will give him this *esrog* as a gift."

The chassidim promised to pass on the message to the rebbe, and assured him that his condition would no doubt be fulfilled. As he handed it to them, he added a clause to reinforce his condition — that if the promise סוכות would not be honored within the year, then the rebbe would not have fulfilled the mitzvah of pronouncing a blessing over one's own *esrog*.

On the very eve of the festival the chassidim arrived with the precious gift. The rebbe was overjoyed. In a year when any *esrog* would have been welcome, he had been blessed with one as perfect as this! All night long he remained awake, waiting on tiptoe for the first glimmering of dawn so that he would be able to perform the mitzvah.

The great moment came, and as he prepared to pronounce the blessing in all the awed rapture of *deveikus*, his chassidim told him of the condition which the man from Preissin had stipulated. The tzaddik's joy wilted into melancholy. Without a word he laid down the *esrog*, and walked up and down in a dilemma for almost the whole day.

Sunset was imminent. Seeing that he would have no other means of fulfilling the mitzvah, the tzaddik said: "Be what may, I'll just have to give him my promise!"

With that, he recited his blessing over the *esrog*. And within a year the wife of the man from Preissin gave birth to a son.

◦§ When to Look at an Esrog

Every year Rabbi Chaim Elazar Wax of Pietrkov would send an *esrog* as a gift to Reb Yechiel of Alexander. On one occasion, however, the tzaddik was not pleased with the *esrog* that he had received. He dispatched his attendant to Pietrkov with the request that it be exchanged for another.

The *rav* of Pietrkov was of course distressed to hear this, the more so since he had nothing better to send.

"There's only one thing I can suggest," he said to the *shammes*. "Not long ago I sent a fine *esrog* to a certain rabbi. Let us call on him together. If he hears that it is for the rebbe of Alexander I am sure he will not send us away emptyhanded."

Their visit in the dead of night awoke the *rav* from his sleep. In fact he was quite taken aback to discover that

SUKKOS his callers were the *rav* of Pietrkov and the *shammes* of the rebbe of Alexander. At first he was unenthusiastic, but when he considered by whom the request was being made, and for whom it was being made, he thought better of it, and handed over the *esrog*.

The *shammes*, all exultant, brought the trophy to the rebbe. But no sooner had he stepped over the threshold than Reb Yechiel addressed him: "What kind of melancholy have you brought me? Tell me, please: what happened to you during your journey?"

When he had heard out the whole story he said: "Please set out at once and return the *esrog* to the *rav* over there."

In the meantime the days were slipping by. Yom Kippur was at hand, Sukkos was only a few days off — and the rebbe was still without an *esrog*.

One day he called his son and said: "You know that every year the *rav* of Pietrkov sends me a box full of plain ordinary *esrogim* — not for the blessing, just to hang in the *sukkah* by way of decoration. Let's open the box. Who knows? Perhaps we'll come across an *esrog* in there that I can use for the mitzvah."

And indeed the rebbe found there an *esrog* that made him very happy. While he was enthusiastically singing its praises, he observed that one of his chassidim who was standing nearby was puzzled at his reaction: it seemed to him unwarranted.

"Now tell me," said the rebbe, "are you a connoisseur of an *esrog*? For in the symbolism of this mitzvah, as you know, the *esrog* corresponds to a man's heart. And tell me: are you a connoisseur of men's hearts?"

The chassidim then gathered that the tzaddik had been shown by the divine inspiration of *ruach hakodesh* that this *esrog* was destined to be his.

"I am always fortunate in having beautiful *esrogim*," he would say. Then, continuing the aggadic theme which relates the *esrog* to the heart, he would add: "When an *esrog* is brought to me, I don't look at it until after we have recited the penitential *Selichos* prayer which evokes the Thirteen Attributes of Divine Mercy. For all the superficial blemishes on an *esrog* are washed away by the contrite tears that are shed during that prayer ..."

koheles

The Book of Koheles is read aloud in many synagogues
on the Sabbath which falls on the Intermediate Days of
Sukkos (Shabbos Chol HaMoed Sukkos).

⇜ Wasting Your Rations

Penniless as he was, this poor jester's tongue never tired: his life was one long frivolous prattle. His one problem was his wife, who lost no opportunity to nag him because there was no food in the house. So, feeling very sorry for himself, he took his sad story all the way to Korets, to Reb Pinchas.

לִשְׂחוֹק אָמַרְתִּי מְהוֹלָל
Of mirth, I said it was frivolous (2:2)

The tzaddik of Korets, advised him in these words: "Control your tongue from jesting, and your financial situation at home will improve.

"Let me explain. Our Sages teach us that — 'A man's income for the forthcoming year is determined for him on Rosh HaShanah.' This does not mean to say that it is decided that he will have so-and-so many measures of grain and so-and-so many measures of some other kinds of household necessities. It means that they allot him such-and-such an amount of pleasure. Now you delight so much in joking that you waste all the pleasure that has been apportioned to you, and you don't leave any for your livelihood!"

⇜ Remedial vs. Symptomatic Treatment

יִתְרוֹן לַחָכְמָה מִן הַסִּכְלוּת כִּיתְרוֹן הָאוֹר מִן הַחשֶׁךְ
Wisdom excels folly as light excels darkness (2:13)

After the passing of Reb Uri of Strelisk, one of his chassidim decided upon Reb Simchah Bunem of Pshischah as his new spiritual mentor.

On his first visit to Pshischah, the tzaddik asked him: "What would you say your rebbe chiefly stressed when

koheLes he used to guide you and your colleagues in the service of the Almighty according to the ways of Chassidism?''

"Above all," replied the chassid, "Reb Uri endeavored to implant in his chassidim the attribute of humility. In fact it was his practice that when anyone came to consult him, even if he was a celebrated scholar or a man of wealth, the visitor was first obliged to bring two large buckets of water from the market place, or some other such chore, in order to inculcate in him this attribute of humility."

"Let me tell you a story," responded Reb Simchah Bunem. "A king once imprisoned three men in a dungeon that was utterly dark. Two of the men were clever, and the other was a simpleton. Every day their jailer lowered them their rations of food and water, but in the pitch-black darkness the simpleton could never make head or tail of the various utensils. In fact he couldn't even manage to feed himself, until one of the clever men taught him by means of signs how to identify the various items. The trouble was that every day they were given different utensils and different kinds of food, so that this lesson had to be repeated afresh every single time. The other clever man, meanwhile, used to sit in silence.

"One day the first man asked the second: 'Why do you always just sit there, and not teach that fool anything? Should it be all *my* responsibility?'

"Replied the second: 'There'll never be an end to all the bother of your teaching. What are you going to do if tomorrow they give him some other kind of plate, and so on the next day, and the next? I'm busy doing something else. I'm sitting here and thinking how we can dig a hole through this wall so that the sunlight will find its way in here, and then without any further effort he'll see everything ...'"

◆§ A Season for Everything

לַכֹּל זְמָן
For everything there is a season (3:1)

When praying, Reb Chaim of Zanz used to serve his Maker with all his might and with all his soul, cleaving to Him in the ecstasy of *deveikus* to the point that he virtually left his body quite behind him. He would stamp one foot and break out into dancing, even though one leg was diseased. Once when he was still a youth he visited Reb Naftali of Ropshitz, and while staying in his household prayed with such enthusiasm that he stamped his foot vigorously. The *rebbitzin* of the tzaddik came to her husband with a complaint: 'Why do you let him stamp like that with his bad leg, instead of telling him to stamp with his good one?''

Replied Reb Naftali ''If he were aware of which leg he was stamping with, then of course I would do as you advise. But what is to be done if when he is praying he doesn't feel which leg is which? ...''

❀ ❀ ❀

On another occasion Reb Chaim was visiting Reb Eliezer of Dzikov, and before his morning prayers he engaged the sons of the tzaddik in the demanding intellectual exercise of a halachic duel. Immediately thereafter he began his prayers, which were as ecstatic as always.

"How is it possible to pray with such fire, "Reb Eliezer of Dzikov asked him, "immediately after the cool-headed exertions of logical *pilpul* which occupied your brain just a moment before?"

"When I begin to pray," answered Reb Chaim, "I forget that there is such a thing in the world as Torah study, and when I am engaged in Torah study, I forget that there is anything else in the world apart from Torah study."

❀ ❀ ❀

Reb Chaim was once called upon to adjudicate in a lawsuit being heard before a rabbinical court of three, the other two members of which had been chosen by the respective litigants. The three members of the *beis din* were all engaged in the deliberate examination of the *Shulchan Aruch* and the other large tomes of legal literature which covered the table. All of a sudden one of the other two scholars looked up from his books, and in an outburst of piety exclaimed: — "Master of the Universe! You are One, Unique, and a Unity!"

Reb Chaim turned to him and said: "When you are engaged in determining the outcome of a lawsuit ac-

koheles cording to the Torah, please leave the Master of the Universe alone, and concentrate instead on what's written in the *Shulchan Aruch* and *Ktzos HaChoshen* and the other halachic codes and commentaries ..."

◦§ A Time and a Place

Silence, an awesome silence, reigned in the *beis midrash*. Reb Yitzchak Aizik of Zhidachov was at the head of the table at the Third Meal of *Shabbos*, chanting his pensive melodies, expounding the mysteries of the Torah, and no man there moved nor breathed aloud.

Such a profound yearning for repentance and for spiritual elevation did the tzaddik arouse in the souls of his listeners that on the morning following one such occasion, not a single one of the merchants and shopkeepers who had come to visit him for the duration of *Shabbos* came to take his leave. In the state in which he had left them, it did not occur to them that they should now be returning to their homes and livelihoods. Not knowing this, the tzaddik asked his sons why no one had come to take his leave. When they duly asked, they received the following answer: "Only yesterday our rebbe, your father, made all the things of This World so unworthy and uninviting in our eyes, that we are ashamed to face him with our problems and requests about our oxen and donkeys and businesses and whatever."

The tzaddik was told of this, and smiled.

"Something similar once happened with Reb Menachem Mendel of Rimanov," he said, "so he passed on a message to his chassidim: '*Shabbos* is one thing, weekdays are something different. Let the businesmen return to their homes and engage honestly in their commerce.' Now please tell my chassidim the words of the Psalmist: 'The heavens are the heavens of God, but the earth He has given to the children of man.'"

Hearing this, each chassid folded up his *tallis*, packed his bags, and returned to his home and his daily affairs.

◆§ Can You Spare a Minute?

R eb Avraham Mordechai of Ger (who passed away in Jerusalem in 1948) once said: "A certain fellow once got the better of me. I had just entered my study, and along comes a man and hands me a *kvitl* with a request.

"I said: 'Believe me that I haven't even one minute to spare.'

"So he answered: 'I can spare more than twenty years to take care of my sick daughter, and can't my rebbe spare for her even one minute?' "

◆§ To Live for This Day

I n the course of a long journey, the Chozeh of Lublin and his disciples once arrived on the eve of *Shabbos* at a crossroads. Not knowing what directions to give the wagondriver, the tzaddik advised him instead: "Let go of the reins, and let the horses go wherever they like."

On the outskirts of a town they found out from a stranger that this was neither the town nor the road that they were seeking.

Said the Chozeh (a Hebrew title which means "the Seer"): "Today I am not a rebbe."

His disciples knew that if they had to depend on his own resources they would be at a loss, for the tzaddik never kept as much as a copper coin overnight: whatever money he was given he always distributed to the poor on the very same day. So they asked him: "If we don't tell people here that you are a rebbe, where will we spend *Shabbos*?"

He replied: "We will go to the local synagogue and be invited to the homes of various householders, as is the universal custom among Jews."

And so indeed, each of his disciples and attendants was invited for *Shabbos* to the home of a different townsman, while the rebbe, according to his wont, stayed on late in *shul* until he had completed his prayers at his own pensive pace. He then saw an old man of about eighty sitting in *shul* and reciting *Shabbos* hymns from his prayer book.

וְעֵת לָמוּת

And a time to die (3:2)

koheles   "Where are you going for *Kiddush?*" the old man asked.

"I don't know," said the Chozeh.

"I would suggest that you go to an inn for your *Shabbos* meals," said the old man, "and after *Shabbos* is over I will go about and collect the money needed to pay the innkeeper."

"They don't light *Shabbos* candles there," replied the tzaddik. "I won't make *Kiddush* at the inn."

"But in my house there's barely enough wine and bread for my wife and myself," said the old man.

"I neither eat much nor drink much," the tzaddik reassured him.

After he had made *Kiddush* and eaten a little *challah* in the cottage of the old couple, his host asked him: "Sir, where do you come from?"

"From Lublin," said the tzaddik.

"And do you know *him?*" asked the host.

"I — am always with him," said the tzaddik.

"In that case," the old man pleaded, "tell me something about him."

"And why do you want to hear about him?" asked the tzaddik.

"When he was a little boy I was his schoolteacher," said the old man. "At that time he was no different than all the other children, but now I'm told that he is a great man and works wonders. In fact, on one day every week I fast and pray that I may be privileged to set my eyes upon him, for you see I am poor and weak, and I cannot make the long journey to Lublin."

"Did you notice anything about him when he was little?" asked the tzaddik.

The old man recalled: "Every day when I would call him to take his turn to read from the *Siddur* I wouldn't find him, and when he would turn up later I would give him a spanking. One day I got it into my head that I'd like to see for myself where he went. I followed him quietly at a distance. He walked right into the forest, sat down in the midst of those ants that sting you, and cried out: שְׁמַע יִשְׂרָאֵל ה' אֱלֹקֵינוּ ה' אֶחָד — 'Hear O Israel, the Lord our God, the Lord is One!' From that day on I never spanked him again."

The tzaddik now understood the reason for which קֹהֶלֶת
Divine Providence had directed him to this town. He
said: "I am he."

The old man heard, and fainted. When he came to, the
tzaddik asked him to reveal to no man that he was in this
town.

When *Shabbos* was over, the Chozeh and his disciples
left the town. The old man accompanied them for part of
the way, and returned to his cottage.

Later that evening the tzaddik and his chassidim arrived at a village where they sat together at the *Melaveh
Malkah* meal which farewells the departing *Shabbos*
Queen. When that was over, the tzaddik said to his disciples: "Let us go back to that town, so that we can pay
our last respects to the old man who has departed for
another world and deliver the eulogy which is his due."

◆§ Now I Understand

Any experienced reader of chassidic *mayses* knows
that a good story presupposes the knowledge of a little introductory mishpachology.

Well, the children of Reb Shneur Zalman of Liadi in-
cluded a son, Reb Dov Ber of Lubavitch, and a daughter,
Devorah Leah. And the daughter of the former, Chayah
Mushka, married the son of the latter, Reb Menachem
Mendel of Lubavitch (known as the author of *Tzemach
Tzedek*).

Once Reb Shneur Zalman asked his granddaughter to
show him some of the manuscript pages that her husband was writing for himself. She did not know exactly
which ones her grandfather wanted, but seeing a rather
thick stack of sheets she brought him those. These pages
contained the long exposition which has since become
renowned under the title *Shoresh Mitzvas HaTefillah*
("The Root of the Mitzvah of Prayer"), and appears in
the book entitled *Derech Mitzvosecha*.

As soon as he had studied it, Reb Shneur Zalman
called for his brother, Reb Yehudah Leib, and for an
elder chassid by the name of Reb Pinchas Reizes, and
told them that he would like to pronounce the blessing of
thanksgiving which is recited on the receipt of glad

koheles tidings. He told them of the exposition he had read, stood up and pronounced the blessing of *Shehecheyanu* in full, and the two listeners responded with "Amen."

When the young author of the discourse discovered what had happened, he became so angry at his wife that he said that he would divorce her. She pointed out that she had heard that respect for one's father's father was an even greater obligation than the mitzvah of respecting one's father — for one's father is likewise obligated to respect *his* father. Since her grandfather had told her to bring the manuscript, what could she do? — especially since her husband, Reb Menachem Mendel, was obliged to honor him as much as he would honor his own father; for was not her grandfather also *his* grandfather, and his teacher as well?

Reb Menachem Mendel said that he would have to look up the *halachah* on this whole question, for what he had said about divorcing her could possibly come under the heading of a vow or an oath. Until he had studied and clarified their situation, therefore, they would not be able to continue living together.

For a few days the poor young woman wept. Finally, after two months of waiting, she told the whole story to her father.

Reb Dov Ber duly raised the subject with his son-in-law, but found that his mind was so firmly made up that he in turn told the story to his father, Reb Shneur Zalman.

On *Shabbos*, after he had delivered his traditional discourse at the table and all the chassidim had taken their leave, Reb Shneur Zalman said to his grandson: "I understand that you have a halachic question under perusal. Since you are an interested party, so that it will be difficult for you to arrive at the truth, let us look up the query together. That way we are sure to be able to arrive at the true intention of the *halachah* in this matter."

After they had investigated the subject and had established that the words uttered were in no way binding, Reb Shneur Zalman said to his grandson: "In order to remove from your heart any trace of irritability towards your wife — better: in order that you should gladden her heart — from now on I will study regularly with you, both in the revealed and in the concealed areas of the קְהִלַּת Torah. In your lives will the promise of the Prophet then be fulfilled."

And paraphrasing the words of Isaiah, Reb Shneur Zalman said: "You shall plant pleasant plants, you shall cause your planting to flourish, and your seed to blossom."

He paused to rest his forehead on his arm, as was his wont, sighed deeply, and concluded with the continuation of the passage from Isaiah: ... נֵד קָצִיר — "The harvest shall disappear in the day of grief and desperate pain."

This incident took place in the year 1807. Fifty-four years went by, and in the month of Teves, 1861, the wife of Reb Menachem Mendel passed away.

An old memory stirred Reb Menachem Mendel. He said: "Now I understand what my grandfather told me fifty-four years ago: ... נֵד קָצִיר (for the numerical value of the letters נ"ד is 54). And now I understand the deep sigh which he then uttered. For the harvest has disappeared in the day of grief."

And he too sighed.

◆§ A Passing like This

In the summer of 1827, Reb Dov Ber ("the Mitteler Rebbe") of Lubavitch made the long journey to Haditch, to pray at the burial-place of his father, Reb Shneur Zalman of Liadi. All the way there he refrained from delivering the chassidic discourses that his followers anticipated expectantly; he did not even desire the company of his chassidim; and whenever he wanted to commit his teachings to writing some mishap always intervened, such as the pen falling from his hand. This he saw as an indication of stern judgment On High, and when speaking to his chassidim he hinted at his imminent demise.

On one such occasion he said: "My father was fifty-four years old when he was imprisoned in St. Petersburg for the second time. At that time two alternatives were offered him from heaven: suffering, or death. He chose suffering. It seems that the other he left for me."

koheles   Reb Dov Ber arrived at Haditch in time for the Days of Awe late in 1827, visited the burial-place of his father several times, and on many occasions expounded the philosophy of *Chabad* Chassidism in the *beis midrash* that had been built at that holy site. On one such visit he returned after quite some time, his face smiling with joy.

"I have secured a promise from my father that they will free me from my position as rebbe," he said.

The chassidim who had accompanied him assumed that his intention was now to travel to the Holy Land, a thing which he had long yearned to do. So they said: "Rebbe, why should you speak like that? How will you leave us like sheep without a shepherd?"

"Why," he reassured them, "you have my son-in-law, Reb Menachem Mendel. He will be a faithful shepherd for you." And indeed, when the time came, the mantle of leadership was taken over by his son-in-law, the author of *Tzemach Tzedek*.

Soon after he began the journey home via Niezhin, but there he fell ill and could not proceed. His chassidim secured the services of the most competent physicians, but none could prescribe a remedy. They warned him to refrain utterly from delivering his accustomed discourses to his eager listeners. This was so bitter a restriction that he said: "I am weary of my life."

His condition deteriorated so seriously that as soon as he was touched he would faint into a stupor, and his doctors tried to bring him to with pungent herbs. By the beginning of Kislev, a week before his passing, his doctors saw that he lay in bed with no apparent bodily vitality, and could not fathom what kept him alive.

While he was in this state one of them said to his colleagues: "Let me show you something strange. You see how he lies here, quite devoid of vitality. Let us allow him to deliver a discourse on the teachings of Chassidism, and his life-force will be restored to him at once."

This they did. He sat up immediately, his face aflame, and asked to have a chair set up for him. The chassidim from all around filled the house to overflowing.

"Now," said the rebbe, "I will teach you secrets of the Torah that I have never before revealed."

But heaven intervened. One of the disciples who

crowded around was standing with others on a bench קהלת
behind the rebbe's chair, leaning forward and straining
to hear every word. His hat fell down, and interrupted
the rebbe's train of thought.

"It seems that in heaven they don't want me to reveal
those teachings," he said.

And he began to expound a different subject.

On the eve of the ninth of Kislev he lost consciousness
several times — and for once they could not bring him to.

There was a great outcry in the house. More chassidim
flocked there, together with other townsmen, and the
men of the *Chevrah Kaddisha* (burial society). Someone
had already said that it was time to cease in their at-
tempts to bring the rebbe back to consciousness, for all
hope had vanished. Suddenly, though, he opened his
eyes. A smile lit up his face, and he said: "I heard a voice
calling: 'What does a soul like this need in This
World?' "

He then asked to be dressed in a white shirt, and was
soon dressed all in white — the picture of an angel.

Then, as if addressing the Heavenly Court, he spoke
in defense of the House of Israel, pleading their cause.
How lovingly did they obey the commandments of their
Maker; how generous were they toward their needy
brethren! For did not even the poorest Jew give charity
beyond his means?

He now instructed the chassidim and his family to be
joyful — for joy sweetens the bitter words of the
prosecuting angels in heaven. He asked that the scholars
present be called near to him, for he desired to expound a
concept in Chassidism. The house was resplendent with
light and joy: surely the rebbe was about to regain his
health and strength. He prepared to speak, and said to
one of the chassidim at his bedside: "While I am expounding, watch over me carefully; for it could be that I
will fall asleep, and if so, touch me with your hand and I
will wake up."

In a state of sustained ecstasy he delivered three discourses, twice expounding the verse "After God shall
you go", and the third time the verse "The remembrance
of Your abounding goodness". He asked a few times
whether it was yet dawn. Just before dawn he reached

koheles the words — כִּי עִמְּךָ מְקוֹר חַיִּים מֵחַיֵּי הַחַיִּים: " 'For with You is the source of life' — You Who are the Life of life ...'' And as he breathed these words, his soul took flight and soared heavenward.

In his lifespan one can see the fulfillment of the verse: "The number of your days shall I fill," for he had been born on that very day, the ninth of Kislev 1773, *exactly fifty-four years earlier.*

Concerning his last moments on earth, his son-in-law Reb Menachem Mendel said: "A passing like this has not been known since the passing of Rabbi Shimon bar Yochai. For it is recorded in *Idra*, in the *Zohar*, that when Rabbi Shimon bar Yochai said the words כִּי שָׁם צִוָּה ה' אֶת הַבְּרָכָה חַיִּים — 'For there God ordained the blessing of life,' while he was saying the word חַיִּים ('life') his soul returned to its Source."

⤳ My Request has been Granted

It is the custom of the townsfolk of Niezhin to mark the anniversary of the passing of Reb Menachem Mendel of Lubavitch (the *yahrzeit* falls on the ninth of Kislev) by praying in the *beis midrash* which stands next to his burial-place, and studying selections from the Mishnah whose initials spell out the letters of his name.

One year a certain man spent the whole day at the holy site, weeping bitterly, until after the evening prayers. The tzaddik's son, Reb Nachum, who was also there, took him home in his wagon, and on the way asked him what was it that made him weep so long.

Though reluctant at first to explain himself, the man finally said: "I will reveal to you my secret. I feel a close bond with the rebbe, and I could not bring myself to leave his resting-place. I therefore came to a firm decision: I would not budge from this place until my soul left me, and I would be buried here, and my bones would lie near that beloved holy spot. It was this that I requested all day, until with the Almighty's help I succeeded. My request has been granted."

"But how do you know that?" asked Reb Nachum. "How do you know that my father answered you?"

"Rabbi," replied the other, "why trouble yourself in

investigating the matter? With your own eyes you will קהלת
see and understand that what I said is true, that (thank
God!) I have been promised what I sought."

When they arrived at home of Reb Nachum, the guest
declined to join him in his evening meal, nor would he
taste anything. Reb Nachum gave him a room alone in
which to sleep — but when at dawn he went to visit him,
he found his guest lying there, lifeless.

Soon after he was buried with all due honor — next to
the resting-place of his rebbe.

◄§ Lifespan

In the month of Iyyar 1834 Reb Shmuel ("the
Maharash") of Lubavitch was born. His father, Reb
Menachem Mendel, asked the household to rise early on
the eighth day for morning prayers, and by ten all the
relatives were assembled in readiness for the circumcision — but the rebbe had not yet come out of his study.
When it was nearing two o'clock and there was still no
sign of the rebbe, people started becoming anxious. His
uncle, Reb Chaim Avraham, said: "He is busy right now
with invitees of loftier stature than ourselves" — and he
sighed.

Half an hour later the rebbe appeared at the door of
his study. There were tears in his eyes, and he held a red
handkerchief in his hand.

"The *bris* will take place today," he said.

He returned to his room, but the anxiety of the waiting
guests was even greater than before. Half an hour later
he again came out of his study, his face exultant. He told
the guests to be glad of heart: the circumcision would
take place that day. Again he returned to his room, rejoined his guests after a few minutes, and the ceremony
began.

In the course of the festive meal following the circumcision the rebbe quoted a verse from *Psalms:* "The years
of our life number seventy" (literally: "the days of our
years — in them [בָּהֶם] are seventy years"). And he continued with a puzzling comment: "A lifespan may
belong to one of several levels — some men live eighty
years, some seventy years, and some live בָּהֶם, with its
letters."

koheles Decades passed, and the infant grew to manhood. Toward the end of the month of Sivan 1882, nearly four months before his passing, Reb Shmuel said: "My father said that some people live 'בָּהֶם, with its letters.' That means (adding together the numerical *value* of the letters of this word, 47, and the *number* of its letters, 3): fifty" — and he uttered a deep sigh.

And indeed, though in actual months lived his life came to forty-eight-and-a-half years, his lifetime spanned the years 5594 to 5643 — according to the Jewish calendar, fifty years.

ᴥ§ Ready and Able

Two years after the passing of Reb Simchah Bunem of Pshischah, his son and successor Reb Avraham Moshe traveled to Biala. Arriving there he quoted the verse from Psalms: "Here will I dwell, for I have desired it." And to his mother he said: "I would fain die."

His mother replied: "I heard from your father that a man has to learn in order to know how to die."

"I have already learned how to die," he said.

"But I heard from your father that a man has to learn a great deal in order to know how to die!"

"I have already learned enough to die," he said — and passed away in Biala soon after.

ᴥ§ In Black and White

As the reader may or may not know, there is a passage in the Mishnah which considers the case of a person who on the eve of a festival prepares black pigeons for use on the festival, but when *Yom-Tov* comes he finds white ones in the nest instead. The question involved is the permissibility of using them, in view of the restrictions of *muktzeh*. At any rate, the expression used there is זְמֵן שְׁחוֹרִים וּמָצָא לְבָנִים — "If he prepared black ones and found white ones ..."

Now in 1833, the year which was to prove to be his last on earth, the chassidim of Reb Noach of Lechovitch wanted to have a new black outfit tailored for him. So they arranged for a tailor to call on their rebbe in order to take his measurements. קהילת

The tailor walked into the study, and found the rebbe walking up and down his room in a state of agitated ecstasy, and repeating to himself in the singsong in which the Mishnah is traditionally studied: "If he prepared black ones and found white ones ..."

⋆§ Nothing More to Do Here

Seeing how desperately ill their rebbe was, the chassidim wanted to summon a medical specialist: perhaps he would still be able to do something. The patient was Reb Yekusiel Yehudah Teitelbaum, the author of *Yitav Lev*, and the grandson of Reb Moshe Teitelbaum of Ujhely. He would not hear of the suggestion, and said: "Let me tell you a story that happened in Poland about two hundred years ago."

This is the story he told his chassidim.

❁ ❁ ❁

Rabbi Yoel Sirkes, the celebrated author of *Bayis Chadash*, one day visited his renowned son-in-law, Rabbi David ben Shmuel HaLevi, the author of *Turei Zahav*. (The two scholars are commonly known by the acronyms of the titles of their legal commentaries, as *Bach* and *Taz* respectively.) The entire town turned out to welcome him. One young scholar alone did not step forward to extend the traditional greeting of *"Shalom."*

"How is that possible?" Rabbi David ben Shmuel protested. The young man answered that he had been informed by the mouth of Eliyahu the Prophet, of blessed memory, that the visiting luminary had been placed by heaven (God forbid!) under a ban. The reason was that when he was once passing through a certain town he encountered two men who were arguing about a wagonful of wood that one of them had bought from the other. The purchaser held that the agreed price was three gold coins, while the seller claimed that they had agreed on three gold coins and one-tenth. Seeing Rabbi Yoel Sirkes, they had asked him to adjudicate their lawsuit.

"What sum is under dispute?" the famed rabbi asked.

"A tenth of a gold coin," they said.

"And should I be held up in the middle of a journey," he protested, "for litigation involving a tenth of a coin?"

The accusing angels in heaven made much of his retort, for the rule the Sages teach us is, "A suit involving one copper coin is to be treated as earnestly as a suit involving a hundred coins."

Having now heard such a story about his father-in-law, Rabbi Shmuel asked him whether the account of it was true — and indeed it was. It was clear to them both that this young man had been caused by Divine Providence to be present at this time and place in order that the misdeed should be set right, and a rabbinical court of three was immediately constituted, and charged with annulling the ban.

Rabbi Yoel then said to the young man: "Since I see that in the eyes of heaven you are a man of some stature, I would ask a favor of you. I would like to give you the manuscript of my commentary on the *Arba'ah Turim*, which I plan to publish under the title *Bayis Chadash*. Before it goes to press, I would like you to look over it and to give me your opinion on it."

Some time later Rabbi Yoel asked him if he had completed his perusal of the manuscript and if he was ready to return it.

"I won't want to return it to you even in twenty years' time," said the young man.

"Why so?" asked Rabbi Yoel. "If the book does not meet with your approval, then please tell me, for did I not give it to you in order to hear your critical comments?"

"Your book *is* good and *does* good," the young man assured him. "However, as soon as you publish it and distribute it around the world, you will have completed your life's task of *tikkun*, of setting yourself in order: you will have nothing more to do in This World. And that is precisely why I want to delay its publication — so that you should continue living with us here."

"If that is what is holding you back," said Rabbi Yoel, "then I hereby commit my soul to my Creator, and will not delay the publication of the book for the reason you give, because the world needs it."

The young man had no option but to return the קְהִלּת manuscript to its author, who proceeded to have it published, volume by volume, beginning in 1631. And in 1640, soon after the appearance of the final volume, Rabbi Yoel Sirkes passed away.

❀ ❀ ❀

Reb Yekusiel Yehudah had completed his story.

"And so it is with me, too," he said to the chassidim who stood anxiously around his sickbed. "If with the help of the Almighty I have already set my spiritual affairs aright, then I have nothing more to do in This World — and I do not want you to call another doctor."

ᴥ§ Tuesday Turns and Goes

One Chanukah evening in the last year of his life in This World, Reb Meir Horovitz of Dzikov, the author of *Imrei Noam*, was playing with his sons at the traditional game of spinning the *dreidel*-top. Every time it was his turn, the *dreidel* would fall in such a way that the letter facing upwards was *gimmel*, the third letter of the alphabet.

"Watch how Tuesday turns and goes," he said, referring to the day by its Hebrew name, *yom gimmel*, the third day of the week. This cryptic comment he repeated twice more, and stopped playing.

Neither his sons nor the other people present had any idea what his remark hinted at, until half a year later, on the eighth of Tammuz, he passed away — on a Tuesday.

ᴥ§ A Great Darkness

One day in 1850 a chassid called on Reb Meir of Premishlan and, as often before, handed him a *kvitl*. The tzaddik took the note on which the man's requests were noted, leaned his head on his arms, and was soon deep in thought. Then he said: "You should know that you stand in serious danger, and are in need of the mercies of heaven. But I have a way in which you may be saved. Every year I send to our needy brethren in the Holy Land 702 gold rubles — the numerical value of the

koheles letters that make up the word *Shabbos* (שַׁבָּת). Half of this sum I send before Pesach, and half before Rosh HaShanah. Now Pesach is already approaching, and I haven't a single penny. Provide me with the 351 gold rubles that are needed now, and you will spared from all evil."

The man trembled in awe.

"Rebbe, of course I want to fulfill your wish," he said, "but I haven't got that amount with me. Let me therefore journey to Lvov to borrow the sum, and I will bring it to you."

"If you haven't got the money," replied the tzaddik, "then your redemption will come through another means. Take a message from me to Reb Yisrael of Ruzhin, who lives in Sadigora, and you will have no need to give me that sum of money."

The chassid agreed at once. In fact he was quite delighted with the opportunity of not only visiting the tzaddik of Ruzhin, but of passing on to him a message from his own rebbe as well.

"Very well," said Reb Meir. "Travel straight from here to Sadigora. As soon as you arrive there go directly to the household of Reb Yisrael, and tell his attendants that you have a message from me. You will arrive there on Friday morning, and when you enter the tzaddik's study you shall address him in these words: 'Meir has given you the following order. Our passports have already been signed, giving us free passage through all the borders. It is true that eighty thousand souls are waiting to welcome you, but for Meir many more are waiting — except that Meir's passport expires before yours.' "

The chassid went pale with terror. He begged to be excused, and tried to explain to his rebbe that he could not undertake a mission such as this. He would be prepared to contribute the sum needed for the poor folk in *Eretz Yisrael* — so long as he would be freed of this mission. Nothing helped. The tzaddik entreated and directed him to carry out his mission in full.

Much against his will the chassid set out for Sadigora. When he arrived on Friday morning the attendant on duty refused him entry: this was not one of the times at

which the tzaddik received callers. But as soon as he said קִהִלַּת
who had dispatched him, the attendant asked his rebbe,
who asked that he be admitted at once.

The chassid approached Reb Yisrael with a *kvitl* in
hand.

"This is not the time for receiving *kvitlach*," said the
tzaddik. "Tell me, therefore, what mission brings you
here."

"Before I do that," said the chassid, "I would like to
receive your blessing, for my holy teacher in Premishlan
has told me that he sees ominous things destined for me.
For this reason I would request you to accept my *kvitl*
and to give me your blessing."

Reb Yisrael blessed him, and the chassid faithfully
passed on Reb Meir's message, word for word. All this
while the tzaddik of Ruzhin sat motionless in his place,
as if the message in question did not involve himself at
all.

One Thursday some months later Reb Meir said to all
the chassidim who were with him: "Whoever does not
want a disturbed *Shabbos* had better make the journey
home."

Though no one understood what he could be alluding
to, they all went home. One man only — a tzaddik by the
name of Reb Yisrael of Kalisz — requested the permission of Reb Meir to stay on for *Shabbos*.

"If you want to be here," anwered Reb Meir, "you
may do so. But just remember that Shabbos is — *Shabbos.*"

And on that *Shabbos* he departed This World.

On *Motzaei Shabbos*, when the Day of Rest was over,
and Reb Yisrael of Ruzhin was sitting at his table on
which stood two lighted candlesticks, one candle suddenly went out. Someone lit it again, but the other one
went out.

"There is a great darkness in the world," said the tzaddik. And the next day the bitter tidings from Premishlan
reached them.

A few months later Reb Yisrael too passed away.

ᴥᔥ A Rebbe's Reasons

The elders of Zvichvust once invited a chassid by the name of Reb Moshe of Razvodov to accept the post of rabbi of their town. Reb Moshe asked the advice of Reb Menachem Mendel of Kotsk, who on no account would agree to the proposal.

Many years passed. Reb Moshe was now an old man, and was again visiting the tzaddik of Kotsk. Before he left, the tzaddik said: "I think you once told me that Zvichvust wants you. What is it to you? Travel there and rest there."

On his way home he therefore headed first for Zvichvust, but as soon as he arrived he fell ill. A few days later he died, and was buried there. It was then that his colleagues understood why the tzaddik of Kotsk had restrained him from accepting the rabbinical post there many years earlier.

ᴥᔥ Chassidic Tactics

וְעֵת לִרְפּוֹא
*And a time
to heal
(3:3)*

The *rav* of Chodorov, the eldest grandson of Reb Yitzchak Aizik of Zhidachov, was once desperately ill. His father, Reb Sender Lipa, who was the tzaddik's firstborn son, requested his father several times to intercede for the young man in heaven, but there was no improvement in his condition.

One day a messenger arrived from the town where the patient lay to inform the family of the tzaddik that the young man was at the very gates of death. It was very late at night, an hour at which Reb Yitzchak Aizik was closeted alone in his room, engrossed in the service of his Creator — a time at which he allowed no one, not even his sons, to disturb him. His sons consulted with each other as to who should pass on the grave news. Eventually they decided on one of his grandchildren, who was later to become renowned as Reb Yehudah Zvi, the rebbe of Dolina, but was at that time a child much loved by his grandfather.

They lit a lantern for him, and he climbed up the flight

of stairs that led to the rebbe's attic. When he arrived at קְהִלַּת the door he coughed once or twice. The tzaddik opened the door, and asked him: "*Nu?*"

The precocious boy chose his words carefully, and said: "*Zeide*, I have come to tell you that the condition of your grandson, the *rav* of Chodorov, is improving. You should therefore ask for the mercies of heaven, so that he should become completely well."

The tzaddik's face beamed. He beckoned the child into his study, gave him a handful of tea-leaves from the cupboard, and said: "Let them brew this tea and give it to the patient to drink. He will perspire a great deal, and the illness will pass away completely."

The tea was of course sent off at once, and after a few hours the young man indeed felt better. The very next day another messenger arrived from there bringing these glad tidings, and the young man's father, Reb Sender Lipa, went upstairs to pass them on to the tzaddik.

Reb Yitzchak Aizik rebuked him gently: "You need to take a lesson in Chassidic thinking from my little grandson Yehudah Zvi. For whereas you added anguish to my anguish, this little fellow was clever enough to animate my soul with some good news. It was this that gave me the spirit to draw down upon the patient the blessing of a *real* return to health."

◄§ Do a Man a Favor

163
וְעֵת לִשְׂחוֹק
And a time to laugh (3:4)

When the Baal Shem Tov first revealed himself, much of the active opposition to him and to his teachings proceeded from the *kloyz*, a circle of eminent scholars in Brody headed by Rabbi Chaim Tzanser (not to be confused with the chassidic rebbe, Reb Chaim of Zanz).

Once Rabbi Chaim sent one of his prominent students to fathom what manner of man the Baal Shem Tov was. The student spent some time in the company of the tzaddik, and ultimately became an admiring disciple.

When it was time to return to Brody and he came to take leave of the Baal Shem Tov, the tzaddik said: "I hereby order you to report to your teacher on anything that you have seen here which you do not view favorably. You see, Rabbi Chaim is one of the learned

koheles and righteous men of this generation. He is a spiritual descendant of Rabbi Yochanan of the Talmud, and throughout his life has never once laughed, in accordance with the teaching of Rabbi Yochanan, 'A man may not fill his mouth with laughter.' Now whoever can give him such pleasure that he laughs will earn himself a portion in the World to Come. And since Rabbi Chaim is an antagonist of ours, perhaps when you speak of me you will do him this favor, and make him laugh."

◄§ And I Laughed Too

עֵת רְקוֹד
*A time to
dance (3:4)*

Serene and tranquil, the Baal Shem Tov sat at the head of his long Friday night table, facing all the venerable disciples who made up the *Chevraya Kaddisha*, the holy brotherhood. He rose to recite *Kiddush* over a goblet of wine, and immediately thereafter broke out in joyful laughter. After sitting for a little while at the table, he again laughed, and then a few minutes later, once more. The chassidim sat in silent wonderment, but did not dare to ask for an explanation. They waited until the Day of Rest was over, and asked Reb Wolff Kitzis to put their question to the rebbe, for it was his custom on *Motzaei Shabbos* to visit the rebbe while he was smoking his pipe, and to raise with him the queries that had arisen during the holy day.

He visited, and the tzaddik answered: "I shall show you what lay behind that laughter."

Calling for his gentile wagon-driver to harness the horses — for the tzaddik often went driving out of town on *Motzaei Shabbos* — he summoned all the disciples and invited them to climb up onto the wagon. All through the night they journeyed, though their destination was unknown to them.

As night lifted, they arrived at a large town called Koznitz. The Baal Shem Tov took up lodgings in the home of the *parnas hachodesh*, the communal functionary who was rostered for duty that month. When after the morning prayers he asked that Reb Shabsai the bookbinder be called to the house, his host asked: "What could you, rebbe, have to do with that old man? He's an honest fellow, it is true, but quite unlettered, and far from being a Torah scholar."

The Baal Shem Tov said that he nevertheless wanted to see him, and when he arrived the tzaddik said: "Could you please call your wife here too?"

When the wizened little old couple now stood before him the Baal Shem Tov said: "Reb Shabsai, tell me please what you did this past Friday night. Tell the truth, and hide nothing."

"Rebbe," the good man trembled, "I will hide nothing of what I did. And if I have sinned, then I ask you now to teach me how to repent.

"Since my young days," he began quietly "I have earned my bread through plying my craft as a bookbinder. So long as I had the strength to work I made a good living, and every Thursday my wife and I would buy whatever was needed for *Shabbos*. On Friday morning I would bar up the shutters of my little shop at ten o'clock and walk across to the synagogue, where I would recite the *Song of Songs* and various passages of Mishnah and *Zohar* which speak of the sanctity of *Shabbos* so as to prepare myself to receive the holy day. And there I would remain until the conclusion of the evening prayers.

"But I'm an old man now, rebbe. Things are different. I no longer have the strength to make a living from my craft, and we have no child to lend us a hand. I live the life of a pauper, and when Thursday comes around I can no longer afford to bring home all that's needed for *Shabbos*. But one thing I don't neglect — my mitzvah of going to *shul* early on Friday. Come what may, I will follow my custom at ten o'clock every Friday morning."

The bookbinder paused, and before resuming, sighed a deep sigh.

"Last Friday morning ten o'clock came around, and I didn't have as much as a single copper coin with which to buy food for *Shabbos*. In fact on Thursday we hadn't even prepared flour for *challos*. I saw that I had no chance of buying what was needed. At the same time, though, in all my life I have never requested the charitable favors of mortal man. I decided therefore that this day too I would request nothing, neither from an individual nor from the community chest. Better that I

koheles should fast on the holy day than to receive the gifts of flesh and blood. I told my wife of this too, and in fact did not leave the house until she had given a handshake to confirm her promise. Even if our good neighbors were to sense that we had nothing prepared for *Shabbos*, and would no doubt want to give us *challos* or fish or meat, she was not to accept anything from their hands. Rather, we would accept lovingly whatever was decreed for us in heaven.

"At ten o'clock I walked across as always to the local *shul*, and stayed there until late in the evening. I didn't go home together with all the other worshipers. For what would I answer if one of them would ask: 'Excuse me, Shabsai, why are there no candles burning in your house tonight?'

"Now while I was at shul that morning, my wife swept out the bare house in honor of the oncoming *Shabbos* Queen. She cleaned away the dust from every nook and cranny — and that is how she stumbled across an old pair of gloves that she had forgotten about for decades. It had little buttons and flowers of silver, just like the fashion was once upon a time. She snipped them off and straight away sold them to the silversmith up the road. There was enough money for *Shabbos*, and even for Sunday too. She quickly bought braided *challos*, and meat, and fish, — everything, and cooked it all in time for *Shabbos*. In the evening, when I was sure everyone had already gone home from all the synagogues in town, I stole out quietly too. From a distance I could see candle-light through the windows of our cottage, so I said to myself: 'No doubt my poor little old lady couldn't summon the strength to restrain herself, and she went ahead and accepted the gifts of flesh and blood.'

"I opened my door and saw a table set with all kinds of good things. I said to myself: 'If I utter any word of complaint now I will disturb the holiness of *Shabbos*.' So I held my peace. I recited *Kiddush* over a cup of wine, and washed my hands, and pronounced the blessing of *HaMotzi* over the sweet braided loaves. After eating the fish my wife had served me, I turned to her as gently as I could: 'It seems that it is too much for you to accept the evil ...'

"She didn't even let me finish the sentence. She said:
'Shabsai, do you remember that coat we used to have with the silver buttons, which had matching gloves that we lost ages ago?' 'Of course,' I said. 'Well,' says my good wife, 'when I was cleaning out the house in honor of *Shabbos* I found them! And with the money that the silversmith gave me for the buttons I bought all these goodies for *Shabbos.*'

"Rebbe, what shall I tell you? When I heard these words I wept for sheer joy, and thanked the good Lord with all my heart. So happy was I that I took my little wife here by the hand, and danced with her around the table. After the soup my heart surged again with the joy of thanksgiving, and again I led her out in a little dance. And after the dessert we danced again. In brief, I could not contain all that joy within me — for the Mericiful One had granted it to us that we enjoy the delights of *Shabbos* directly from His holy hand, without resorting to the gifts of flesh and blood."

Shabsai's face grew serious.

"And now, rebbe," he said deliberately, "if I have sinned in this I would ask you to prescribe me a means of penance. I will follow whatever you instruct me to do."

The Baal Shem Tov turned to his disciples and said: "Believe me, all the hosts of heaven laughed in joy and danced with this man — and I laughed too."

He then addressed the old lady: "Which would you prefer — to live the rest of your days in wealth and comfort, or that you give birth to a son in your old age?"

"How much longer can we have on this earth?" she said. "We are getting on in years; what good is wealth to us? But it would be beautiful to leave behind us an upstanding son!"

"These tidings, then, are for you," said the tzaddik. "At this time next year you will give birth to a son. You shall give him my name, Yisrael. And when you have passed on to the World of Truth, you will yet bask in his radiance. Let me hear when he is born: I will come to the circumcision and be his *sandak.*"

And so it was. A year later the bookbinder's wife gave birth to a son whose name was to be renowned far and wide — Reb Yisrael, the Maggid of Koznitz.

The Chicken or the Egg?

Every Friday night Reb Chaim of Kosov would dance exuberantly, his face like a beacon aflame. It once happened that a bench fell on his feet, and because of the pain he felt he stopped dancing for a while.

A few weeks later he was dancing again with the same fire as before, as if nothing had happened. His chassidim wanted to persuade him not to resume his custom yet, for they knew that his legs were still painful.

But Reb Chaim said: "Do you think I stopped dancing because my feet were hurting? On the contrary: my feet were hurting because I stopped dancing."

A Waste of Shoe-Leather

While his chassidim were engaged in prayer — ignited by pious ecstasy, according to their custom — Reb Naftali of Ropshitz used to walk up and down between them across the length and breadth of the *beis midrash*, with his *tallis* resting on his shoulders, scrutinizing them one by one.

One morning after *davvenen* he commented: "Today I passed between all the rows of chassidim to observe them in their service of the Creator, and I saw Reb Zvi the Beadle dancing in holy rapture! He can dance, and his dancing isn't in vain. He will grow to be a mighty tree, in whose shade many great men will shelter. But I also saw this other fellow dancing (and he named him). What a pity to wear out a good pair of shoes on dancing of that sort!"

Self-Made Men

עֵת לִקְרוֹעַ
וְעֵת לִתְפּוֹר

A time to rend and a time to sew (3:7)

The match was about to be sealed in a document — between the son of Reb Avraham Yaakov of Sadigora and the daughter of Reb Zvi HaKohen of Rimanov. When they were about to sign the *tenaim*, the bridegroom's paternal grandfather, Reb Yisrael of Ruzhin, addressed the bride's father as follows: "Mechutan! It has always been my custom on such occasions

to converse with the father of the other party on the sub- קהרלת
ject of our family lineage. Now, too, I would like to do
this. Well, my *yichus* is as follows. My great-
grandfather was Reb Beirish; my grandfather was his
son Reb Avraham HaMalach ('the Angel'); my great-
uncle was Reb Nachum of Chernobyl; my uncle was his
son Reb Mordechai of Chernobyl." (And in listing them
he merely mentioned their names, without adding any of
the traditional epithets of honor.)

"Well, then, my dear *mechutan*," he concluded, "now
it's your turn to tell me of *your* lineage."

"My father and mother passed away when I was a boy
of ten," said Reb Zvi. "I did not know them well enough
to be able now to enumerate their praises. One thing I
know: they were upright, honest-hearted people. After
their passing, a relative apprenticed me to a tailor, with
whom I worked faithfully for five years. Even though I
was only a lad, I was always scrupulously careful about
two rules: *not to spoil anything new*, and *to fix anything
old*."

Reb Yisrael of Ruzhin understood his meaning, and as
he prepared to sign the *tenaim*, joyfully announced to
the whole festive gathering: "Gentlemen, the match is
approved and upheld by both parties!"

◈ A Graceless Thing

A certain Jewish tailor who lived not far from
Pshischah was very much in demand by the
fashion-conscious dandies among the gentile nobility.
One such *paritz* bought himself a length of material in
Paris, and on his return told the tailor: "This fabric is
very expensive, so make sure that the cloak comes out as
well as such a fabric deserves."

The tailor laughed out loud, and protested: "Sir, why
do you say such a thing? Am I not known to be the most
expert tailor in the entire province?"

When in due course he brought back the completed
garment, the squire tried it on — and at once began (with
the help of his raucous henchmen) to abuse the poor
tailor, claiming that he had ruined the precious fabric.
They drove him violently out of the household, and for

koheles good measure threw the hapless garment after him in disgust.

In a short time, needless to say, the wretched fellow found himself out of favor and out of work. One day his wife said: "Look here! Everyone who is in trouble travels to town to speak to Reb Yerachmiel, the son of the Yid HaKadosh of Pshischah. Take my advice and do the same."

To cut a long story short, this is what Reb Yerachmiel advised him: "Undo all the stitches in the cloak, then sew it together again with the very same stitches, and bring the garment to the *paritz.*"

In his heart of hearts, the tailor scoffed a little at this piece of advice, but he had no alternative, so he followed it. He brought the reconstituted cloak to the squire, who called his wife in to give her opinion too. They were both so pleased with his handiwork that they apologized for their earlier treatment of him, and even affirmed their goodwill by adding to the agreed fee.

The little man was stupefied. He came back and told the tzaddik, who explained as follows: "When you came here last, I could tell that when you made the cloak the first time you had made it out of arrogance — and arrogance is a graceless thing. That's why they didn't like your work. By the time you came here I saw that you were considerably more humble, and that's why I told you to undo the arrogant stitches and to sew the cloak anew — *in humility,* for then it would acquire grace."

◆§ Reasons for Speaking

עֵת לַחֲשׁוֹת
וְעֵת לְדַבֵּר
A time to be
silent, and a
time to speak
(3:7)

The tzaddik of Brahilov, who wrote *Mayim Kedoshim,* once spent *Shabbos* in the household of Reb Baruch of Mezhibuzh. When at the Friday night table Reb Baruch asked his guest to expound on some learned Torah subject of his choice, the latter declined, saying: "When we are in the presence of our rebbe all the wellsprings of wisdom are stopped up: I can say nothing."

The next day, the guest turned to his host and said: "Rebbe, you always expound beautifully; do say some *divrei* Torah!"

Reb Baruch expressed his refusal by punning on three

words from a well-known *Shabbos* table-hymn: קְהִלַּת דְּרוֹשׁ נָוִי וְאוּלָמִי. In their context, they mean: "Seek Thou my Abode and its holy chamber" — in reference to the *Beis HaMikdash*. Reb Baruch, however, used each of the three words in an alternative meaning, thus: "If a person sermonizes (דוֹרֵשׁ) for the mere sake of sounding beautiful (נָאֶה), better by far to remain dumb (אִלֵם)!"

And he held his peace.

◀§ *Out of Pity*

Nag and scream as she might, the *rebbitzin* Sheindl could never manage to rouse any irritated reaction from her long-suffering husband, Reb Yaakov Yitzchak, the Yid HaKadosh of Pshischah. He would just listen, and remain silent. Once, for the first time ever, he answered her, and she lashed out at him with redoubled fury; he answered a second time, and once again she did not remain in debt ...

Present during this exchange was the rebbe's disciple, Reb Simchah Bunem. He was amazed that on this occasion his rebbe had apparently forsaken his lifelong policy of being one of "those who are abused, but do not abuse in return".

"Why are things so different today?" he asked.

"You see," said the tzaddik, "I realized that she suffers even more because of my silence. I felt sorry for her — so I answered her."

◀§ *Worth a Copper Coin*

During the period that Reb Menachem Mendel of Kotsk was a disciple of Reb Simchah Bunem of Pshischah he was walking down the street with his friend Reb Yitzchak of Vorki, and they encountered an old woman who was peddling knives. Reb Yitzchak wanted to buy himself a small knife, for which the old woman asked for four copper coins. Reb Yitzchak offered her three — but the deal was interrupted by the loud voice of his friend, calling him by his nickname: "Itshe! The Mishnah teaches us: 'Do not converse excessively with women.' Now isn't *that* worth one copper coin?"

◄§ Counting One's Words

An old man who had been a disciple of Reb Zvi of Zhidachov once called on the tzaddik's cousin, Reb Yitzchak Aizik, during the time that the latter succeeded him as rebbe in the same town.

Reb Yitzchak Aizik received him with a heavy heart.

"You were privileged to know a tzaddik of the stature of our late rebbe," he said plaintively, "and now you come to me?"

The old man then shared his distress with the rebbe: one of his grandchildren had contracted a fearful disease, and he had come to ask the rebbe to pray on his behalf. The tzaddik held his peace, and said not a word in reply.

This was on Friday, the eve of *Shabbos*. On the next day, after the *Shabbos* prayers, the tzaddik told the elderly chassid to worry no more, for his grandson's condition was (thank God) already improving. He went on to apologize for not having answered at all on Friday, and explained that every *Shabbos* heaven granted him a certain number of words for the ensuing week. By the time of the visit he had already used up the allotment of words that had been apportioned him — but now, with the arrival of *Shabbos*, he made use of his new harvest of words to bless the grateful old man.

◄§ To Speak, and Not to Speak

Reb Nasan David of Shidlovitz was spending one of his many *Shabbasos* in the household of Reb Chaim of Zanz. In the course of the festive meal on Friday night Reb Chaim asked his guest to deliver some *divrei* Torah. The learned man was faced by a dilemma. On the one hand he did not want to contravene the wishes of his illustrious host; on the other hand, it was not easy to hold forth in the presence of the great man, and at his own table.

He had an idea, and proceeded as follows: "It was the accustomed way of Moshe Rabbeinu to *teach* Torah, and his brother Aharon was usually the *listener*. But in the famous interchange that takes place immediately after

the death of Aharon's two sons, where Aharon humbly קְהִלֹת
and eloquently answers the challenge of Moshe Rabbeinu, it is written: 'And Moshe heard, and it was good
in his eyes.' That is, now that their accustomed roles
were reversed, with Aharon the speaker and Moshe Rabbeinu the listener, we see that *Moshe heard, and it was
good in his eyes ...*"

And in this way the tzaddik of Shidlovitz accommodated his two conflicting interests — both at once.

◄§ The Eloquence of Silence

With Reb Menachem Mendel of Vorki, silence was a
way of divine service. He spoke very little indeed,
and on one occasion sat with his chassidim throughout a
long night without a solitary word being spoken — and
they sat there in humble awe.

Among those at his table one day was Reb Beirish of
Biala. The *tish* — the Yiddish word for "table," used by
chassidim to signify an inspirational gathering at the
rebbe's table — lasted for some hours. No one breathed a
word, neither rebbe nor chassidim. You could have heard
a fly.

After the Grace after Meals the guest from Biala exclaimed: "That was some *tish* we had today! He taught
me a lesson in Torah, and with his questions tore me
apart sinew by sinew. But I didn't take it sitting down: I
answered him every single thing he asked me!"

◄§ Steam Power

The railway station was bustling with chassidim: Reb
Yehudah Aryeh Leib of Ger, the author of *Sfas Emes*,
was about to leave the country, and they had all come to
see him off. They traveled with him as far as the border,
and as they were taking their leave one of the elder chassidim asked him for a farewell gift — just one more little
dvar Torah to mark their parting.

The rebbe said: "Do you know why the railway
engine out in front has the strength to draw along all
those carriages? — It's because he restrains his steam
within him ..."

◆§ Of Hosts and Horses

שֶׁהֶם בְּהֵמָה
הֵמָּה לָהֶם
They
themselves
are but as
beasts (3:18)

During the years of their self-imposed wanderings, whenever the brothers Reb Elimelech of Lyshansk and Reb Zusya of Hanipoli passed through Ludmir, they would lodge in the humble cottage of a certain poor chassid by the name of Reb Aharon, who was related by marriage to Reb Aharon of Karlin. In the course of time, when they had become renowned, they once drove towards Ludmir in a horse-drawn carriage, accompanied by a band of chassidim. As soon as they arrived at a nearby village a wealthy burgher from Ludmir came out to greet them there, and to invite them to lodge in his mansion when they reached the town. They asked him to ride on ahead to his home without waiting for them; they would arrive alone. When he discovered soon after that they had headed directly to the cottage of their former host, and had declined his invitation, he complained to them.

"Look," they said, "we are exactly the same people we were before. Nothing about *us* has changed, so there is no reason that we should change our lodgings. There *is* a change however in our carriage and horses, and that is why you would like us to take up lodgings with you. Very well, then: you may take the horses and the carriage, and *they* will take up lodgings with you."

◆§ Horse Sense

An overly-pious ascetic who lived not far from Apta used to engage in self-mortification. He ate neither meat nor any product from the animal kingdom, never slept in a bed, and kept himself awake through much of the night. He decided one day to visit the Ohev Yisrael, Reb Avraham Yehoshua Heschel of Apta. If the tzaddik would prove to be canny enough to recognize his exemplary virtue, then he would remain in Apta and become his chassid. If, however, the tzaddik failed to value his saintliness, then he would go straight home and never visit him again.

Arriving in Apta he found the tzaddik eating his mid-

day meal, not stopping to greet him nor to show him any קְהִלַּת
noticeable marks of respect. The young man was taken
aback, and turned to go. Clearly this tzaddik was no
competent judge of men. The Ohev Yisrael however sent
someone after him, asking him to wait until he completed his meal, for then he would speak with him.

When the young man re-entered, the tzaddik greeted
him and took him for a stroll in the garden. There he
proceeded to show him stables.

"Rebbe," mused the guest, "if I may ask: why are you
showing me your stables?"

The tzaddik replied: "You see these horses? They
sleep very little; and when they sleep it is only on the
ground; and they eat nothing that comes from the animal
kingdom. In a word, they undergo all the conventional
forms of self-mortification. But in the end what are they?
— Horses …"

The young man decided to stay in Apta after all,
where in the course of time the tzaddik guided him in the
service of God according to the teachings of Chassidism.

◆§ Fair Exchange

The wagon-driver had a problem: his horse refused to
eat. So he called on Reb Yisrael Yitzchak of Alexander and poured out his distress.

"And how do *you* eat?" asked the tzaddik?

"Why, I eat like all wagon-drivers eat," said the simple fellow. "When I wake up in the morning I wash my
hands, and at night, before I go to sleep, I recite the
Grace after Meals."

The tzaddik rebuked him: "Because you behave like
an animal, your horse behaves like a man. You start
behaving like a man, then your horse will start eating
like an animal!"

◆§ Undoing My Work

When Reb Ben-Zion of Bobov arrived in Cracow, a
group of over-eager chassidim wanted to unbridle
the horses of his carriage, and to harness themselves to it
instead.

The tzaddik refused, saying: "All my life I toil in the hope of changing horses into men — and would you want to change men into horses?!"

◄§ The Western Light

יֵשׁ אֶחָד וְאֵין
שֵׁנִי
There is one
and no
second (4:8)

On the fifteenth day of Tammuz 1743, Rabbi Chaim ben Attar, the author of *Or HaChaim*, passed away in Jerusalem. At sunset on the same day, the *Shabbos* on which the weekly Portion of *Pinchas* was read from the Torah, when the Baal Shem Tov in the far-off Ukraine had just recited the blessing over bread at the beginning of the Third Meal, he said to his disciples: "The western light has gone out."

On *Shabbos* the Baal Shem Tov spoke only the Holy Tongue, and since on that day he spoke very little altogether, his disciples asked him no questions. On *Motzaei Shabbos*, when the Day of Rest had passed, he told them that Rabbi Chaim ben Attar had passed away; since he was from the western lands (the Mughreb), he had referred to him as "the western light" — a term borrowed from the *Menorah* in the Temple.

In answer to the question of the disciples as to how he knew what had happened to the lamp which had been extinguished in North Africa, the Baal Shem Tov answered: "There is one mystical *kavannah* underlying the commandment of washing the hands before meals, which heaven reveals to but one man in each generation. Until this day that secret was entrusted to Rabbi Chaim ben Attar. Then today, while I was washing my hands for the Third Meal, this secret was revealed to me. That was my sign that Rabbi Chaim is no more with us."

◄§ One Mission

יֶלֶד מִסְכֵּן וְחָכָם
A poor and
wise child
(4:13)

The daughter of Reb Yisrael, the Maggid of Koznitz, had an unusually precocious child who lived only to the age of seven. At the meal of *Seudah Shlishis* on the *Shabbos* before he died — it was a week when the portion of *Chukas* is read — he walked up to the head of the long table and, for the first time, sat down next to his grandfather.

The Maggid at the time was discussing the subject of קהלת the waters over which Moshe Rabbeinu was punished for having struck the rock. At this the young prodigy opened his mouth and astounded all those present by presenting an original explanation of Moshe Rabbeinu's action.

The following Tuesday morning, the chassidim who were in the *beis midrash* of the Maggid observed that the little fellow was praying the silent *Shemoneh Esreh* prayer at great length and with visible exertion. When his grandfather asked him why he had taken so long to finish, the child said: "*Zeide*, I was told by heaven that I am about to leave This World. Do not exert yourself too much in praying for me, for the order is final and cannot be undone."

From there he went home. He fell ill immediately, and by Thursday was no more. The next day, when the Maggid found his daughter weeping, he consoled her with these words: "If only you could see the joy that radiated throughout *Gan Eden* when your little son arrived there, you would not weep."

◆§ The Value of Chutzpah

An old *misnaged*, who was both learned and violently opposed to the ways of the chassidic movement, once posed a provocative question to Reb Mordechai of Lechovitch: "Why is it that when any one of our *misnagdish* young men sits and studies Torah in the *beis midrash* he is always so polite and well-mannered; but if he should join up with you chassidim, he immediately becomes impudent?"

מֶלֶךְ זָקֵן וּכְסִיל
An old and foolish king (4:13)

The tzaddik answered patiently: "I am sure you know that the Evil Inclination is both old and learned. How do we know that he is old? — Because King Shlomo calls him 'an old and foolish king.' How did he pick up enough scholarship to become learned? — Because he is the steadfast companion of all scholars. Now when this old scholar approaches some young man and tries to seduce him to heed his blandishments — if that young man is shy and polite and well-mannered, he won't have *koheles* the audacity to drive him away. And that is why chassidim have to be impudent!"

◄§ He's No Fool

In Ropshitz there lived a sanctimonious individual who, in a fit of pious ostentation, decided to go about town wearing the classic garb of the ascetic — sackcloth. The townsfolk used to call him "Leibele the fool."

Once this self-styled saint called on Reb Naftali of Ropshitz, and as he approached the door he pulled out a corner of this undergarment here and there. For otherwise, how would the tzaddik see what he was wearing?

As soon as Reb Naftali caught sight of him at his door he muttered as if to himself: "No! He's no fool, he's no fool!"

Assuming that these words referred to himself, the pious one stepped forward to the tzaddik's table and said: "Rebbe, I see that you too hold that I'm no fool. In that case, why do people call me a fool?"

"No, no, my friend," the tzaddik was quick to correct him. "I didn't mean you. I was talking about the Evil Inclination. King Solomon referred to him as 'an old and foolish king,' and I certainly do not regard *him* as a fool — not if he can fool a man like you into a *sack!*"

◄§ An Informed Preference

טוֹב לִשְׁמֹעַ
גַּעֲרַת חָכָם
מֵאִישׁ שֹׁמֵעַ
שִׁיר כְּסִילִים
Better to hear the reprimand of a wise man than [to be] a man who hears the song of fools (7:5)

The communities of Frankfort on the Main and Nikolsburg offered their rabbinical posts at the same time to the celebrated brothers, Reb Shmelke and Reb Pinchas. They did not specify which post was offered to which of them, deciding instead to leave the decision to the brothers themselves. Reb Shmelke was the older brother, but argued in his modesty that his younger brother was better suited to the position in Frankfort, which was a far more prominent community. Reb Pinchas for his part refused to encroach on what he saw as the rightful prerogative of his older brother. They decided therefore to visit Reb Dov Ber, the Maggid of Mezritch, and to follow his advice.

They were still standing outside the door of the tzaddik's study, each insisting that the other enter first, when the Maggid himself opened the door and said: "The *rav* of Nikolsburg shall enter first, for he is the older brother."

They now had their answer.

Reb Shmelke arrived in Nikolsburg, where the community eagerly anticipated a series of *Shabbos* afternoon sermons on the traditional themes — Talmudic argument and ethical teachings. Instead, their new *rav* amazed them by choosing as his subject the Seven Worldly Wisdoms, one per week.

Sensing their surprise, Reb Shmelke explained: "We read in *Koheles,* טוֹב לִשְׁמֹעַ גַּעֲרַת חָכָם מֵאִישׁ שֹׁמֵעַ שִׁיר כְּסִילִים — 'Better to hear the reprimand of a wise man than [to be] a man who hears the song of fools.' Now this raises a problem. For surely we would have expected the second half of the verse to read: מִשְּׁמֹעַ שִׁיר כְּסִילִים — 'than to hear the song of fools.' The verse however is really trying to imply the following: 'From whom is it good to hear the reprimand of a wise man? מֵאִישׁ שֹׁמֵעַ שִׁיר כְּסִילִים — from a man who hears as well the song of fools.' For if the wise man who reprimands is not familiar with worldly knowledge, his listeners might challenge him and say: 'You do not know it, and that is why you reject it.' Whereas if a man is familiar with the Seven Wisdoms and nevertheless urges people energetically to invest their time in the study of the Torah alone — to such a man they will listen."

And he proceeded at once to expound his favorite themes of Torah law and ethics.

◆§ The Good Old Days

אַל תֹּאמַר ...
שֶׁהַיָּמִים
הָרִאשֹׁנִים הָיוּ
טוֹבִים מֵאֵלֶּה
Do not say ... that the former days were better than these (7:10)

It was so pleasant sitting around in the rebbe's *beis midrash* telling stories of tzaddikim of bygone years that the chassidim of Reb Chaim of Kosov did not realize that it was almost midnight. One of them had just told a miraculous story about the Baal Shem Tov. He came to the end of the story, and one of his friends sighed and said: "Where in the world could one come across such a Baal Shem Tov today!"

koheles The little group turned at the sound of footsteps coming downstairs from the attic where the rebbe had his study. Who could this be coming to join them at this hour?

The door of the *beis midrash* opened, and there in the doorway stood Reb Chaim.

"Fools that you are!" he said. "In every generation there is a Baal Shem Tov — except that in those days he was revealed, and now he is hidden."

He left, and his chassidim mused in silence over the *ruach hakodesh* that had made him aware of their words.

✦§ To Test the Patience of an Angel

וְאִשָּׁה בְּכָל אֵלֶּה לֹא מָצָאתִי

But a woman among all those I have not found (7:28)

The Yid HaKadosh — Reb Yaakov of Pshischah — once told his chassidim the following story.

✿ ✿ ✿

Once upon a time there was a chassid who passed away, and appeared forthwith before the Heavenly Court. Hosts of good angels vied with each other in singing his praises, for he was free from sin. But at the very moment when the Court was about to declare his utter innocence, in flew a very influential angel and pointed out that this man had committed one particular transgression.

"Why did you do it?" they asked.

"I was forced to," he replied. "My wife nagged me into doing it."

The prosecuting angel burst out laughing.

"What kind of an excuse is that — that he took notice of his wife?!"

The Heavenly Court thereupon issued its verdict. The chassid would be duly punished for his sin. As for the prosecuting angel, because he had laughed at the excuse given by the chassid, he would be sent down into This World in the incarnation of a man and would marry a woman — and then they would see how *he* managed.

✿ ✿ ✿

When the chassidim heard this story, they said that in

speaking of that angel, their rebbe was referring to קֹהֶלֶת himself.

[See: *Out of Pity*, p. 191.]

⋅§ The Lesser Evil

The following episode was recounted by Reb Avraham of Slonim, the author of *Yesod HaAvodah*.

The wife of Reb Zusya of Hanipoli, as everyone knows, had the tongue of a shrew. One day he bethought himself: "Our Sages say that, 'He who has an evil wife will never see the gates of hell.' But who knows? Perhaps hell is easier to take than a wife like my Gnendl ..."

For a moment the Heavenly Court gave him a glimpse of hell. At once he shouted: "Curse, Gnendl, curse!"

⋅§ A Disciplined Body

In the last year of his life Reb Yehudah Aryeh Leib of Ger, the author of *Sfas Emes*, suffered from an illness for which no cure was known. Except for his arms, his body was paralyzed, and his physicians said that certain of his internal organs were in the same state.

אֲשֶׁר עָשָׂה הָאֱלֹקִים אֶת הָאָדָם יָשָׁר

God has made man upright (7:29)

Once when one of his doctors came to examine him he told him to raise his hands. This he did.

"Higher," said the doctor, "higher than your head."

"Higher than my head?" mused the tzaddik. "That I am incapable of doing, because it is written in the *Zohar* that it is forbidden to raise one's arms higher than one's head."

⋅§ Nothing but the Truth

A certain individual once commited an offense that according to Ukrainian law was punishable by the death penalty. Finding it difficult to prove his guilt, the judges decided that if two of the great tzaddikim of the time — Reb Moshe of Savran and Reb Raphael of Bershad — swore that they knew that this Jew had not committed the offense, they would acquit him.

כַּאֲשֶׁר שְׁבוּעָה יָרֵא

Who fears an oath (9:2)

Seeing what lay in store for the hapless fellow, Reb

koheles Moshe of Savran decided that the saving of a life over-
rode the prohibition of taking a false oath in the Ukrainian court. He decided furthermore that even if his
calculation contravened the *Halachah*, he would choose
knowingly to be punished for it in hell, so long as he
would save this man from death. Besides, not only his
life was at stake, but the lives of his wife and children
would otherwise be left in jeopardy.

Reb Raphael, however, could not bring himself to
promise to take such an oath. He was a faithful disciple
of Reb Pinchas of Korets, for whom the attribute of truth
was the entire basis of his divine service, and all his days
had fled from the faintest shadow of falsehood. The accused man's wife and children gave him no rest. Night
and day they wept before him, pleading with him to save
their lives. And he, who all his life had never turned
anyone away emptyhanded, and was always willing to
abandon his life and possessions to save anyone of his
brethren from shedding a tear, this time hardened his
heart and did not listen to them. This went on day by
day, until the very last day before the time fixed for the
oath.

That night the tzaddik spent closeted in his study,
without one moment's peace of mind. On the one hand
he knew that he had an opportunity of saving the lives
of this man and his wife and children — and the saving of
another's life overrides all the prohibitions in the Torah.
Moreover, the Talmud teaches: "Whoever saves the life
of a fellow Jew, it is as if he saved the whole world." On
the other hand, how could he bring himself to do this
despicable thing, from which he had scrupulously kept
his distance all his life? What exertion he had undergone,
what toil of soul he had invested, in order to cleanse
himself of the merest whisper of anything smacking of
falsehood! And now, was it conceivable that he should
take a false oath? He, who all his life had never given the
name "yea" to what he knew in good faith was "yea",
nor had said "nay" of that which he knew to be "nay" —
lest he discover that he had erred; he, who had never
worn clothes that were dyed for the very notion suggested deceit; he, who had taught and ruled that
faleshood was the primary source of all impurity, and

that truth was the source of all that is holy; — would he קְהִלַת
now go and tell a lie on oath?

But what of the woman and her children? The blood
of an entire family?

He broke out in tears and cried: "Master of the
Universe! You are my witness as to how I have always
been prepared to sacrifice my very soul for the sake of
truth. And yet now that I have grown old and grey you
have brought me into this trial. Take my soul from me,
dear God, take me from the world, and let me not see my
downfall!"

And so he wept with all his heart, until at length his
soul left him.

Early in the morning his chassidim came to inform
him that the accused had himself confessed his guilt, so
that there was no longer any point in the two tzaddikim
taking an oath. But they found their rebbe lying in bed
motionless, his soul having flown away.

◁§ Feasting and Supplication

The town of Ostrov once boasted a wealthy and אֱכֹל בְּשִׂמְחָה
generous citizen by the name of Reb Yospe, who לַחְמֶךָ
maintained ten scholars in full-time study at his expense *Eat your bread*
in his private *beis midrash.* Once, when his daughter fell *with joy (9:7)*
ill, he entered the House of Study and gave each of the
scholars a gratuity, and asked them to fast and recite
Psalms on behalf of his child. One of these men was Reb
Yitzchak of Drohovitch, who was later to introduce his
saintly son Reb Michel of Zlotchov to the teachings of
the Baal Shem Tov.

Reb Yitzchak took the additional grant home and said
to his wife: "Take this extra money that I was given today, and please go off to the market right away to buy
meat and fish and all the rest, and prepare a festive meal
just like you do for *Shabbos.*"

The rich man's daughter was soon healed, and her
father expressed his thanksgiving by setting up an appropriate festive meal. Reb Yitzchak's colleagues in the
meantime had maintained certain hard feelings toward
him, because he had not fasted. They even reported the
fact to their joint benefactor. When they were all seated

koheLes at the *seudah* of thanksgiving, therefore, Reb Yospe asked Reb Yitzchak to explain why he had conducted himself in this way — for he knew that he was a man of stature.

"If I too had fasted," replied Reb Yitzchak, "that would have made absolutely no impression on the Heavenly Court, because up there they are already quite used to me and my fasting and self-mortification. But when instead of that I set up a festive meal in the middle of an ordinary weekday, there was a whole tumult in heaven. 'What's making Yitzchak so happy?' they asked each other. Then the whole story came out — that Reb Yospe's daughter was dangerously ill, and that he had distributed large sums of charity, including the sum that I received. So they ruled in heaven that she would be defended against all evil, by virtue of that *tzedakah* that her father had given out."

⊷§ One Duty Overlooked

Seeing that he was dangerously ill, a certain tzaddik dispatched his two sons to Reb Pinchas of Korets to ask him to pray on his behalf. Reb Pinchas promptly asked his wife to prepare a meal worthy of such guests, and to make them *kreplach* filled with cheese.

In the course of the meal, every time he would taste the *kreplach*, he would say: "What a fine delicacy this is!"

For a tzaddik this was strange behavior indeed — but the guests said not a word. And when they were about to leave, their host said: "Go in peace, and your father will be well, God willing."

The story behind this is that their father had never in his life eaten cheese. This species of food therefore raised a complaint in heaven: since the tzaddik had never eaten it, he had never elevated the divine sparks hidden within it and thereby brought its spiritual potential to fulfillment. Now that he was ill this voice of accusation was raised more insistently than ever before. But now that his sons had eaten the cheese and Reb Pinchas had spoken up in its praise, the accusing voice was silenced, and the sick man regained his health.

קהלת

✦§ An Honest Day's Work

Just before he fell asleep one night, Reb Chaikl of Amdur, one of the disciples of the Maggid of Mezritch, fainted. When after some time he came to, his chassidim asked him what had happened.

בְּכָל עֵת יִהְיוּ
בְגָדֶיךָ לְבָנִים
*Let your
garments be
always white
(7:8)*

"A certain king," he began, "had many servants, each with his own tasks of cleaning and repairing. He ordered them to come to him every evening with the implements and garments that they had repaired that day, and to put them away in his storehouses; the next day they would be apportioned new items to fix.

"Now among these servants there was one lazy fool. Not only did he have nothing to show for his day's work, but in addition he had soiled the clothes that had been given him. When evening came he too showed the king his day's work. But when he looked about and saw that his friends had all presented the king with beautiful objects worthy of storing in the king's treasure-house, he was confounded by shame ..."

✦§ But He's Not Thine

Before Reb Menachem Mendel of Vitebsk, the senior disciple of the Maggid of Mezritch, left Russia for *Eretz Yisrael* in 1777, the other disciples of the Maggid met and divided up amongst themselves their respective spheres of influence in the spreading of the teachings of Chassidism. In the course of this discussion, Reb Shneur Zalman of Liadi was allotted Lithuania and White Russia. The disciples allowed special permission to Reb Shlomo of Karlin to visit the three towns Beshenkovitz, Tzeshnik and Liepli — all of them in the Vitebsk region which was to be under the influence of Reb Shneur Zalman — for this would allow Reb Shlomo to maintain his traditional connection with these towns as he had done since the time Reb Menachem Mendel of Vitebsk was still in Horodok.

אִם רוּחַ הַמּשֵׁל
תַּעֲלֶה עָלֶיךָ
מְקוֹמְךָ אַל תַּנַּח
*If the spirit of
the ruler rises
up against
you, do not
leave your
place (10:4)*

Some time later Reb Shlomo of Karlin wanted to reside in Beshenkovitz, so he first asked the sanction of Reb Shneur Zalman for the move. The *Rav* made his consent

koheles contingent on three conditions. Firstly, Reb Shlomo was not to speak lightly of those who devoted themselves to the assiduous study of the Talmud, the *Halachah*, and the other revealed levels of the Torah; secondly, he was likewise not to speak disparagingly of those who were endowed by nature with the fear of God; thirdly, he would inculcate his own chassidim and disciples with a sense of obligation to do their own toil in the service of God — as opposed to the approach which demands of the individual chassid only that he should have faith in his rebbe's ability to elevate him spiritually.

Though Reb Shlomo was prepared to accept the first two conditions he could not bring himself to agree to the third, for he taught that those who are bound up with a tzaddik are raised up by *his* efforts in divine service. The task of such chassidim, therefore, is only to be enthusiastic in the practical observance of the Torah and its mitzvos. The *Chabad* school of thought founded by Reb Shneur Zalman, by contrast, demands of each individual chassid (in keeping with his ability) an intellectual endeavor — to contemplate the manifestations of divine light and power in the universe. Thus through intellectual effort, he is expected to generate the emotive experience of the love and fear of his Creator.

At any rate, Reb Shlomo did not move to Beshenkovitz, though he continued to make his periodic visits.

In 1783 he visited Reb Shneur Zalman in Liozna in connection with some matter of communal concern. The *Rav* treated his guest very respectfully, and when he left, sent several of his scholarly chassidim to see him on his way. One of them was Reb Binyamin of Kotsk, a man with a rich soul and a profound intellect. On the way he and his colleagues attended to Reb Shlomo's every need with the greatest respect. He, for his part, discussed with them *divrei* Torah on all its revealed and concealed planes, and was most impressed with the depth of their scholarship. Reb Shlomo's destination was Beshenkovitz, and the party of young men intended to accompany him part of the way there, as far as Vitebsk. As they arrived there and took their leave of him, he turned to Reb Binyamin of Kotsk and said that if he would agree to continue with him as far as Beshenkovitz, he would be most grateful. The young man agreed.

On their way there Reb Shlomo asked the wagon-driver to draw rein in a certain field, for he wanted to recite the afternoon *Minchah* prayers. He climbed down, but could find no water with which to wash his hands before praying. He climbed up again, and sat for a while in the wordless ecstasy of *deveikus*. Suddenly the horses began to gallop along no known road, and no one could stop them. Across fields and hills and valleys they galloped, until they reached a stream, and there they slowed down and stopped. Reb Shlomo smiled, climbed down, washed his hands, and recited the *Minchah* prayers with all the fire and enthusiasm which characterized his divine service. When he took his seat again, the wagon-driver said that since this region was utterly unknown to him, he had no idea which direction to take. Reb Shlomo thereupon told him to allow the horses to choose their own direction. On they galloped until they reached a highway. Arriving at an inn Reb Shlomo gave the order to stop, and they climbed down. There they prayed the evening service, the midnight service of *Tikkun Chatzos*, and when morning came, the *Shacharis* prayers. Resuming their journey, they arrived at Beshenkovitz in time for the *Minchah* prayer before sunset. This was a Thursday, and by this stage it would be quite impossible for Reb Binyamin to return to his rebbe in Liozna in time for *Shabbos*. He therefore stayed in Beshenkovitz, where he encountered many fellow chassidim of Reb Shneur Zalman. When they saw how their rebbe held Reb Shlomo in such esteem that he had sent a young scholar of the standing of Reb Binyamin to accompany him on his journey, they too honored the visiting tzaddik more than they had previously done.

For two whole days after *Shabbos* Reb Binyamin walked around like one in a daze, from all that he had seen and sensed in Reb Shlomo's divine service. It even occurred to him that he should stay on and spend some time in his company. When he finally called on Reb Shlomo to take his leave, the tzaddik spoke to him for a few hours, entreating him to stay with him. He promised that he would reveal to him the most dread mysteries in the Torah, and that he would prepare for him a circle of *koheles* disciples who would be worthy of his teaching.

Reb Binyamin listened quietly to everything he said. When it came to giving his reply, he did so by quoting a Ukrainian folk-rhyme (for Reb Shlomo too would often flavor his conversation with folk adages in Ukrainian):

"The master's a master — but he's not mine;
The lad's but a lad — but he's not thine."

And he returned to his rebbe in Liozna.

⊸§ Healing to the World

There was once a chassid who for years had found joy and enlightenment by being in the presence of Reb Yisrael of Ruzhin. It once happened that in a moment of weakness, when he was back in his hometown, he erred and transgressed in a somewhat serious matter. His shame was so deep that he could not bring himself to allow the rebbe to lay eyes on him. For a long period he remained at home instead of paying his accustomed visits to Ruzhin for *Shabbos* and festivals, until one day he decided to shake himself out of his predicament, and said to himself: "How long is this business going to continue to deprive me of the holy delight of greeting my rebbe? Come what may, I'm going to set out for Ruzhin!"

Arriving there he began explaining himself to the rebbe: a certain obstacle had prevented him from coming all this time.

"When you leave," said the rebbe, "look up how the *Targum* paraphrases the verse: — 'If the spirit of the ruler rises up against you, do not leave your place.'"

Immediately upon leaving the tzaddik's presence, the chassid looked up the *Targum* to the Book of *Koheles* and found the following: "If the spirit of the Evil Inclination prevails in you and gathers strength to rise up over you, do not forsake the good place in which you were accustomed to stand, for the words of the Torah were created in order to bring healing to the world, and to cause grave sins to be ignored and forgotten in the presence of God."

◆§ The Life of a Leaf קֹהֶלֶת

In 1896, while Reb Shalom Ber of Lubavitch was staying at a summer resort in the country, he once went strolling with his son Reb Yosef Yitzchak, who was later to succeed him as rebbe. As they passed through fields of near-ripe grain, the ears of corn and the wild grass nodded and danced in the breeze.

כַּאֲשֶׁר אֵינְךָ
יוֹדֵעַ מַה דֶּרֶךְ
הָרוּחַ

As you know not the way of the wind (11:5)

"Behold divinity!" exclaimed Reb Shalom Ber." Every movement of each ear of corn and stalk of grass was conceived of in the primal thought of Him Who gazes down to the end of all generations; every movement is now actualized by Divine Providence for the sake of a purpose known to heaven."

They continued to stroll into a forest, and Reb Yosef Yitzchak was engrossed in contemplation of the concept of Divine Providence which he had just heard from his father. Still deep in thought, he happened to pick a leaf from a tree as he passed, and as he walked on he tore off little bits from it from time to time, with no particular intention.

"How can one relate so lightmindedly to a thing created by the Almighty?" his father rebuked him. "Just now we were speaking of Divine Providence, and yet you pick a leaf from a tree, which was created by the Almighty for a particular purpose, and which has vitality and a body, and you tear it into little strips and spread it out in various places. In what way is the leaf's 'I' worse than your 'I'? True enough, it belongs only to the vegetable kingdom and you are a human being, and there is a big difference between the two. But just as the human being has his task to fulfill, so has this representative of the vegetable kingdom *its* function to perform — and both have a divinely-directed purpose.

"This is what our Sages meant when, discussing the laws of damages, they said 'Man is always liable to cause damage, whether awake or asleep.' A person who is asleep does not see, but a person who is awake does see. You were awake, and I roused you to see the Divine Providence in the creation — but 'man is always liable to cause damage ...' "

❧ How to Lose One's Temper (i)

וְהָסֵר כַּעַס
מִלִּבֶּךָ

*Remove
anger from
your heart
(11:10)*

R eb Mordechai of Lechovitch was marrying off one of his children or grandchildren, but when he rose from the table to make his way to the *chuppah* where the ceremony was to take place, he found his way blocked by one of his chassidim by the name of Reb Nachum the *shochet*.

"Nachum," asked the tzaddik, "What is it you want?"

"Rebbe," answered the chassid, "I once hear from your mouth that when a king is rejoicing, that is a good time to entreat him for mercy. Very well: I want to rid myself of anger."

The tzaddik gave his promise that his request would be fulfilled. And from that time Reb Nachum found it impossible under any circumstances to become angry.

❧ How to Lose One's Temper (ii)

S o warmly did Reb Yitzchak of Vorki love all his fellows that he never grew angry at anyone. On one occasion, however, a certain woman provoked him so insistently that he was compelled to rebuke her.

"In order to grow angry," he said, "I must first put on a different *kapote*."

So he asked Feivl, his attendant, to bring him his other coat. When he had put it on he said: "Feivl, now rebuke her for me, please."

❧ How to Lose One's Temper (iii)

T his story was told by Reb Avraham Shalom of Stropkov.

Two litigants once appeared in a lawsuit before Reb Menachem Mendel of Linsk, the father of Reb Naftali of Ropshitz — but one of them refused to accept the verdict that he handed down.

"When I was appointed as *rav* of this town," said Reb Menachem Mendel, "I brought with me a little box which lies on top of a chest. In that box lies anger. When I am obliged to be angry for the sake of the name of

heaven, I climb up on a bench and reach up to the top of קֹהֶלֶת
the chest until I get to the box. I open it up, I take out a
little bit of anger, and am angry. Now if I get angry at
you, nothing will be able to cure you of the consequences. Be warned!"

Both litigants were overcome by awe and agreed to accept the decision which was legally binding.

Reb Avraham Shalom of Stropkov concluded: "That
is what is meant by the verse in *Koheles*, 'Be not hasty in
your spirit to be angry, for anger rests in the bosom of
fools.' That is to say: with fools, anger is in their bosom,
ready for immediate use; with tzaddikim, it lies in a
box."

⧉ Sight-Saving

Reb Menachem Mendel of Kotsk once said to his עַד אֲשֶׁר לֹא
chassid Reb Zelig of Shrintzk that it is a good idea for תֶּחְשַׁךְ הַשֶּׁמֶשׁ
a man to know one Talmudic tractate thoroughly by וְחָשְׁכוּ ...
heart, because one day he could need it. Reb Zelig went הָרֹאוֹת בָּאֲרֻבּוֹת
off, and duly studied the whole of Tractate *Taanis* until *Before the*
he knew all of its 59 pages by heart. Immediately after *sun is*
that his eyes weakened, and he lost his vision complete- *darkened ...*
ly. *and the eyes*
in their orbits
He wrote a *kvitl* at once to the rebbe, asking him to *are dimmed*
pray on his behalf. The rebbe replied: "Why didn't you *(12:2-3)*
study Tractate *Bava Basra* instead [with its 350 pages]
for then you would have had your eyesight for a far
longer time."

⧉ Three Parables

Reb Menachem Mendel of Kotsk held the Maggid of וַאֲזֵן וְחִקֵּר וְתִקֵּן
Dubno in high esteem, and was fond of saying that מְשָׁלִים הַרְבֵּה
three of his parables hit their target unerringly. *He weighed*
and sought
❈ ❈ ❈ *out and set in*
order many
The subject of the first parable is the verse: "Not upon *proverbs*
Me have you called, O Yaakov, for you have been weary *(12:9)*
of Me, O Israel."

Two merchants hired the same wagon-driver to
deliver goods back from the fair to their respective ad-

koheLes dresses. One had a small casket of precious stones; the other — a cumbersome crate full of iron and lead. When the wagon arrived at their hometown the porter who unloaded it confused the two boxes, and delivered the heavy crate to the home of the gem merchant. When the latter offered him a token fee for the delivery of a small casket, the porter protested: "Is that how much you offer me for lifting such a mammoth crate?"

"My good man," the gem merchant corrected him. "If the box you brought here was hard to carry, then it most certainly isn't mine. *My* goods involve no exertion whatever!"

"And this," said the Maggid of Dubno, "is what the Prophet says in God's name: 'Not upon Me have you called, O Yaakov'; and the proof of this is the second half of the verse: 'For you have become weary of Me, O Israel.' From My merchandise one doesn't grow weary."

❀ ❀ ❀

The second parable illustrates the verse in which Moshe Rabbeinu, having entreated the Almighty to forgive his brethren for the sin of the Golden Calf, begs as a last resort: "And if not, erase me please from Your book which You have written."

A certain courtier was constantly embarrassed by the habit of one of his relatives of stealing from the king's treasure-house, because after every such escapade he would have to intercede. Once the relative stole such a vast sum that the courtier could find nothing to say in his defense. So he said to the king: "I have only one solution to my predicament. Your Majesty, depose me from my position of honor — because my relative takes the liberty of committing his various indiscretions only because he depends on my intercession. If I no longer occupy a favored position, it will never occur to him to repeat what he has been doing."

And this was what Moshe Rabbeinu said to the Almighty: "Erase me please from Your book" — and then Israel will not depend on my intercession on their behalf.

❀ ❀ ❀

The subject of the third parable is a verse which קֹהֶלֶת decries Israel's fickleness in straying from her loyalty to God: "Has ever a nation changed their gods, even though they are not gods? But My people have exchanged their glory for that which does not profit."

There was once a well-to-do householder who married off his daughter to a learned young man, and promised to follow the custom of supporting him for the first few years of their marriage.

A few years passed, and he approached the young man with a query: "Nu, young man, when are you going to start shifting for yourself? I'd suggest you try your hand at merchandising, and earn something that way."

"But I don't know the first thing about buying and selling," protested the young man.

"Here," said his father-in-law, "take this money off to the market-town over there, where you'll find big-time merchants dealing in all kinds of merchandise. Before you buy anything, drop into some shop and ask how much that particular item costs retail. If you then buy up goods in quantity from one of the wholesalers, then of course you should pay less than what the shopkeepers charge, in order to make a profit. Especially if you buy a whole wagonload of goods, then of course you should buy at a low price. Clear?"

The green young man headed dutifully off to the market-town, and on the morning of the big regional fair asked the seasoned dealers what bargains they could offer him. Keeping a straight face they brought him an entire wagon-load of *shofaros*. He paid a low price for them, and trundled proudly home.

His father-in-law was aghast. "Are you out of your mind?" he shrieked. "Sure you bought cheap — but how long it is going to take you to *sell* this bargain of yours? No town needs more than *one* ram's horn for Rosh HaShanah, or two at the most!"

"I told you I was no expert in business," said the meek young man.

It was too late to do anything now, so the father-in-law stacked away the *shofaros* in some storeroom in the back yard, and the young man returned to his books.

A few years later the father-in-law raised the delicate

koheles subject again: "What's going to be with *tachlis*? When are you going to learn to stand on your own feet? Here, take some more money, and buy up some merchandise. But do me a favor: promise me you won't invest in any more *shofaros*. Okay?"

The young man was careful to bear this warning in mind, so this time he bought something else: an enormous wagonload of toothpicks. Nor did he forget to check up first on the retail price — and he was heartened to see that this time he was paying something like one percent of the price in the shops.

His father-in-law hurried outdoors to see what goods were these that were loaded sky-high on the huge wagon that creaked its way towards his house.

"Schlemiel mine, where's your head?" he wailed. "Don't you realize that to sell this mountain of toothpicks you'll have to live as long as Methuselah?"

"But I told you I'm no businessman," the young man quavered.

His father-in-law found another storeroom and filled it with this new acquisition.

Months passed, and he decided that sooner or later he would have to do something about the whole matter. So he called on the services of an experienced merchant, and told him that he could sell the *shofaros* on his behalf for whatever price was offered, whether in money or in chattels. Soon after he called in another veteran merchant, and empowered him likewise to sell the toothpicks for whatever exchange he could manage. Neither knew of the other, and they each went their separate ways in search of suitable customers. After some weeks they happened to meet, and each offered his bargain to the other. In a word, they exchanged their respective wagonloads, and each set out happily to report on his success ...

To add to the father-in-law's vexation at seeing this double surprise, along came his son-in-law with a complaint: "This isn't fair! You said I was a clumsy *batlan*, a no-hoper in business affairs. But these two merchants are expert and experienced. And what did they bring you? — *Shofaros* and toothpicks, just like me!"

His father-in-law's patience burst: "Fool that you are!

they exchanged nonsense for nonsense. But as for you, you had good solid currency. You could have bought all manner of good things, yet you bought nonsense!"

And this is what the verse means: "Has ever a nation changed their gods, even though they are not gods?!" That is to say: when the heathens do change, then at worst they exchange nonsense for nonsense. But "My people have exchanged *their glory* for that which does not profit."

קֹהֶלֶת

✑ Quick Quill

R eb Shmuel of Lubavitch recounted an interesting observation concerning his grandfather, Reb Dov Ber of Lubavitch: "My grandfather, the 'Mitteler Reb-be,' used to write his chassidic discourses at a prodigious speed and in a very compact handwriting. Each sheet compromised fifty or sixty lines, but when he reached the foot of the page the ink of the first line was not yet dry. His chassidim used to say that he wrote by means of an incantation uttered over his quill. God forbid — this is not true. My grandfather never made use of such things. It was simply that his hand was bound to the faculty of thought, so that he wrote at the speed of his thoughts."

וְכָתוֹב יֹשֶׁר
דִּבְרֵי אֱמֶת

And words of truth written properly (12:10)

✑ Bedfellows

M odesty was basic to the lifestyle of Reb Eliezer Horovitz of Dzikov. He abhorred self-importance; he refused to succeed to the position of his father Reb Naftali in Ropshitz; and he did not allow his chassidim to repeat accounts of his own wondrous exploits.

Likewise, he did not publish the novel expositions of Torah subjects on which he had lectured and which he had committed to writing. When passing this on as a prohibition to his sons, he gave his reason: "You see, there are certain so-called chassidim who after they have enjoyed a square meal on *Shabbos* lie down to rest, and they take some sacred book with them to read until they fall asleep. But I don't want to share a bed with them."

וְיֹתֵר מֵהֵמָּה בְּנִי
הַזָּהֵר עֲשׂוֹת
סְפָרִים הַרְבֵּה

And most of all, my son, be wary of making many books (12:12)

הושענא רבה

hoshanah RaBBah

◆§ Humbled in Body, Buoyant of Soul

Dependent on the goodwill of his father-in-law, as
was usual in those days in the first few years after
marriage, the young Reb Moshe of Kobrin suffered exceedingly. There were times when his father-in-law gave
vent to his opinions on Chassidism by depriving the
young man of his daily bread. On one such occasion he
was compelled by sheer want and misery to spend the
festival of Sukkos with his poverty-stricken mother,
with whom he shared a daily diet of black bread and sour
milk. This in itself did not disturb him, for he used to say
that in that menu he could taste all the delicacies the
world had to offer.

On another occasion he was in the household of his
father-in-law for Hoshana Rabbah — that dread day on
which the verdict handed down on Yom Kippur is sealed
with ultimate finality. A man like himself would fain
spend the day in soul-searching and prayers of suppli-
cation. His father-in-law however dispatched him to
market to buy up a quantity of oats from the local peasants. This would then be stored for later resale. After
some hours he dutifully returned with the goods, exhausted and famished. Not even water was prepared for
him with which he could wash his hands. After drawing
water from the well he ate what was offered him for the
festive meal of the holy day — a slice of bread, and a
wretched serving of sour milk. Night fell, and the
festival of Shemini Atzeres beckoned to all and sundry to
be light of step, and to dance in the synagogue with the

Torah at the *Hakkafos.* So, with such a Hoshana Rabbah הוֹשַׁעְנָא
behind him, off he went to *shul.* רַבָּה

Years later, when he was already renowned as a tzaddik, he once said: "Would that the Almighty grant me
now such elation of spirit at the *Hakkafos* as I experienced that year!"

❧ A Man of Principle

A simple villager once tied together his little bundle of
five willow twigs on the morning of Hoshana Rabbah, and with his *hoshana* in hand took the road to Vorki
in order to pray with his rebbe, Reb Yitzchak.

On the way he was accosted by a surly squire who
asked him: "What's that in your hand?"

"A *hoshana,*" said the simple Jew.

"Say: *broom!*" shouted the stranger, and beat him
mercilessly in order to force the word out of him — but
the little man was not intimidated.

The stranger tried a new question: "Where are you
heading?"

"To the rebbe of Vorki," answered the villager.

"Say: *to Itchke!*" shouted the stranger, and again
belabored him with his cudgel.

The chassid was no man to be so disrespectful as to
refer to his rebbe by his first name, so with every blow he
repeated: "To the rebbe! "

And the stranger vanished.

Aching but upright, the chassid arrived at Vorki.
There the rebbe asked him what had happened on the
way, and the chassid told him the whole story.

"The squire," said the tzaddik, "was the Evil Inclination in person. His aim was to ruin you by two means —
that you should abuse a mitzvah, and that you should
refer to your rebbe by name. But you withstood the trial.
Know, therefore, that a fearful verdict that was hanging
over your head was at that moment annulled. A blissful
year has been inscribed and sealed for you in the Book of
Life!"

And so it was: the chassid indeed enjoyed a year of
blessings.

שמיני עצרת
shemini atzeres

❦ A Free World is Yours!

עֲצֶרֶת
תִּהְיֶה לָכֶם
You shall
have a day
of solemn
assembly
(Numbers
29:35)

A young chassid was once at the table of Reb Avraham of Sochatov, the author of *Avnei Nezer*, during one of the festive meals of Shemini Atzeres. As was usual on such occasions, the tzaddik was rapt in a state of *deveikus*.

All of a sudden the young man's mind was overwhelmed by a turbulent onrush of impure thoughts. Alarmed, he exerted himself by every feat of mind he knew, but he felt himself beleaguered. In his desperation he recalled the words of the Psalmist: שִׁוִּיתִי ה' לְנֶגְדִּי תָמִיד — "I have set God before me always," and pictured before his eyes the four letters of the Divine Name. Relentlessly these thoughts attacked him still, and conjured up before his eyes the most despicable images. He was enslaved. His world was dark. What else could he do? And in the anguish of his soul he thought: "Master of the Universe! If only my rebbe knew of the battle that is raging within me right now, he would *surely* be able to help me!"

While he lingered on this thought, the tzaddik opened his eyes, roused himself from his *deveikus*, and began to expound on the verse which gives the festival its name: בַּיּוֹם הַשְּׁמִינִי עֲצֶרֶת תִּהְיֶה לָכֶם. These words are commonly translated, "On the eighth day [i.e., of Sukkos] you shall have a day of solemn assembly." The tzaddik, however, interpreted עֲצֶרֶת as meaning "withholding." In support of this he cited comparable usages of the word, such as כִּי אִם אִשָּׁה עֲצֻרָה לָנוּ ("Women have been withheld from us"); and וְעָצַר אֶת הַשָּׁמַיִם וְלֹא יִהְיֶה מָטָר ("And he will **שְׁמִינִי** hold back the skies so that there will be no rain"). Ap- **עֲצֶרֶת** plying this interpretation to this verse, he explained that the forces of impurity in the world have no claim on the bounty of life-giving holiness that is showered down to God's People on this festival; it is withheld exclusively לָכֶם — "for you," His People, and not for them. For the same reason, he explained, Shavuos is also called "Atzeres." For likewise in the Torah, which was given on Shavuos, the forces of impurity in the universe have no hold.

"Whoever plunges his head into the study of the Torah is granted a free world!" the tzaddik concluded. Then, raising his head to gaze directly on the young man's face, he proclaimed aloud: "In the giving of the Torah they are not *mechutanim* at all; they have no say whatever!"

At that exact moment, the young man later recounted, he sensed how all the unworthy thoughts fled from his mind like men fleeing from a flying arrow. His thoughts became pure and beautifully clear, and he was able to dwell without hindrance in a mind that treasured his soul's delights.

⋘ The Third Mechutan

After the festive meal on the eve of Shemini Atzeres, Reb Chaim of Zanz retired to his room, and a group of his chassidim followed him there.

"Rebbe," one of the elder chassidim addressed him. "Tomorrow, God willing, we will recite *Geshem*, the prayer for rain. Would it not be advisable that our rebbe pray at that time that the Almighty grant everyone a livelihood? Reb Menachem Mendel of Rimanov also used to pray thus on this occasion."

Reb Chaim replied: "One should pray only for life; a livelihood will come of itself. As our Sages teach us, 'He who gives life will give sustenance.' "

The debate continued back and forth for two hours, until the older chassidim became tired and returned to their homes, leaving the younger men to continue.

One of them asked: "What is a man to do when he has

a daughter of marriageable age and he hasn't got a penny with which to marry her off?"

"You're not the only *mechutan*," the tzaddik reprimanded him. "There's a third *mechutan!* For the Talmud, as you know, teaches us, 'There are three partners in the making of a man: his father, his mother, and the Holy One, Blessed Be He.' If so, then in addition to yourself and the bridegroom's parents, the Creator is also a *mechutan* and you therefore have nothing to worry about. Another thing: In the holy books it is written that all the creatures in the universe exert themselves to help the union of a man and a woman to take place. If that is so, then is it conceivable that a match should not materialize because of money? Now let me tell you a story that actually happened:

"When I set out to Russian to marry off my daughter to the son of Reb Yaakov Yisrael of Chercass, I didn't own as much as one lone penny. As I reached the city limits the customs agent there made me a gift of two silver reinish. I proceeded on my way with all my family, just as people do when they are on their way to a wedding. There were a lot of expenses, and thank God nothing was lacking. By the time I reached the town of my *mechutan* on Thursday night I again didn't have a penny to my name. Just then, along comes his *gabbai* and tells me that his master would like to see me now. He wanted to discuss matters ... I thought it over. Money for a dowry I certainly didn't have, so why should I rush ahead and see him right away that evening? I therefore told the *gabbai* that I don't talk at night at all. That way I would give myself a quiet night, at least. Sure enough, in the morning the *gabbai* appears again. Now I had no option but to go.

"As soon as he greeted me I said at once: 'Mechutan! Let it be clear from the outset that I don't have a penny to my name. If you want to set up the wedding — fine. The bride is here with us. If you don't want to, then why should I stay here for *Shabbos?* On the way here we passed through a town nearby and they asked us to spend *Shabbos* with them; so I can go there.'

"My *mechutan* didn't say one more word about money, and the wedding went ahead as planned."

❀ ❀ ❀

At this point a second young chassid raised his query: "But what is one to do when the little ones ask for bread and there is nothing to give them?"

"You're not their only father!" said Reb Chaim. "There's a father in heaven too, and He will surely give them their food when they need it. Let me tell you a story.

"When Reb Michel of Zlotchov was a little boy he once came to his father Reb Yitzchak of Drohovitch who was sitting poring over his books, and cried: 'Father, I'm hungry!' His father slapped him lightly and said: 'You're not hungry!' A moment later, however, the father turned around and saw that there was a coin on the window sill. He called his son back to him and calmed him down, saying: 'I'm sorry, my little one. Now I see that you really *are* hungry — because there's a coin on the window sill.'

"So we see," concluded Reb Chaim of Zanz, "that the Almighty sees to it that there should be food to give one's children when they need to eat."

But the chassidim persisted in their demand that he pray for a livelihood for whoever was in need.

❀ ❀ ❀

A third young man spoke up: "Now what is to be done if a man has to pay his rent, and needs a little money with which to do business, and he simply hasn't got it?"

"One shouldn't worry about anything, and one shouldn't want anything," said the tzaddik. "A man should regard himself as nothing (אַיִן) — and in truth he *is* nothing. As soon as you need something, then you yourself are already something (יֵשׁ), for one who feels himself to be nothing is in need of nothing. A man should only wake up in the morning and say: 'Master of the Universe! You give food to all Your creatures; give me food too.' And after that one should not worry any further. Let me tell you a story.

"Reb Moshe Teitelbaum of Ujhely spent the first years after his marriage in the household of his wealthy father-in-law who supported him. Free of all mundane worries, he was able to study Torah to his heart's con-

tent. When his father-in-law passed away he was left
without any kind of financial support and he had no idea
of how to start providing for his wife and children. He
tried to concentrate on his studies as heretofore, but
could not. One day he had a bright idea. If he had ten
thousand silver reinish, then he could entrust the entire
sum to some merchant who would do business with it,
and he would be supported by the profits. But the way
things were, he did not know how to secure the peace of
mind required for sustained study.

"One day he was sitting over his *Gemara,* though
without concentrating, and began to weep over his situation — until he fell asleep over the open volume. He
dreamed that he was entering a great hall. At the head of
a table sat an elderly scholar who looked up from his
books and beckoned to him to pass into an adjoining
room. Entering there he encountered another man who
asked him: 'Do you know who that is, studying in the
great hall?' Reb Moshe answered that he did not know.
'Why, that is Rabbi Yitzchak Luria, the holy Ariz*al*,' said
the man. The *rav* of Ujhely approached the table where
he sat, and the holy man said: 'Young man! If a person
does have ten thousand silver reinish, is he no longer dependent on the favors of the Creator? Either way he is
dependent — in order that he should be able to eat, and
talk, and walk, and live. And just as the Creator will
grant you these favors, so too will He grant you a
livelihood — even without ten thousand silver reinish!'
The *rav* of Ujhely woke up, and his mind found peace."

Reb Chaim of Zanz had completed his story, but the
debate with his chassidim continued through the night
until daybreak, the tzaddik not budging from his conten-
tion: a man should want nothing, and then the Creator
gives every man his needs.

Suddenly Reb Chaim rose from the bed on which he
had been sitting and said: "Chassidim such as these I can
do without! Please leave the room."

He lay down to catch a nap, but after a short time he
rose and said to someone: "They've confused me, and I
couldn't fall asleep."

שִׂמְחַת תּוֹרָה
simchas torah

⋙ A Canopy of Fire

One Simchas Torah the wife of the Baal Shem Tov אֵשׁ דָּת לָמוֹ
saw that his disciples of the Holy Brotherhood were *A fiery law*
rejoicing and dancing, and drinking a great deal of wine. *for them*
Fearing that there would not be enough wine left for *Deut. 33:2)*
Kiddush and *Havdalah* she said to her husband: "Tell
them please to stop dancing and drinking, for otherwise
you won't have enough wine left."

The tzaddik smiled and said: "You spoke well. Go
along and tell them to stop, and they'll go home."

The *rebbitzin* opened the door and saw the disciples
dancing in a circle, while over their heads hovered a
canopy of fire. Thereupon she herself went down to the
cellar, and brought them as much wine as was needed.

⋙ The Promise

On another occasion the disciples of the Baal Shem
Tov were dancing in a circle on Simchas Torah, and
the Divine Presence rejoiced in their midst. In the course
of the dancing the shoe of one of the disciples came
apart, and he was distressed at not being able to join with
his colleagues in their holy joy.

Adel, the Baal Shem Tov's daughter, who was
watching all the while, turned to him: "If you promise
me that within a year I will give birth to a son, I will give
you a good pair of shoes immediately."

He gave his promise, and within a year she gave birth
to the son who was to become renowned as Reb Baruch
of Mezhibuzh.

simchas
torah

אַתָּה הָרְאֵתָ
לָדַעַת
You have
been shown
to know ...
(Deut. 4:3)

◂§ Hitch Your Wagon to a Star

Reb Shneur Zalman of Liadi, the founder of the Chabad system of chassidic philosophy, was a disciple of Reb Menachem Mendel of Vitebsk until in 1777 the latter left Russia for the Holy Land.

One year at Simchas Torah, when it was time to begin the *Hakkafos* and the entire synagogue was waiting for Reb Menachem Mendel to begin the recitation of the verses of אַתָּה הָרְאֵתָ, he stood in silence. Then he approached Reb Shneur Zalman and said: "I can see a hundred ideas expounded in that passage, but I cannot realize them in practice. I would therefore rather refrain from reciting it."

Reb Shneur Zalman protested: "But a man can never stand at the place which his eyes reach; for when he reaches that place he will see even further, and so on and on without end. So too, rebbe, when you have realized *these* hundred ideas in practice, you will perceive yet more ideas and insights, and there will be no end to the matter."

The rebbe was well pleased with this answer, and proceeded at once to recite the verses.

◂§ An Unwelcome Companion

It happened when Reb Levi Yitzchak of Berditchev was still a very young man, within a year of his marriage, and still supported by his father-in-law. He was not yet known as a tzaddik, but when Simchas Torah came the elders of the congregation honored him with the recitation of the verses of אַתָּה הָרְאֵתָ.

Reb Levi Yitzchak approached the lectern, took up the *tallis* that was on it in readiness to enwrap himself in it — but immediately put it down. He paused a moment, picked it up again, and again returned it to its place. This sequence repeated itself several times. The worshipers were of course waiting impatiently for him to enwrap himself in the *tallis* at long last, and begin the ceremonial reading. But instead, they suddenly heard him say loudly and clearly: "If *you* are a scholar, and a chassid as well, then *you* recite the verses!"

With that he left the lectern and returned to his seat. שִׂמְחַת

The congregation gaped: what kind of mockery was תּוֹרָה this? The young man's wealthy father-in-law, who was one of the respected burghers of the community, was embarrassed. He nevertheless managed to restrain his curiosity — and indignation — until the *Hakkafos* and the dancing were over.

In answer to this query, Reb Levi Yitzchak said: "Let me tell you the true reason for what I did.

"When I approached the lectern and wanted to put on the *tallis* and say those verses, along came the Evil Inclination and said that he wanted to recite them *together with me*. So I challenged him, and I asked: 'Who are you that you should be deserving of that honor?'

"He answered me with a question: 'And who are *you?*'

"I replied: 'At least I am a scholar, a *lamdan*.'

" 'So am I,' he said.

"Then I said: 'A *lamdan?* Where did *you* study the Talmud and the legal codes? I at least studied under these and these sages. But *you?*'

" 'But I was there *together with you,*' he said, 'so I too studied under those same sages.'

"I challenged him again: 'But I'm a chassid!'

" 'So am I,' he claimed.

" 'A chassid?' I protested. 'Where did *you* pick up instruction in the chassidic way of life? *I* spent my time in the company of tzaddikim and was taught by them. But where were *you* during that time?'

" 'There too I was *together with you,*' he insisted, 'so I too gained whatever instruction you gained.'

"Now when I saw that I could cope no longer, that he would not let me go, and insisted on wanting to recite the verses out there *together with me*, I put the *tallis* down, and I said to him: 'If *you* are a scholar, and a chassid as well, then *you* recite the verses yourself!' "

◆§ Faith in a Tzaddik

The winter of 1786 set in so early that by the הַהַקָּפוֹת
Intermediate Days of Sukkos snow was already fall- *The*
ing in Liozna, the hometown of Reb Shneur Zalman, the *Hakkafos*

simchas
torah author of *Tanya*. It was bitterly cold, and to be able to go out into the *sukkah* people had to put on fur coats and padded boots. That year Shemini Atzeres fell on *Shabbos*. Snow fell all Friday night, and in the morning the rebbe asked someone to remark innocently to Kozma, the gentile handyman, that it would be impossible to eat in the *sukkah* as long as the snow was piled up on its roof of green branches. Though he could not be given an explicit instruction because this would constitute a transgression of the holy day, the gentile understood what was desired. He cleared the snow away, and the rebbe went out to the *sukkah* to recite the *Kiddush* and eat the festive meal of *Shabbos* and *Yom-Tov* there.

Most of the chassidim from the surrounding towns and villages who had converged on Liozna in order to spend the last few days of the festival in the company of the tzaddik suffered now from frozen fingers and toes, and many of them had caught cold.

Now on Hoshana Rabbah, the day before Shemini Atzeres, it was the rebbe's custom to have all the Torah scrolls taken out of the Holy Ark and carefully rolled together again, and bound in such a way that the stitches which joined any two neighboring sheets of parchment would fall exactly half-way between the wooden roller (*etz chaim*) on either side. The *sifrei* Torah were then enwrapped in their mantles, in readiness for the dancing in the synagogue in the evening. Each year he would appoint a chassid to supervise this activity, and when it was completed it was his responsibility to report to the rebbe that everything was in order. That year the man chosen to supervise was a chassid of stature by the name of Reb Pinchas Reizes, the son of the learned Rabbi Henich Schick of Shklov.

When Reb Pinchas called on the rebbe in order to report on the completion of the task, he brought to the rebbe's attention the great numbers of chassidim who had caught cold on the way to town and who were ill with fever. The rebbe leaned his head on his arms, remained in that position for some time in a state of *deveikus*, then opened his eyes and said in his characteristic singsong: "Concerning the Torah it is written, אֵשׁ דָּת לָמוֹ — that it is 'a fiery law for them.'

Now today is Simchas Torah. So let everyone come שִׂמְחַת along to the synagogue for the *Hakkafos*, for in the תּוֹרָה Talmud the Divine Presence is referred to as אֵשׁ אוֹכֶלֶת אֵשׁ — 'one fire that consumes another fire.' The fire of Simchas Torah will consume the fire of their fever."

Now in Liozna at that time there lived two aged scholars, both of them learned, both of them God-fearing, and both of them *misnagdim*. True indeed they had the greatest respect for Reb Shneur Zalman, but nevertheless they were *misnagdim* through and through. One of them was known as Rabbi Aizik Mechadesh (מְחַדֵּשׁ), and the second as Rabbi Naftali Zahir (זָהִיר). Now Hebrew has a special verb for the scholarly achievement of hitting upon a novel analysis or conclusion in the course of Talmudic argument — *mechadesh*. Thus it was that Rabbi Aizik acquired his quaint nickname among his deferential *misnagdish* colleagues, for he was always announcing: "Today, thanks to the Almighty, I was *mechadesh* such and such in the Torah." His colleague saw his own chief virtue in the fact that he was scrupulously careful (Hebrew: *zahir)* in questions of *kashrus*, forbidden modes of speech, and so on; hence his pious nickname.

These two elderly gentlemen were lifelong students in the yeshivah of Smilovitz, which had been famous fifty or sixty years beforehand, when it was headed by a sage called Rabbi Shalom Yudel, of whom it was said that the Prophet Eliyahu revealed himself to him. By the time these two students had arrived at the yeshivah this sage was old and blind, and the lectures for advanced students were delivered by his son-in-law, Rabbi Shimon Eliyahu, who was known as "the *ilui* (genius) of Drutzin." Both Rabbi Aizik and Rabbi Naftali had married and settled in Liozna, where they had been enabled by their wealthy fathers-in-law to continue studying.

When Reb Shneur Zalman arrived at Liozna for the first time and delivered a complex Talmudic discourse the two scholars were most impressed, and when he ultimately settled there they often called on him to discuss *divrei* Torah with him. This was at a time when the townsmen of Liozna, like the townspeople from the entire region, were *misnagdim* in all their ways. Their an-

tagonism to the teachings of Chassidism nevertheless
was not violent and bitter like the antipathy that was
shown to the adherents of the movement in the regions
of Vilna, Minsk, Brisk and Slutzk.

The old folk of Vitebsk and Mohilev and the surrounding townships used to describe how it was common in those days for various passersby to drop into the
shul or *beis midrash* in their part of the world, and to
recount to the listeners who grouped around them stories
of a tzaddik and sage who lived in the region of Podolia
who was always exerting himself to better the lot of his
brethren in body and in soul. These passersby included
eminent scholars who were at home in the entire
Talmud, and they too would liken the miracles recounted
of this tzaddik to the miracles recorded in the Talmud of
various *tannaim* and *amoraim* of ancient times.

These passersby were tzaddikim *nistarim*, hidden
saints, the colleagues and disciples of the Baal Shem Tov,
and they used to pass from town to township in order to
make his teachings known among the masses. This explains why a few years later, when the regional councils
of Vilna and Slutzk began to issue bans on the teachings
of the Baal Shem Tov, their proclamations were not
heeded so carefully by the simple believers of the
provinces of Vitebsk and Mohilev; even before they
themselves became chassidim, at least they were not un-
relenting opponents of the movement as were their fellows in Vilna and Brisk, for example.

One day, after Reb Shneur Zalman had visited
Mezritch to see his rebbe, Reb Dov Ber, Rabbi Aizik and
Rabbi Naftali asked him on his return to Liozna why he
had gone to the trouble of traveling so far, especially
since this caused a certain wastage of time from Torah
study. After all Vilna was closer, and in the course of a
visit to Rabbi Eliyahu, the Gaon of Vilna, he could have
clarified any problematic points he had encountered in
his studies.

Reb Shneur Zalman replied: "In Vilna one learns how
a Jew should study Torah, whereas in Mezritch one
learns how the Torah teaches a Jew."

When he began to spread the teachings of the Baal
Shem Tov and the Maggid of Mezritch, the two learned

townsmen gradually lost their accustomed closeness with שִׂמְחַת him, though they continued to treat him with respect. So תּוֹרָה much so, indeed, that when the regional council of Slutzk published a ban against Reb Shneur Zalman, these two sages wrote a letter of protest in which they averred that the rebbe's scholarship and saintliness were beyond question.

Rabbi Aizik had a nephew called Reb Moshe Aptzuger who was a chassid. For the last days of Sukkos, therefore, in the year in which our story takes place, 1786, he came to Liozna accompanied by his two sons and a son-in-law, and they all lodged in the home of Rabbi Aizik. Reb Moshe was a man of weak constitution, and after the ordeal of the arduous journey he was kept in bed by a dangerously high fever. The three younger men likewise fell ill. Reb Avraham the Doctor was summoned at once. He said that they had nothing to fear, but he was doubtful if Reb Moshe, old and weak as he was, would survive his illness. Their host, Rabbi Aizik, was understandably distressed, and complained constantly that the whole idea of traveling to see one's rebbe in such conditions was a mitzvah earned at the expense of a trangression and hence forbidden.

The eve of Shemini Atzeres arrived. At night, immediately after the *Maariv* prayers, three prominent chassidim — Reb Pinchas Reizes, Reb Ephraim Michel of Shklov, and Reb Chaim Eliyahu of Dubrovna — set out with some other young men to the various inns and hostelries in town. Their task: to call all the guests who were ill to come to *Hakkafos* in the synagogue, and to bring those who were unable to walk — in order that they should all be warmed by the fire of the Torah.

The words of the rebbe on this subject had in fact got around among these out-of-town guests during the day, for as soon as Reb Pinchas Reizes had left the rebbe's home he had passed on everything he had heard to all those who were in the courtyard of the synagogue at the time. Word of this had thus taken no time to reach all the inns. Nevertheless, when Reb Pinchas and his friends began on their rounds at night, the lodgers there still asked him to repeat the statement letter by letter, exactly as he had heard it from the rebbe's mouth. This he of

course did. Those who were ill and their families rejoiced
alike, for they were all certain that everyone would now
be cured.

That night was a tempestuous night. Gusts of sleet
alternated with torrents of rain. The streets were
treacherous quagmires. But none of this prevented the
ailing and the sick from defying the elements and going
to *Hakkafos;* and as for those who simply did not have
the strength to plod through the mire, they were carried
to *shul* on the shoulders of a group of husky young
chassidim.

When this enthusiastic little band arrived at the house
of Rabbi Aizik, they found him arguing with the sons
and son-in-laws of his nephew Reb Moshe. The three
young men insisted on asking the visitors who were expected at any minute to help them stumble their way to
Hakkafos, and to carry their old father there. Rabbi
Aizik argued that it was unthinkable they should go outdoors in their state. As for their father Reb Moshe, there
was nothing even to discuss, for he lay all day uncon-
scious, and Reb Avraham the Doctor had said that his
life was in danger. If he would be carried outdoors, the
first gust of wind would extinguish what little life was
left in him, God forbid.

The moment Reb Pinchas and his friends arrived,
therefore, the three young patients cried out happily:
"Thank God! Now we are all saved, our father and all
of us."

And in piercing discord with this exultant chorus, Reb
Aizik was shouting: "A bunch of murderers, that's what
you are! What you are doing is an offense against the
Torah!"

Reb Pinchas stepped in, and warily approached the
elderly patient. Reb Moshe was as still as a log, his eyes
were closed, his skin was dark, and he was obviously in
high fever. What was Reb Pinchas to do?

While he stood in silent vexation, Rabbi Aizik
launched his complaints: "A man in his state you want
to take to *shul* for *Hakkafos?* Even when the Temple was
standing, and Jews were obliged explicitly by the Torah
to make the pilgrimage to Jerusalem, some were not
obliged. As the Talmud teaches us in Tractate *Chagigah:*

'Except for the lame and the sick.' Surely, then, this שׂמחת
limitation applies to a mitzvah instituted by the Sages. If תורה
you carry Reb Moshe outdoors now, you will be guilty
of outright murder!"

At this point Reb Moshe's sons chimed in: "Since the
rebbe said that this visit will cure everyone, then we
believe with perfect faith that if these young men carry
our father to *shul* for the *Hakkafos* he will be utterly
cured."

Reb Pinchas faced an unenviable dilemma. On the one
hand, according to mortal reason Rabbi Aizik was completely right. A man so dangerously ill should obviously
not be moved from his bed — and out into such a forbidding night! On the other hand he was struck by the
strong and simple faith of the sick man's sons — good,
honest villagers, in whom faith in a tzaddik radiated to
the very point of self-sacrifice, without any calculations
at all.

He pondered on this until he began to feel ashamed of
himself. "Just think a moment," he told himself. "I,
Pinchas the son of Rabbi Henich of Shklov, who was
privileged to study Talmud and *Halachah* and Torah
philosophy at the feet of Shklov's mightiest sages; who
has come to appreciate the stature of the rebbe through
the comprehension of his teachings; who am now enjoy-
ing my eighth year in his radiant company; — and *still*
the Matter in me prevails over the Form, and the natural
intelligence prevails over the intelligence of the soul;
while these simple young men, who came here to the rebbe only out of a God-fearing sense of duty, and who do
not comprehend the profundity of the rebbe's teachings,
— in *them* the Form prevails over the Matter, and the intelligence of the soul radiates within them with all the
sensitivity of simple faith! Be ashamed of yourself,
Pinchas the son of Rabbi Henich, in the presence of these
simple villagers!"

His friend Reb Chaim Eliyahu of Dubrovna roused
him from his reverie by nudging him, and saying: "Look
here, Reb Avraham the Doctor says that the poor old
man is in his last hours, God forbid."

Reb Pinchas had not yet managed to react, when he
heard one of Reb Moshe's sons calling out aloud:

"Father! The rebbe has sent someone to invite you to the Hakkafos! Father, wake up! We have to go to the rebbe's Hakkafos!"

The old man opened his eyes, his face showed signs of life, and he feebly nodded his assent to be taken to *shul*. They dressed him as warmly as they could, and Reb Chaim Eliyahu and his friends lifted him gingerly and carried him off to the rebbe.

The *shul* was steaming hot, and packed from wall to wall with people. Many of them were so sick that they could not even sit on the benches, and had to be propped up against the walls. Some coughed without respite, and others groaned in their misery. The most serious case there was Reb Yaakov Yeshayahu of Chotemsk. He was in his sixties, respected for his mastery of both the revealed and the hidden aspects of the Torah, and a faithful servant of his Maker. He made a living as a *melamed* in the village school and by running a modest hostelry in his house. Needless to say, he was known to be charitable and hospitable. In the course of the years he had several times made his way on foot to Mezritch; after the passing of the Maggid he had gone to Horodok to hear the teachings of Reb Menachem Mendel; and after the latter had left Vitebsk for *Eretz Yisrael* he had instead visited Reb Shneur Zalman. Physically, he was so tall and well-built that his friends used to nickname him "Yaakov Yeshayahu *Kohen Gadol*" — for the Hebrew words for "High Priest" can be taken literally to mean "the big *kohen*." According to Reb Avraham the Doctor, this man's very size had made him more vulnerable, though he predicted that in the long run it would enable him to ward off the Angel of Death. For the moment, nevertheless, he lay there prone and listless.

The custom of Reb Shneur Zalman on the afternoon of Hoshana Rabbah was to pray the *Minchah* prayers early, with a restricted group, in the small annex to the synagogue that was known among the chassidim as "the Lower Garden of Eden". From this time on, the joy of the approaching festival was already in the air. Later in the afternoon the rebbe would deliver a discourse to a select company of guests. When night fell, the "small *minyan*" of the rebbe met again for the *Maariv* prayer, and with this envied group of elder chassidim the rebbe began the Hakkafos. During this time he himself would lead the little congregation in the reading of all the verses of אַתָּה הָרְאֵתָ, he himself led all of the seven circuits around the bimah in the center of the synagogue, and it was he who read aloud the verses which open each of the rounds of dancing. With one hand he would hold a sefer Torah, one hand he would place on the shoulder of one of his elder chassidim, and with him he would dance. While this was going on his chassidim could feel their souls being lit up; it was as if they were standing at the site of the Holy Temple in Jerusalem; it now seemed within their reach to clamber to the loftiest heights of Torah, worship, and repentance; at this moment they experienced the ideal described by the Sages: "From these wellsprings they drew divine inspiration." Or, to express their elevation in chassidic terms, this was a time at which the most subtle, innermost facet of the soul — the yechidah — revealed itself.

Whoever was privileged to be present at that first series of Hakkafos, and saw the rebbe's face radiate with his rapturous love of God, felt that he too was caught up in that wonderful aura of holiness that filled the very air of that modest sanctuary.

"I recall," Reb Pinchas Reizes used to say, "that when I was at those Hakkafos for the first time, I experienced an entire revolution within myself. I actually became a new man. And then I imagined how a Jew used to feel in ancient days, when he made the pilgrimage to the Beis HaMikdash in Jerusalem, and there saw the Divine Presence revealed!"

Only those fortunate people who were named by the chassid in charge were permitted to participate in these Hakkafos. With few exceptions, this opportunity was not granted to any chassid more than once.

After these Hakkafos Reb Shneur Zalman used to go to his sukkah (for in the Diaspora some eat in the sukkah on the evening of Shemini Atzeres), and there he would recite Kiddush over a cup of wine. From there he would proceed to the spacious synagogue that stood in his courtyard, where he would join in the Hakkafos of the entire congregation of chassidim.

simchas torah   That year, when the rebbe entered his *sukkah* for *Kiddush*, he asked that three chassidim be called to him — Reb Michael Aharon of Vitebsk, Reb Shabsai Meir of Beshenkovitz, and Reb Yaakov of Semilian. As soon as they arrived the rebbe addressed them as follows: "You, Michael Aharon, are a *kohen;* you, Shabsai Meir, are a levite; and you Yaakov, are a *Yisrael.* I now need a rabbinical court of three that will compromise a *kohen,* a levite, and a *Yisrael* and that is why I have chosen you to constitute the *beis din.* When you now hear me reciting the *Kiddush,* you are to respond *Amen* after each of its blessings, remembering that the assent signified by your *Amen* is to apply to all the requests and *kavanos* that I shall have in mind."

Before he began to recite, he asked that several large wine vessels be brought to the *sukkah.* After *Kiddush* he poured the wine that remained in his goblet into one of the vessels, and told the *beis din* of three that he now appointed them to be 'emissaries of healing.' They were to take wine from the vessel into which he had poured and mix it with the wine in the other vessels, and then distribute it among the chassidim who were ill. They would then be well. The three chassidim were to take this wine up to the women's gallery as well, and were to give it to those women who were childless, or who had miscarried.

Word of the rebbe's instructions in the *sukkah* spread within minutes, and all the chassidim in the synagogue awaited the three men eagerly. They for their part selected a squad of young chassidim to help in the orderly distribution of the wine. Since this would be no easy matter, the men concerned were chosen for their brawn rather than brain; and the moments that followed were so memorable that their very names have been lovingly passed down from generation to generation in the oral tradition of chassidim. There was Zalman Mottel's and four of his burly comrades from Shklov, Shimon Baruch's and three other young men from Dubrovna, and so on and on, from Horodok, Kalisk, Vitebsk, and other towns — twenty young men in all.

The three elder chassidim appeared at the door of the *shul* followed by their younger helpers — and all those waiting hundreds gazed upon them in silent awe. The

beis din of three stepped up to the *bimah*, and Reb שִׂמְחַת
Yaakov Semilian repeated the rebbe's words aloud, letter תּוֹרָה
for letter.

As he concluded he said: "Thus far is what the rebbe
said. Now I would like to add a few words of my own.

"It is a strong tradition amongst chassidim, handed
down from one generation of elders to the next, that in
order for the blessing of a rebbe to be realized, the one
being blessed has to fulfill two conditions: firstly, that he
should believe in the blessing with simple faith, without
trying to be clever and artful about it; secondly, that he
should be ready and willing to observe faithfully the
desire of the tzaddik who gives the blessing, in matters of
divine service — whether in Torah study, in worship, or
in ethical conduct."

Even though everyone heard the elder chassid clearly,
nevertheless to be doubly sure they asked Reb Michael
Aharon HaKohen, because his voice was louder, to
repeat his words.

The moment now arrived for the twenty young men to
share out the rebbe's wine to all those present. As soon as
this was done the rebbe arrived in the *shul* to celebrate
the *Hakkafos*. For this second series it was his custom to
lead the congregation in the reading of the first and last
verses to be recited before the dancing, and would take a
sefer Torah for the circuit of the first and last *Hakkafah*
with his chassidim.

The next day the entire township was buzzing with
talk of the miracle, for all the sick had been restored to
health. In fact Reb Avraham the Doctor said that he had
already despaired of some of them; for them this could
be called a resurrection of the dead.

As for Rabbi Aizik, the recovery of his nephew Reb
Moshe Aptzuger turned him into an enthusiastic chassid. He had always been a profound and assiduous
scholar, and these traits he now extended to the study of
the discourses on the philosophy of *Chabad* Chassidism
which he heard from Reb Shneur Zalman.

In later years he was fond of recalling that momentous
night: "The uncomplicated faith in a tzaddik which I
saw then in my nephew's sons astounded me. I would

never have believed it possible — unless I had seen it with my own eyes."°

◆§ Slip of the Tongue

"Right in the middle of the sublime hour of *Hakkafos* one Simchas Torah," Reb Simchah Bunem of Pshischah once recounted, "the word 'urn' dropped into my mind. I was perturbed no end, for I had no idea what this worldly digression signified. So I took certain measures, and attended to the matter. The next night, when *Yom-Tov* was over, a simple farmer from one of the nearby villages came to bring me his glad tidings: the thieves had returned his urn.

"Behind this, you see, there's a story. Last summer this villager came to me and with tears in his eyes told me of his lamentable luck: his urn had been stolen. So, in order to comfort him, these words fell from my lips: 'During *Hakkafos* they will return it to you!' In the course of time I forgot about the whole episode; so that when that word reappeared last night I gathered that because I had let drop a sentence which sounded bizarre to the bystanders, heaven had punished me by allowing a mundane thought to disturb me during the *Hakkafos*.

"So you can see, then," he concluded, "how carefully a man has to watch his tongue."

◆§ Echoes

"Once," recalled a certain chassid, "I spent *Hakkafos* on Simchas Torah in the *beis midrash* of Reb Menachem Mendel of Kotsk. According to custom, the tzaddik took a *sefer* Torah in hand, and walked around the *bimah* in the synagogue. When he reached the place where I stood he said aloud the verse: 'And in His Sanctuary, all proclaim His glory.' At that moment my face changed colors. It seemed to me that I

° Reb Yosef Yitzchak of Lubavitch, who passed away in New York in 1950, was told this story by his uncle Reb Zalman Aharon (the son of Reb Shmuel of Lubavitch), who heard it from Reb Nachum (the son of Reb Dov Ber, who was the son of Reb Shneur Zalman of Liadi), who heard it from the lips of Reb Pinchas Reizes — the same Reb Pinchas who figures in the story itself.

was standing in that Sanctuary, and that I could hear all שִׂמְחַת the angels proclaiming: 'Glory!' תּוֹרָה

"Other chassidim told me later that at the moment when they heard other verses from the rebbe, such as, 'Render to God glory and strength' — they likewise seemed to hear these same words from the mouths of the angels and the Patriarchs. In fact some of those present even fainted on the spot."

⋙ Blessings on Credit

On Simchas Torah 1887, when the *gabbai* announced that Reb Shalom Ber of Lubavitch was now to be honored with holding the first *sefer* Torah while making the first circuit of the synagogue during *Hakkafos*, the rebbe said: "I am not yet ready."

He then called across a certain dealer who used to trade on a commission basis, and asked him to explain how his business operated.

"Simple," he said. "I bring merchandise from the big city and supply it to all the little retailers, and whoever pays up for the previous consignment gets his new batch on credit."

Now the Hebrew word for "on credit" is *hakkafah*, the same word that signifies one of the festive circuits in the synagogue, in the course of which people dance with the Torah on the festival of Simchas Torah.

The rebbe therefore said to all those assembled: "After one has paid in cash — by the various distinctive kinds of divine service that characterize the month of Elul, Rosh HaShanah, the Ten Days of Penitence, Yom Kippur, Sukkos, *Simchas Beis HaSho'evah* and Shemini Atzeres — one can take a new consignment of blessings for the new year *on credit (behakkafah)*; and in token of this we will now begin the *Hakkafos*."

⋙ A Case of Conflicting Orders

One may not mingle one joy with another
(Talmud, Tractate Mo'ed Katan).

Reb Asher, a relative of Reb Menachem Mendel of Lubavitch, related that he had once come to Pre-

Now during that period the tzaddik's daughter was so
dangerously ill that by the time Simchas Torah came
around she was at the point of death. The tzaddik, as
always, was dancing exuberantly at the Rejoicing of the
Law, when a group of chassidim rushed into the *beis
midrash* with an outcry, imploring that he do something
to call down the mercies of heaven on his daughter.

The tzaddik (who out of unfeigned humility used to
refer to himself in the third person, by his diminutive
nickname, as "Meir'l") walked into her room. He saw at
once how matters stood, and when he came out he said:
"Master of the Universe! You commanded us to blow
the *shofar* on Rosh HaShanah — and Meir'l blew; You
commanded us to fast on Yom Kippur — and Meir'l
fasted; You commanded us to dwell in the *sukkah* during the festival — and Meir'l dwelt in the *sukkah*; You
commanded us to be happy on Simchas Torah — and
Meir'l is happy. But now You've gone and caused his
daughter to be sick. Meir'l, for his part, has to accept this
state of affairs joyfully, for the Mishnah teaches us, 'A
man is obliged to bless his Maker for grievous tidings *in
the same way* as he does for glad tidings.' And the
Talmud explains that this means, 'to accept *joyfully.*'
Meir'l therefore is accepting his lot joyfully.

"But *Ribbono shel Olam* — Master of the Universe!
Does the *Halachah* not establish the law that 'one may
not mingle one joy with another? ...'"

And immediately after, news came from his home that
his daughter's fever was subsiding, and she recovered.

◆§ March On, Soldier!

Dancing with abandon, singing with joy, the
chassidim of Reb Naftali of Ropshitz celebrated
Simchas Torah in his courtyard, while the tzaddik
observed them through the window of his house.

Suddenly he motioned them to stop. The tzaddik
stood a moment lost in thought, and said finally: "And if
one soldier *does* fall during a war, because of that should
all the soldiers flee from the battle? — No! The battle

must continue! Dance on!"

The chassidim resumed their dancing.

After the festival was over, word reached Ropshitz
that at the very moment that the tzaddik had held up the
dancing the *rav* of Ulianov, one of his foremost disciples,
had passed away.

⋘ *Intoxicated — but Sober*

On joyous occasions such as Simchas Torah and
weddings, Reb Menachem Mendel of Lubavitch (the
author of *Tzemach Tzedek*) used to drink strong liquor
in large quantities. No matter how much he drank, not
only did this not affect his presence of mind, but on the
contrary his intellectual powers were heightened, and it
was during such times that he would deliver lengthy
original discourses on the profoundest concepts of chassidic philosophy.

Once, when his father-in-law Reb Dov Ber was alive,
a group of chassidim were *farbrengen* together with the
rebbe on *Motzaei* Sukkos. Reb Menachem Mendel rejoiced and drank together with them, and his father-in-
law the rebbe expounded vast areas of chassidic
teaching, according to his custom. When it was almost
morning, as soon as the chassidim had gone home, his
father-in-law sent off his attendant with a message to
Reb Menachem Mendel, requesting him to immediately
commit to writing the teachings he had heard in the
course of the night, and to send these notes back with the
messenger. The attendant found the young man's door
closed, and returned to the rebbe emptyhanded. The rebbe told him to go again, and to walk right in without any
delay.

With great effort he got in, and found Reb Menachem
Mendel in a state of sober rapture, lying on the floor
with arms and legs outstretched, and oblivious to his
entry. Though the attendant was alarmed at the sight he
approached him quietly and passed on the rebbe's request. Reb Menachem Mendel rose at once, did as he was
requested, and handed his notes to the attendant.

simchas Some years later, when he had already succeeded his
torah father-in-law as rebbe, he was present at the wedding of
one of his relatives. In the course of a long winter's night
he drank a great deal, and expounded Torah at length.
When at dawn he rode home in his carriage his traveling
companions assumed that he was asleep, inebriated.
They were therefore most surprised when they reached
the gate of his home, and he sat up and said: "I have just
recalled that there is another place where a chassidic discourse ought to be taught — in the home of my son
Yehudah Leib, who is now in mourning over an infant
who (heaven forfend!) passed away."

Instead of going home, therefore, they drove off to the
home of Reb Yehudah Leib (who was later to be rebbe in
Kopust), in order to bring him consolation by the
teaching of Torah to those around him.

❈ ❈ ❈

On another occasion — it was Simchas Torah, after the
morning prayers — a group of chassidim who sat at his
table drank a great deal, as did the rebbe himself, while
he expounded philosophical and ethical subjects in
generous measure. In the course of his exposition he
made frequent mention of his grandfather, Reb Shneur
Zalman of Liadi. Every time his name came to his lips his
face became fiery, and tears streamed down his cheeks.

This *farbrengen* continued through the afternoon,
into the night and almost until dawn. When the chassidim finally went their separate ways and the rebbe
retired to his study, a few daring individuals amongst
them peeked through the cracks to see what he was doing.

He was sitting at his table, studying the logical intricacies of the Talmud with gusto.

ראש חודש

rosh chodesh

◄§ Forget It!

Soon after the Baal Shem Tov became known as a tzaddik, a certain conference of rabbis and heads of communities decided to summon him to appear before them in order that they should be able to see what manner of man this was.

When he arrived — it was a Rosh Chodesh — one of the rabbis addressed a question to him which was so simple as to be insulting: "If on Rosh Chodesh a person forgets to say the paragraph beginning *Yaaleh VeYavo*, is he obliged to repeat his prayer or not?"

"This question," replied the tzaddik, "is relevant to neither yourself nor to me. You will forget to say it even if you do repeat the *Shemoneh Esreh* prayer; I won't forget it even the first time."

And so it was. On that same day the questioner forget to insert the paragraph *Yaaleh VeYavo*, and when he repeated the *Shemoneh Esreh* he forgot it again.

◄§ Self-Righteousness

A *misnaged* who was well known for his antagonism to chassidic teachings once happened to arrive at the household of Reb Ber of Radoshitz at a time when the tzaddik was seated with a group of his chassidim for the festive meal which they held in honor of Rosh Chodesh.

"Tell me," said the tzaddik to his guest, "why do *misnagdim* not make a point of holding a festive *seudah* like this to mark the New Moon? After all, it is an explicit *halachah* appearing in the Code of Jewish Law (*Orach Chaim*, section 419): 'It is a mitzvah to make one's meal finer in honor of Rosh Chodesh.' "

When the *misnaged* did not reply, the tzaddik resumed: "Let me tell you the reason. The difference between a chassid and a *misnaged* is like this. When a *misnaged* performs a mitzvah then he knows that he has done a mitzvah, and files it away in his portfolio of mitzvos. And if (God forbid) he commits a sin, then he

knows that he sinned, and files away the offense in his
portfolio of sins. A chassid, however, is forever in doubt
as to whether he has discharged his obligations, for he is
constantly anxious lest he sinned; and as to the mitzvos
which he has fulfilled he is not convinced that he has
done them properly — for perhaps they were marred by
some self-serving motive.

"Now our Sages teach us: 'When the *Beis HaMikdash*
was standing, the altar (i.e. the sacrifices) used to atone;
but now, a man's table atones for him.' As you know,
different sacrifices used to atone for transgressions of
different categories, some of which may have been committed unwittingly, whether before or even after the
event. And in this very connection we have an explicit
statement in the Mishnah: 'And for a sin of which is
known neither when it is begun nor when it is completed, ... the offerings of goats sacrificed on Rosh
Chodesh atone.'

"You can therefore understand why chassidim are
more particular in the observance of a festive *seudah* on
Rosh Chodesh than are *misnagdim*."

This explanation was so warmly received that the *misnaged* became a steadfast chassid of the Sava Kaddisha
of Radoshitz. Every month thereafter, when he made his
own *seudah*, he would repeat these words, remarking
fondly that it was because of this *dvar* Torah that he had
the good fortune of join the ranks of the chassidim.

◄§ *Starting with Oneself*

When Reb Meir HaGadol ("the Elder") — the
grandfather of Reb Meir of Premishlan — was still a
young man, he was once passing through a town where
he was invited to the festive meal following a circumcision. At the head of the table at this *seudas* mitzvah sat
the local *rav*, who was ideologically opposed to the Baal
Shem Tov. Reb Meir sat at one side of the table at the far
end, surrounded by a little knot of his chassidim who
crowded around him in order to hear anything he might
say. Since it was Rosh Chodesh, he followed the chassidic custom in those parts by giving them the cue to
begin singing the Psalm of that day (בָּרְכִי נַפְשִׁי).

Resenting this evidence of the influence of the Baal
Shem Tov, the local *rav* began to lecture on some learned
subject in a manner that was designed to register his dis-
approval of Reb Meir.

After the Grace After Meals the *rav* regretted this expression of pique, and sought a way to make the peace.
He therefore took a seat next to Reb Meir and said: "People say that you are a man of learning. Let me hear a *dvar*
Torah, if I may."

"Well," said Reb Meir, "here's a thought that is
topical: it comes from the Psalm that we just sang now in
honor of Rosh Chodesh.

"It is written there יֵצֵא אָדָם לְפָעֳלוֹ וְלַעֲבֹדָתוֹ עֲדֵי עָרֶב.
Now in its plain meaning this verse of course means: 'A
man goes forth to his work and to his labor until evening.' But at a different level the verse could be read so as
to imply the following instruction in the service of the
Creator: 'A man should first go forth to *his* work and *his*
labor; and only when he has set *himself* in order should
he proceed with his next task — עֲדֵי עָרֶב, to see to the
mutual responsibility (עָרֶב means 'evening'; עֲרֵבוּת
means 'guarantorship') which binds all Jews. For indeed
the Sages have taught that all Jews are guarantors for
each other. But so long as a person has not set himself in
order, he is unable to do this for others and to guide them
in the service of their Maker.'"

These words found their way into the listener's heart.
He asked Reb Meir to direct him in an approach to
repentance and to give him guidance in the service of
God according to the teachings of the Baal Shem Tov,
but Reb Meir told him that the only way to learn this was
to visit the tzaddik personally. They set out there
together at once, and in the course of time the *rav* became
attached to the Baal Shem Tov and remained a faithful
chassid of his.

◦§ *Of Stories and Scholarship*

One of the prominent chassidim of Reb Menachem
Mendel of Lubavitch was Reb Yitzchak Aizik Ep-
stein of Homil, the author of a profound work on
Chabad philosophy entitled *Chanah Ariel*.

Dispatched once as an emissary of his rebbe to speak
with Reb Yisrael of Ruzhin on a matter of public concern, Reb Aizik utilized his visit to study the ways of the
chassidim of Ruzhin, but most especially to observe the
conduct of the tzaddik himself.

It was the custom of Reb Yisrael not to be alone at certain times — when greeting his chassidim briefly on their
arrival (*kabbalas Shalom*); when receiving them for an
interview (known in Yiddish as *praven-zich*, among
Polish chassidim); and when reading the notes on which
they recorded the subjects of their requests for his intercession (*kvitlach*, in Yiddish). On these occasions, on
his right side stood one of the elder disciples (known as
the *mekurav*) who was chosen by the tzaddik to convey
his words to the chassidim; on his left stood his senior
functionary (*gabbai rishon*).

Among the chassidim who visited Ruzhin at that time
was one of the respected *rabbanim* of Bukovina who had
come in order to secure the rebbe's approbation
(*haskamah*) on the manuscript of a learned work which
he had just completed. Another chassid had arrived for a
similar reason, except that his manuscript was an
anthology of stories about tzaddikim and memorable
chassidim which he had collected over the years. When
the time came for the reception of guests, these two chassidim stood before the tzaddik with their compositions in
hand. On an instruction from Reb Yisrael, the *mekurav*
first read out several passages from the scholarly tome,
and then several stories from the anthology.

For some time the tzaddik was faraway in a state of
deveikus. He then spoke in praise of the telling of
stories of tzaddikim, an activity in This World which
raises echoes in the palaces of the tzaddikim in the World
Above. From this he proceeded to develop a lively
learned argument based on the *chiddushei* Torah
propounded by the author of the first book. That completed, he instructed the *mekurav* to write down his approbation of both books — the anthology and the
scholastic work.

Reb Aizik, the veteran *Chabad* chassid, was deeply
impressed by the line of original thinking pursued by the
tzaddik, but puzzled by the precedence he showed to the

stories over the learned work — both in offering his reactions, and in granting his approbations.

A couple of days later he found himself invited to the festive meal which was held in Ruzhin in honor of Rosh Chodesh. In the course of the *seudah* the tzaddik addressed himself to Reb Aizik in the third person, according to polite usage in certain rabbinic circles: "The sage from Lithuania was surprised that we spoke first of the stories of tzaddikim and then of the *chiddushei* Torah, and that the approbations were likewise given in this order. Now in fact this query is an ancient one, and has been dealt with by *Rashi*, who was a luminary in both the revealed and the hidden spheres of the Torah. He raises it on the very first verse in *Genesis*, where he comments as follows: 'The Torah should not have started before, 'This month is for you the first of the months' (the verse in *Exodus* which, in introducing the subject of the Pesach sacrifice, gives the first mitzvah which the Jews in particular were commanded to observe). Why then does the Torah begin with *Bereishis (In the beginning)?* — For the reason expressed by the verse in *Psalms:* 'He has declared to His People the power of His works.' "

The tzaddik of Ruzhin now proceeded to interpret this comment by *Rashi*.

" 'The power of His works' refers to the soul that lies within all created things at all times. My grandfather, the Maggid of Mezritch, was instructed by his rebbe, the Baal Shem Tov, how to perceive the soul that lives within the body of everything. What I did with the two books brought before me follows the same order in which the Almighty gave us the Torah. First comes the Book of *Genesis*, which tells stories of tzaddikim — the lives of the Patriarchs. (Likewise we find in the Midrash: 'When the Almighty was about to create man, With whom did he consult? — With the souls of tzaddikim.') *Only thereafter* comes the Book of *Exodus*, in which the commandments with all their legal requirements first appear."

A wealthy chassid by the name of Reb Leib Koshmirk, who was a follower of Reb Shmuel Abba of Zichlin, once passed through a town called Kutna. In the course of conversation with the governor of that province, whom he knew well, the gentile asked the chassid whether he knew the rebbe of Zichlin personally. Suspecting trouble Reb Leib answered that he did not, and proceeded to ask the governor what business he had with the rebbe of Zichlin. The governor explained that he had received an order from Warsaw that he should crossexamine the rebbe, for some informer had notified Warsaw that the rebbe was antagonistic to the Russian government and was even aiding and abetting the Polish rebels. (If the truth is to be told, incidentally, this suspicion was not without foundation.) Reb Leib immediately told the governor that he could report back to Warsaw with the reassurance that he himself had investigated the matter and had found no cause for pursuing the matter further. Since the governor respected Reb Leib, he followed his advice.

Soon after Reb Leib arrived at Zichlin, and found his rebbe sitting at the head of a festive table with a group of chassidim, at a *seudah* in honor of Rosh Chodesh. He thought it would be an impertinence to tell of his encounter with the governor now, at the table, and decided to wait until the *tish* was over.

In the meantime the tzaddik offered his listeners an original insight on two verses from *Hallel,* the series of Psalms of thanksgiving which had been read in that morning's prayers in honor of Rosh Chodesh.

"In one verse," he said, "it is written: 'Praise God, all you nations.' In the next verse it is written: 'For His kindness to us has become great.' Now if He has been kind to *us,* why should the *nations* praise Him?

"Sometimes," he answered his own question, "it happens that a Jew is about to fall into a snare set by a gentile, and the Almighty shows that Jew an act of lovingkindness by sending an emissary through whom the evil decree is annulled before it can be realized. At the time, the man saved does not even know that evil plans ראש had been laid against him. Thus he does not even know חודש that he has any particular reason to thank the Almighty. The gentiles, however, who know that they had the possibility of harming that Jew, and the Almighty out of his kindness to His People frustrated these designs — *they* are the ones who should praise Him!"

Reb Leib listened in awe: there was clearly no need for him to tell his rebbe why he had come to Zichlin.

◆§ Saved Unawares

The Chozeh of Lublin once told of a certain anti-Semitic noble whose particular target was a chassid who spent his days and nights in study and prayer, and who rose before daybreak summer and winter to make his way in his *tallis* to the *beis midrash*.

Seeking out ways in which he could rid himself of this Jew in his neighborhood, he decided to send one of his henchmen to dig a deep pit across the very path which the chassid passed every morning. In the dark, he would no doubt not notice it.

That night the Omniscient One arranged for a respected guest to visit the chassid, with whom he exchanged learned table talk for long hours together. By the time the host woke up it was already daylight, so that on his way to the *beis midrash* he saw the pit and walked around it.

The noble was so confident that he had by now gotten rid of the chassid that he strolled out to relish the evidence with his own eyes. On the way there he was amazed to encounter his prey, looking hale and hearty, about to enter the *beis midrash*.

"Why did you set out late this morning?" he asked.

And when he heard the explanation a change overcame him, and he broke out in praise to Him who finds ways to save His People and His pious ones.

❀ ❀ ❀

"In this sense," said the Chozeh, "we can understand the two consecutive verses: 'Praise God, all you nations, ... For His kindness to us has become great.' We ourselves are not aware of the miracles which are performed for us. As the Talmud says: 'The one to whom a miracle happens is not aware of it.' It is the gentiles who know what designs they have made against us — and the Almighty saves us from their hands."

◄§ Come Back Tomorrow

שַׁבָּת
רֹאשׁ חֹדֶשׁ
Rosh
Chodesh
which falls
on Shabbos

It was the practice of Reb Avraham Yehoshua Heschel of Apta to eat in relative quantity, for spiritual reasons which were part of his distinctive approach to the service of God. Reb Mordechai of Chernobyl, by contrast, used to eat exceedingly little. At a *Shabbos* meal which they once happened to spend together, the tzaddik of Chernobyl tasted a morsel and left the remainder of his meal untouched; the Ohev Yisrael of Apta did likewise.

Said Reb Mordechai: "Sir, is it not your practice to eat more than this? Why then depart from your custom this time?"

Reb Avraham Yehoshua Heschel replied: "*Shabbos* enjoys a prestigious status in relation to all other holy seasons — but, as our Sages say, 'In the very place of her greatness, there you find her humility'. Accordingly, she honors her guests graciously. When Rosh Chodesh arrives, for example, she defers to him, and the congregation worships *his* version of the *Musaf* prayer instead of hers; when it is *Yom-Tov* that falls on *Shabbos*, she gives way in *all* the festive prayer services; when Yom Kippur falls on *Shabbos*, she even waives her right to the three festive meals. And since it has been my privilege to share a meal with yourself, who eats little, I have learned from the example of *Shabbos*, and I do as you do."

❀ ❀ ❀

On another occasion one of the tzaddikim of the Chernobyl family spent *Shabbos* in a certain town, where another guest had also arrived — a *darshan*. Now chassidim have been traditionally impatient of itinerant preachers of this sort, one reason being the demoralizing influence of their eloquent preoccupation with the agonies of hellfire. Anyway, the whole town found its way on *Shabbos* afternoon to the lodgings of the tzaddik

in order to hear an encouraging word from his mouth, so רֹאשׁ
that when the other guest ascended the pulpit to deliver חֹודֶשׁ
himself of his sermon, he found he had no audience.
This could not be: the sermon was all prepared, itching
to be delivered. So the *darshan* went along to the inn,
and asked the tzaddik to tell those present that they
should now adjourn to the synagogue in order to listen to
his sermon.

The tzaddik replied: "*Shabbos* knows how to honor
each guest — whether it is Rosh Chodesh, or *Yom Tov*,
or Yom Kippur (as detailed above). When is this the
case? — With a respectable guest, such as these. But
when a *mournful* guest arrives, such as the fast of
Tishah BeAv, and wants to be accommodated in the
midst of the joy of *Shabbos*, then *Shabbos* says: 'Do me
a favor, old chap; go away today, and come back tomorrow ... ' "

ৰ৾ৄ Spurning a Gift

And they shall bring all your brethren from
among all the nations as an offering to God
(*Haftarah* of Rosh Chodesh).

Whenever Reb Menachem Mendel of Liska — the
father of Reb Naftali of Ropshitz — signed a letter,
he always added the words *Ohev Yisrael* ("the one who
loves his fellow Jew"). Once, when he was about to ap-
pend these two words, the pen fell from his hand. He
picked it up and tried again. But when once more some
such mishap occurred, he gathered that it was not
heaven's will that he should now sign this, and he wept
sorely: "One good trait I had of which I could be proud
— *ahavas Yisrael*, the attribute of loving one's fellow —
and now that too has been taken from me!"

He scrutinized his actions carefully, lest he had of-
fended someone — but found nothing. He called his
family and asked them to do likewise. It transpired that
the same morning there had been a caller — some coarse
and unspiritual fellow who wore the kind of hat that was
favored by the vulgar yokels of those provinces. He had
asked to be admitted to the tzaddik, but the family had
not allowed him this.

Reb Menachem Mendel at once instructed his attendants to find the man and to bring him to his study. They
hunted about in vain from one corner of the town to the
next, from one inn to the next tavern. Finally someone
gave them a lead: he had seen such a man, but he had
been seen entering a place of unsavory reputation. They
headed straight there, and found him. They told him that
the tzaddik wanted to see him and talk to him, but he
refused. So they took hold of him and brought him bodily to their rebbe, mentioning meanwhile where they had
found him.

The tzaddik took no notice of their comment. Instead,
he received the stranger with a smiling countenance and
requested his forgiveness for the incident that had taken
place that morning. He honored him in every possible
way, seeing to it that the members of his family who had
not admitted him in the morning should now serve him
vodka and cake. As for the stranger, when he saw with
what affection and respect the tzaddik related to him, he
found room in his heart for some second thoughts about
his lifestyle, and with time became a penitent in all his
ways.

When he had left, and the tzaddik observed how his
family and his chassidim were amazed that he should
give this kind of treatment to a hardened sinner, he said:
"Think for a moment on a prophecy of Yeshayahu that
speaks of the days of the Messiah. It is written: 'And
they shall bring all your brethren from among all the nations as an offering to God, upon horses, and in chariots,
and in litters, and upon mules, and upon camels, to My
holy mountain Yerushalayim.' So the question arises:
Who are those Jews who will wait until the *Mashaich*
brings them? As far as chassidim are concerned, as soon
as they hear that the *Mashiach* is here they will run of
their own accord to greet him. Those who are not chassidim, — well, if they won't run, at least they will walk;
and without any doubt even they will not wait until the
goyim bring them to greet the King *Mashiach*. So to
whom must our verse be referring? — It must be the sinners who are sunk deep in iniquity. Concerning *them* the
verse tells us, that when the *goyim* hear that the
Mashiach has arrived, they will go and bring them to

Jerusalem 'as an offering to God'.

"Now today we insulted an 'offering' such as this. ראש
Shall I then not be grieved over it? And now that this 'of- חודש
fering' has returned to my hands, shall I not love him?"

י"ט כסלו

yud-tes kislev

⋙ The Liberation of Reb Shneur Zalman

For chassidim, the Nineteenth of Kislev is a dual festival. Among *Chabad* chassidim it is the day that celebrates the liberation from imprisonment of Reb Shneur Zalman, the founder of the Lubavitch dynasty and the author of *Tanya*; for other chassidim it marks the anniversary of the passing of his teacher, the disciple of the Baal Shem Tov — namely, Reb Dov Ber, the Maggid of Mezritch. (The Kabbalah teaches that each soul in the World Above is admitted to ever loftier heights of spiritual perceptiveness on each anniversary of the day on which it left its bodily abode on earth. Accordingly a *yahrzeit* is celebrated amongst chassidim as a day not only of remembrance, but of rejoicing — הִלּוּלָא — as well.) Those who celebrate the day as a *yahrzeit* only, observe the Nineteenth of Kislev alone; but for those who in addition celebrate it as the day of the Alter Rebbe's liberation, the rejoicing overflows into the next day too, for reasons which will presently become apparent.

The actual events of the Nineteenth of Kislev — the way in which the Rav was betrayed to the authorities by informers, his imprisonment, and his release — are related at length in various books: *Shivchei HaRav* (Lvov, 1924), *Beis Rebbe* (Berditchev, 1902), *HaRav MiLiadi U'Mifleges Chabad* (Warsaw, 1914), *The Arrest and Liberation of Rabbi Shneur Zalman of Liadi* (New York, 1964), *Rabbi Shneur Zalman of Liadi* (New York, 1971), and others. The sequence of episodes which appears below concerning the events of the liberation and the festival which marks it is culled from other sources — the accounts handed down orally by the tzaddikim and elder chassidim of *Chabad*, and recorded in large measure in the published talks of Reb Yosef Yitzchak Schneersohn of Lubavitch.

R eb Dov Ber, the Maggid of Mezritch, once said to his
disciple, Reb Zusya of Hanipoli: "Write to our sage
(gaon), Reb Zalmanyu Litvak ('the Lithuanian'), and tell
him to come here."

And from that time on his colleagues of the Chevraya
Kaddisha, the holy brotherhood of the disciples of the
Maggid, called Reb Shneur Zalman of Liadi "the Rav."
One of them, Reb Avraham "the Malach" ("the angel"),
the son of the Maggid, told his father of this, and this
was the answer: "The holy brotherhood have spoken the
truth. A name carries significance and in the Halachah,
the law is settled according to him who is called 'Rav'.
The Shulchan Aruch (Code of Jewish Law) of the Rav
will be accepted throughout all the communities of the
House of Israel."

When the Rav arrived soon after at Rovno, where the
Maggid lived for the last few years of his life until soon
before his passing, Reb Zusya of Hanipoli told him that
the Maggid had referred to him as "our gaon." Reb
Shneur Zalman sighed deeply, and fainted. When he
came to he was exceedingly weak, and had to remain in
bed.

This took place in the summer of 1772. His disciples
were afraid to tell their rebbe, the Maggid, of what had
happened with his beloved disciple. Indeed Reb
Menachem Mendel of Vitebsk — one of the elder disciples, leader of the group that settled in Eretz Yisrael, and
who passed away in Tiberias — held that it was out of the
question for them to do so, because of the anguish involved. The members of the brotherhood would have to
find some means themselves of making a pidyon for
their ailing colleague. Reb Levi Yitzchak of Berditchev
argued otherwise, and ultimately persuaded the disciples
to inform the Maggid. This they did through a deputa-
tion of three: Reb Menachem Mendel of Vitebsk, Reb
Susya of Hanipoli, and Reb Levi Yitzchak.

The Maggid answered in the following words: "And
God hid it from me! He has the sensitivity of a son. I was
like a son to my rebbe, the Baal Shem Tov, and he is like
a son to me."

The disciples could not guess what these cryptic words conveyed — until the middle of the month of Kislev, at the very end of 1772, a few days before his passing, the Maggid told them: "What you sense now, Reb Zalmanyu already sensed last summer ... "

And before his passing he took the Rav's hand in his own and said: "*Yud-Tes Kislev is our hillula*" (day of rejoicing).

On Tuesday of the week in which the Portion of *VaYeishev* was read, on the Nineteenth of Kislev, 1772, the Maggid passed away. Twenty-six years later — on Tuesday of the week in which the Portion of *VaYeishev* was read, on the Nineteenth of Kislev, 1798, the Rav was liberated from his incarceration in St. Petersburg. Since that year, the day has been celebrated as a festival among *Chabad* chassidim around the world.°

⮒ The Black Wagon

On Rosh Hashanah, 1798, the chassidim of Reb Shneur Zalman of Liadi sensed a somber note in their rebbe's divine service. A few weeks later, on Simchas Torah, they again sensed something similar — when he was at *Hakkafos*, when he read the Torah, and in the subject-matter of his discourses. All of this dampened their accustomed joyfulness and left them uneasy.

Late during the night after *Yom-Tov* word got around that a special armed officer had arrived in Liozna to arrest the rebbe. Deciding that it would be advisable at this point to fulfill the verse "Hide yourself for a brief moment", the rebbe slipped out of a side door and found himself a quiet haven. The officer returned to his headquarters emptyhanded, but he repeated his attempt two days later. The night before, the rebbe consulted with Reb Shmuel Munkes, one of the elder chassidim, and

---

°This episode was recounted by Reb Yosef Yitzchak Schneersohn of Lubavitch, who heard it from his father Reb Shalom Ber, who heard it from his father-in-law the rebbe of Ovrutch, who heard it from his grandfather Reb Mordechai of Chernobyl, who heard it from his father Reb Nachum of Chernobyl — who was a member of that same holy brotherhood that figures in the above episode, and was an eye-witness to it.

they decided that if the agent were to appear, the rebbe would allow himself to be arrested.

Thus it was that when the officer in fact appeared the next day Reb Shnuer Zalman did not hide, but within a few hours was already seated in the infamous black wagon which was reserved by the Czarist regime for rebels who were under capital sentence. Covered on all sides with heavy black metal panels, and with no windows whatever, it was designed to cast dread on all those who saw it. Guarded by gendarmes, the iron-clad black wagon clanked its fearsome way down the highway to St. Petersburg.

His chassidim were vexed — but did not despair.

৭§ Collective Self-Discipline

On the same night that Reb Shneur Zalman was arrested, his chassidim assembled to consider possible paths of action. First of all it was agreed that all those present, as well as other chassidim who were named, were to free themselves from all their business and domestic affairs, and devote themselves — physically, spiritually, and materially — to the rescue of the rebbe and the salvation of Chassidism.

The meeting elected a committee which was charged with co-ordinating all the efforts aimed at saving the rebbe, maintaining all the activities which he had organized, and strengthening the morale of his chassidim wherever they were scattered. It was further decided that all of *Anash* (an acronym for *anshei shlomeinu* — "the men of our brotherhood"), old and young alike, were obliged to take their orders from this committee without question, on pain of exclusion from the chassidic fraternity.

The committee's first act was to issue a protocol, to be binding on *Chabad* chassidim everywhere so long as the rebbe would remain imprisoned: (1) all the chassidim were to fast every Monday and Thursday, unless physically unable to do so; (2) on weekdays they were to eat only bread and drink hot water, and on *Shabbos* only one cooked dish was to be eaten at each meal; (3) no engagements and weddings were to be fixed for this period; and weddings which had already been arranged

would be solemnized with one meatless meal for ten people only; (4) every *melamed* was to recite *Psalms* with his
pupils every day; and before this he was to explain to
them the episode of the libelous accusations leading to
the arrest, for the tzaddik of a generation is brought to
account for the sins of his generation; (5) each chassid
was to tell his wife and young children and any other
member of his household of the whole story, pointing
out the extent of the rebbe's suffering, the villainy of his
libellers, and the praiseworthiness of those who share in
the anguish of a sage and tzaddik; (6) each chassid was
to be punctilious in paying his regular *maamad* for the
upkeep of the rebbe's household, as well as his other
contributions for the maintenance of the brethren who
had moved to *Eretz Yisrael*; (7) each man was to list all
the silver and gold vessels and jewelry that he owned; (8)
each community of chassidim was to choose one trustee
who would superintend the fulfillment of all the above
orders, and would collect funds [as in (6) above] and lists
[as in (7) above]; (9) If, God forbid, one of Anash were to
pass away during this period, all the men of that community were to assemble and immerse themselves in a
mikveh. After the deceased had been prepared by
taharah and clothed for burial, his soul was to be solemnly adjured to ascend as an emissary of the community to
the abode in heaven of the Baal Shem Tov and the Maggid of Mezritch, and to tell them that the rebbe was in-
carcerated and the teachings of Chassidism were under
threat. Three times were they to administer this oath —
after the deceased was clothed, on arrival at the place of
burial, and before the grave was closed. On that day,
moreover, all were to fast.

The committee then set up three groups of activists:
(a) those entrusted with rescuing the rebbe; (b) those
committed to raising the funds needed for this, as well as
for the maintenance of the rebbe's household, and for
the members of the fraternity in the Holy Land through
the Rabbi Meir Baal HaNess Fund; (c) those charged
with protecting the survival of the teachings and
customs of Chassidism, and with sustaining the morale
of the chassidic communities.

The first group was subdivided into three cells: one

based in St. Petersburg in order to assemble intelligence
and to take action according to their findings; one based
secretly in Vilna in order to be apprised of developments
mooted among the *misnagdim;* a third cell in Shklov
with the same task. These three cells were to com-
municate only through their own appointed liaison
agents, never through the mail, and all their activities
were to be kept utterly secret.

The second group raised its funds according to assess-
ments made by the trustee and two elder chassidim of
each locality. They made lists of all the silver and gold
vessels and jewelry in the possession of each household,
and secured documents of sale from their owners, who
were notified that if after a certain period the rebbe was
still (God forbid) in prison, they would all be obliged to
transfer these objects into the safekeeping of the trustee,
so that if funds were needed there would be no delay.
While these lists were being drawn up, accounts were
also drawn up of all the dowry moneys held in trust by
the communal treasurers. With these funds, too, the
owners furnished the local trustee with documents en-
titling him to use them on demand. Exact copies of all
these lists and documents were forwarded to the committee.

The third group undertook its task of defending and
spreading the teachings of Chassidism by traveling
through cities, villages and rural settlements, explaining
the rebbe's philosophy and the way of life upheld by the
movement to the masses among whom they moved.°

⋖§ *A Tree of Life*

It was a Thursday night when the black wagon took
Reb Shneur Zalman from Liozna on its way to St.
Petersburg. At half past ten the next morning, on the eve
of the *Shabbos* when the Portion of *Bereishis* is read —
some six hours before candle-lighting time — the rebbe
asked that they stop where they were until after *Shab-*

°These details were all passed on by an eye-witness — Reb Nachum, the son of Reb Dov Ber
of Lubavitch (and the grandson of the rebbe who was imprisoned) — to Reb Zalman Aharon
(the son of Reb Shmuel); the latter made notes of them, which were copied by his nephew Reb
Yosef Yitzchak of Lubavitch.

bos. The gendarmes ignored his request. A moment later י״ט כסלו the axles of the wagon broke. No sooner had they repaired them, than one of the horses collapsed and died. Fresh horses were brought, but they could not move the wagon from its place.

By this time the gendarmes gathered that it would be impossible to press on with their journey against the rebbe's will, so they asked their prisoner if they could detour to a nearby village, and spend the next day there. The rebbe did not agree. He did however agree to their second suggeston — that the wagon should be taken off the highway into a field.

The spot at which the Alter Rebbe spent that *Shabbos* is about three miles from the village of Rudnia, which is near the town of Nevel. An old chassid who survived into this century — Reb Michael of Nevel — used to relate to chassidim now alive that he knew chassidim who were able to point out the exact spot at which the rebbe had spent that lonely *Shabbos*. He had gone there himself to see it with his own eyes. All the way there he had seen old and drooping trees on both sides of the road, but that memorable spot was marked by a tall tree with luxuriant foliage.

Reb Yosef Yitzchak of Lubavitch records that when this old man from Nevel used to recall that moment, and would describe the spot in detail, his soul would light up with a noble awakening of pious awe. And the rebbe adds that the sight of the tree did more for arousing the soul of this chassid of a bygone age, than the study of a moral tract does to certain chassidim today ...

◆§ The Blessing in a Gold Frame

On his arrival at St. Petersburg, Reb Shneur Zalman was at once escorted to the secret cells of the dread Peter-Paul Fortress, where he was to spend over seven weeks. For the first three weeks he was held under the severe conditions which were the lot of those impeached for rebellion against the Czar. The rationale for this was simple. One of the principal charges against the rebbe was that he had treacherously raised funds for Russia's traditional enemy, the Turkish sultan. *(Read:* He had

collected money through the charity boxes of the Rabbi
Meir Baal HaNess Fund for the support of his chassidim
in the Holy Land, which was then under Turkish rule!)

This interrogation took place not there, but in the
headquarters of the *Tainy Soviet,* the Secret Council, on
the other side of the Neva River, so that the Alter Rebbe
had to be taken across each time by ferry.

On one such occasion the rebbe asked his ferryman to
stop the ferry so that he could stand and recite *Kiddush
Levanah,* the blessing recited over the New Moon.

When he refused the rebbe said: "If I want to, I can
stop the boat myself."

And indeed, after the official again refused to oblige,
the boat stopped in the middle of the river. The rebbe
then recited the verses of *Psalm* 148 which are said
before the blessing, but did not pronounce the *berachah*
itself. The ferry then proceeded on its way.

When the rebbe again asked the gentile to stop the
boat, he asked: "What will you give me in exchange for
the favor?"

And in reply Reb Shneur Zalman gave him a blessing
which he recorded on a note in his own handwriting. In
later years, when that official rose to a position of power
and enjoyed an old age of honor and prosperity, he
treasured that note, which he kept under glass in a heavy
gold frame. Indeed, it was seen and read by a renowned
chassid by the name of Reb Dov Ze'ev of Yekaterinoslav. How he came to see it is a story all of its own.

Before Reb Dov Ze'ev was appointed *rav* of the chassidic community in Yekaterinoslav, he lived in Stradov,
where he was the community's *mashpia* —that is, the
elder chassid charged with the teaching of chassidic
philosophy and the guidance of the brotherhood in
worship and self-refinement. There were two old men
there who were hard of hearing, so Reb Dov Ze'ev was
obliged to lecture at the top of his voice. In appreciation
of this effort, one of these old-timers would tell him an
anecdote drawn from his priceless memory — for he had
himself several times visited the Alter Rebbe, then his
son Reb Dov Ber, and then his successor Reb Menachem
Mendel. One of these recollections was that not too far
from Stradov there lived a gentile squire who was the

son of the official who had received that written blessing
from Reb Shneur Zalman halfway across the River
Neva. The son too revered the note in the frame, he said.
Hearing this, Reb Dov Ze'ev made it his business to
locate that *paritz*, and was thus able to see the note.

❧ ❧ ❧

One *Yud-Tes* Kislev, on the anniversary of Reb
Shneur Zalman's release, Reb Yosef Yitzchak related the
above episode and added that as a boy he had been left
with a question. Since the Alter Rebbe had already
stopped the boat, why did he not recite the *berachah* as
well, and then he would not have to depend on the favor
of the gentile? When he had grown older, he continued,
and had grasped the approach of Chassidism more pro-
foundly, he understood that there was a point of principle involved. The Alter Rebbe had been obliged to act as
he did, for a mitzvah is made to be performed *only when
it is clothed in the ways of nature*, and not through
supernatural miracles.

He added incidentally that the very fact that a
manuscript page of the Alter Rebbe's handwriting
should be found in the hands of a gentile is a mystery
known only to the Knower of Secrets.

✎§ Say it with a Smile

In the course of his crossexamination at the *Tainy
Soviet*, Reb Shneur Zalman was asked twenty-two
questions. These included the following: Why had he introduced alterations in the accepted formula *(nussach)* of
prayer? What was the point of Chassidism? Why in the
chassidic interpretations of the Kabbalah was the term
malchus (literally: "sovereignty," but in this context
relating to one of the divine attributes) referred to as the
attribute furthest removed from the Source of divine
light? — And did this not imply a disrespect for the
imperial regime of the Czar? Why did he send funds to
Eretz Yisrael, which according to the informers was
nothing less than a bribe to the Turkish authorities, as
part of a brazen attempt to overthrow the Czar's rule?
(On this last allegation, see *The Blessing in a Gold*

Frame, above.) The last question involved a statement
which appeared at the end of the first chapter of his
Tanya, which made an unflattering comparison between
the spiritual source of the souls of gentiles as opposed to
the spiritual source of the souls of Jews.

The Alter Rebbe gave detailed and reasoned replies to
twenty of the questions, and they were presented in a
manner which made them find ready acceptance. To the
question on the attribute of *malchus* he gave a lengthy
written reply which — after translation by two censors —
was likewise accepted and approved. But when his interrogators came to their last question he remained silent,
and only smiled. They received his silent smile as an
answer to their question, and asked no more.

After his liberation the rebbe told his elder disciples
that his intention at the time had been as follows: "You
have seen, gentlemen, that I have provided satisfactory
answers to your twenty-one questions. You have thus
proved to yourselves that what I have said is true. This
being the case, if I now give a reply to your last question
you will doubtless find that it too is true. Why then do
you seek to make this so clear? Would it not be better
that this question remain unanswered? ..."

And he added that his interrogators understood his
meaning well, and gave their tacit approval to it.

Interestingly, the above episode is recorded in *Beis
Rebbe* (Part I, p.33) in the following cryptic formula:
"This smiling silence carried with it a profound meaning. This, however, is a dread secret that cannot be
revealed. But a word to the wise is sufficient ... and the
interrogating ministers understood his answer." The
reason for keeping this as a "secret" was simply that *Beis
Rebbe* was published under the heavy hand of the
Czarist censor in Russia, in 1902 — hardly a time and a
place for publishing such "secrets."

When the rebbe finally arrived home to Liozna he
delivered a discourse based on the verse: "Because you
did not serve the Lord your God with joy." In this lecture
he explained the Kabbalistic theme that joy mollifies the
severity of the stern judgment which, according to the
letter of the law, a person might otherwise deserve. And
he later commented that this principle he saw clearly

realized in practice in the *Tainy Soviet* in St. Petersburg י"ט כסלו
— and what he had in mind was that smile at a critical
moment.

◄§ Inspired Exultation

On his way home from St. Petersburg, Reb Shneur
Zalman was accompanied by thousands of chassidim. On Tuesday, the second day of Chanukah, thousands of people were waiting to greet him on his arrival
at Vitebsk, and here he remained for all of Chanukah. By
the time he reached Liozna a vast multitude of chassidim
from the nearby towns had converged on the town, and
travelers had reported that all along the road they had
seen throngs of people from faraway communities who
were meeting and coming to welcome him home.

There were chassidim who desired to write a scroll telling the remarkable story of his deliverance, and to have it
read annually like the *Megillah* of Esther. In fact a select
group of elder chassidim had already prepared drafts for
such a chronicle, and after secret consultation had
decided to arrive in Liozna as a delegation between
Pesach and Shavuos in order to request the rebbe's approval of their project.

When they approached the rebbe on this question, he
did not agree to it, and answered as follows: "This day
will be fixed as an everlasting festival for Israel, a day on
which the great Name of God will be exalted and hal-
lowed. The hearts of thousands of Jews will be aroused
in *teshuvah* and in worship, for this episode is engraved
in the hearts of the Israel of the World Above (a Kabbalistic term for a certain lofty level of divinity), and inscribed in the heart of Israel in This World."

◄§ The Password is Truth

A kind Providence has preserved the mellow pastoral
letter which Reb Shneur Zalman sent out to his chassidim on his liberation — in order to restrain and re-direct
the understandable reactions which some of his ardent
followers must have contemplated. It appears as the second epistle in *Iggeres HaKodesh* in his *Tanya*, and opens

with the words uttered by the Patriarch Yaakov at a moment in which he was considering the abundance of divine favors for which he felt humbly grateful: "I am unworthy of all the acts of lovingkindness."

It is the custom for chassidim to study this letter in groups on *Yud-Tes* Kislev, and it sometimes serves as a text for learned and inspirational discourses.

After having given his interpretation of the verse, Reb Shneur Zalman draws towards his conclusion thus: "Therefore I come with a general announcement to inform all the men of our brotherhood regarding the multitude of favors — 'the great things that God has done for us': to hold on to the attributes of Yaakov, ... not to become haughty-minded in relation to their brethren, ... but to subdue their heart and spirit before everyone according to the attributes of 'truth unto Yaakov'."

Reb Shneur Zalman's great-grandson, Reb Shmuel of Lubavitch, was once studying this epistle with his son, Reb Shalom Ber, and he commented: "If the Alter Rebbe had not added the words ('according to the attribute of *truth unto Yaakov'*), he would have had another fifty thousand chassidim. But the Alter Rebbe demanded the attribute of truth!"

⊷§ *An Eye-Witness Recalls*

An eye-witness of the events of this stormy period used to describe it in all its details year after year — Reb Nachum, the son of Reb Dov Ber, and the grandson of Reb Shneur Zalman of Liadi, the protagonist of the *Yud-Tes* Kislev epic. He used to begin as follows.

"For ten years my grandfather was a disciple of Reb Dov Ber, the Maggid of Mezritch, and for five years the leader of the holy brotherhood — until he became renowned as the preacher of Liozna. For twenty years he toiled in a number of tasks. The first of these was the establishment and consolidation of the three celebrated *chadarim*. In the first of these study halls, which he founded in 1778, he taught his disciples for five consecutive years. The entrance requirements included a thorough familiarity with the Talmud, Midrash, *Sefer Halkkarim* and *Kuzari*, and a knowledge of *Zohar*. The

second cheder was established in 1780, and the third in
1782; the usual period of study in each of these more advanced stages was three years.

"My grandfather's other tasks in this period included
the guidance of his chassidim, and his endeavors at
spreading and explaining the doctrines of his teachers,
the Baal Shem Tov and the Maggid of Mezritch. When
the various regions were allocated to the disciples of the
Maggid for this purpose, my grandfather undertook the
most difficult, for this area was nearest to Lithuania.
When *Tanya* first appeared — and by that time there
were already (thank God) tens of thousands of chassidim, including scholars and halachic authorities who
followed his legal decisions (as in the construction of the
mikveh, the insistence on honed slaughtering-knives for
shechitah, and so on) — that was when the libelous accusation took place."

(Incidentally, the word in fact used by Reb Nachum
for *Tanya* was *Kuntressim*. Before *Tanya* was first
published as a book in 1796, its subject matter was disseminated among the chassidim in the form of single
handwritten chapters and even half-chapters, which
were called *Kuntressim* — 'leaflets'. For this reason, the
older chassidim who remembered those days continued
to use this name for the work even after it was printed as
a book with a title.)

At this point Reb Nachum would proceed to describe
in detail the libelous accusation which the *misnagdim*
brought to the Czarist authorities and the exultation in
their camp when the rebbe was taken to St. Petersburg.
For example, when on Sunday, the twenty-seventh of
Tishrei 1798 word reached Vilna, Minsk and Shklov that
he had been taken off to St. Petersburg in the black
wagon, guarded by gendarmes with swords drawn, it
was announced publicly that on the next day, Monday,
all the synagogues should introduce the Psalms of the
Hallel into the morning service and the townsmen should
conduct a festive meal to mark the occasion. This announcement encountered opposition from some of the
older sages in the *misnagdish* camp, for in each of these
three towns there were scholars who had the opportunity
of getting to know Reb Shneur Zalman, and they exerted

whatever influence they could have to restrain these ex-
pressions of vindictiveness. Thus it was that in the ma-
jority of synagogues in these three towns the announce-
ments encouraging merrymaking were ignored.

From this Reb Nachum would move on to the Alter
Rebbe's stay in prison, the liberation, the way in which
the glad tidings spread, and the itinerary from St. Petersburg to Liozna.

All this was recounted clearly and succinctly. When
he recalled the arrest his voice would drop unawares, as
if he were weeping; when he reached the liberation, his
voice would rise with the joy of a remembered triumph.
He adopted the rule which obtains with the reading of
the *Megillah* on Purim — once at night and a full repetition by day. Moreover, if one of the dignified old chassidim would join the gathering after he had begun, —
why, he would go back to the very beginning and start
all over again.

๙ It's My Privilege

The elder chassidim of Rèb Shneur Zalman's
generation used to enumerate ten tribulations (*yis-
surim*) which the tzaddik underwent: (1) his journey to
Mezritch; (2) and (3) the two ideological attacks made on
him by Reb Pinchas, the author of Sefer *Haflaah*; (4) the
objections raised against his going to Mezritch by his fellow sages of Shklov and Mohilev and other towns; (5)
the difficulty of determining the practical application of
the *Halachah* in his *Shulchan Aruch*; (6) the misgivings
expressed by veteran disciples of the Maggid of Mezritch
(chiefly by Reb Baruch of Mezhibuzh) over the doctrines
of the *Chabad* school of chassidic philosophy which he
founded; (7) the disputations with the *misnagdim*; (8)
the complaints raised by his colleagues, the tzaddikim of
Volhynia, because he refused to join them in issuing a
cherem (ban of excommunication) on the *misnagdim*
who battled against his lifework; (9) the difficulties in
maintaining his chassidim in *Eretz Yisrael*; (10) the complaint of Reb Shlomo of Karlin that Reb Shneur Zalman
opposed Napoleon in his Russian campaign.

When Reb Yosef Yitzchak of Lubavitch once

recounted the above at a public gathering, one of his listeners asked: "Why did they not count the Alter Rebbe's imprisonment in the Peter-Paul Fortress as one of the ten tribulations?"

The tzaddik answered: "This used to be enumerated by the elder chassidim as one of the merits (zechuyos) which the Alter Rebbe was privileged to have. And these are the ten: (1) the writing of his edition of the *Shulchan Aruch*; (2) the editing of the prayer rite (*nussach*); (3) the regulations he issued governing the construction of the *mikveh*; (4) the institution of the honed slaughtering-knife for *shechitah*; (5) the dissemination of the teachings of Chassidim; (6) maintenance of the chassidic community in the Holy Land; (7) his imprisonment and deliverance; (8) the acceptance which his works won in scholarly circles, achieving a status normally reserved for the works of *geonim* of earlier generations — as evidenced by the name "the Rav" with which he was graced; (9) the ten melodies (*niggunim*) which he composed, which foster *deveikus* and arouse a desire for *teshuvah*; (10) his blessing: that wherever chassidim would earnestly endeavor to strengthen the position of the Torah and the *mitzvos*, they would succeed — so that one man would have the power of ten thousand."

◄§ Whose Festival is This?

One year at a *Yud-Tes* Kislev celebration, a chassid of scholarly stature called Reb Yitzchak Aizik of Homil posed the question: "Who was granted a salvation on *Yud-Tes* Kislev? The Alter Rebbe? — For him it made no difference where he was. Even in the rigors of *Tainy Soviet* he lacked nothing. Did someone say that he didn't have *Shabbos* clothes to change into? — Even that was not lacking, because he had a handkerchief, and every Friday afternoon he would tear off two tiny strips with which to keep his socks up, so you see that each week he had new garters in honor of *Shabbos*."

"Who then was granted a salvation of *Yud-Tes* Kislev? — It was the *Almighty* who was granted a salvation (לה' הַיְשׁוּעָה), because through the Alter Rebbe's release the light of Godliness has been revealed and disseminated far and wide in This World! Now isn't that enough reason to make you want to dance?"

And the exuberant throng broke out into a lively dance at once.

ᴈᵍ Orders are Orders

It is the custom in every community of *Chabad* chassidim throughout the world to share out the tractates of the Talmud every year according to the instruction of Reb Shneur Zalman of Liadi in one of the pastoral letters which are collected under the title *Iggeres HaKodesh*, and which are published as Part IV of his *Tanya*. Though the Alter Rebbe himself does not set a particular date, the division is made afresh every *Yud-Tes* Kislev, by which time each chassid has made it his business to complete the study of his tractate.

A famous chassid by the name of Reb Yitzchak Aizik of Homil used to ask each participant individually if he had studied the tractate for which he had signed up the previous year, and each chassid in turn would of course answer that he had.

It once happened that as he was reading down his list, he reached a certain tractate and asked the individual concerned: "Have you studied it?"

"Yes," was the reply.

"The *whole* tractate?" asked Reb Yitzchak Aizik.

"Yes."

"The whole tractate *this year?*"

The chassid now faltered, and explained: "Last year, some days before *Yud-Tes* Kislev, when I had already made up my mind which tractate I wanted to undertake, I decided to go ahead and begin studying it at once."

Reb Yitzchak immediately apportioned the first few pages of the tractate among those present, to be studied on the spot. He explained his action by pointing out that the Alter Rebbe in his epistle writes that the entire Talmud had to be completed "each and every year" — and that was why this had to be done *in the course of one year.*

In St. Petersburg there lived a very wealthy man of about fifty who was born into a family of *Chabad* chassidim from Mohilev. He himself was by now not only far from the traditions of his family, but indeed far from observance of the mitzvos altogether. At the age of fourteen he had already found his way somehow to the big city where he had succumbed to the pressures of the time and the place, until eventually he even desecrated the *Shabbos* publicly, ate *trefah* food, and so on. Nevertheless, since his roots had been in a family of prominent disciples of the tzaddikim of the *Chabad* dynasty, when pictures of the Alter Rebbe and his grandson, Reb Menachem Mendel, first became available, he commissioned a celebrated artist to make copies for him, which he framed and hung in his private library.

The more he prospered, the more he became assimilated. His sons were given Russian names, they received secular education, and the only callers in his house were either Christians, or Jews who had forgotten their background.

One day the urgency of a certain business matter involving a local chassid demanded that he go to see the other man personally at home. As he walked inside, he saw tables set as if for a festival, and the whole household rollicking with joyful singing. Seeing his guest arriving, the host immediately rose to welcome him, ushered him into his office, and they discussed their business affairs.

That done, the guest took the liberty of asking: "Excuse me, but what is the celebration in there? Is it perhaps a family occasion, for which I could wish you *Mazel Tov?*"

"Yes," replied the host, "it is indeed a family *simchah.* Right now we are conversing by telephone with our fathers and grandfathers in the Garden of Eden. And we were so glad to hear regards from there that we decided to turn on a feast ..."

The guest, of course, had no idea what he was expected to say in response to this kind of talk.

yud-tes   Seeing his embarrassment the host continued: "Today
kislev   is *Yud-Tes* Kislev. In *Gan Eden*, in the abode of the Alter
Rebbe, there is a great deal of rejoicing. All the tzaddikim
have assembled there in order to wish him *Mazel Tov* on
his liberation, and on the tens of thousands of people
who have become chassidim. Our fathers and grandfathers who used to travel long distances to visit the rebbes of their respective generations are there too for the
big celebration, and we, their children and grandchildren, are rejoicing together with them over this festival
which is both theirs and ours."

These words drove deep into the heart of that
magnate. He recalled his childhood, when chassidic
farbrengens just like this one used to take place in his
own father's house. He felt a violent urge to join in with
those happy chassidim, if only for a moment. But then
again, he felt himself to be so strange and remote from
their lifestyle that he could not summon the strength to
express his wish. He almost felt ashamed of himself.
How could he, who ate *trefah* food and who desecrated
the *Shabbos*, join in with this pious brotherhood of chassidim?

The host had the sensitivity to rise to the occasion un-
asked, and while inviting him to join the celebration for a
moment, said: "By the way, my friend, while you're in
there you'll get regards from your father and your
grandfather too ..."

And he saw to it that his guest should feel as if —
literally — at home.

An hour passed, two hours, three. The magnate forgot
altogether that he had booked theater tickets for himself
and some important officials of his acquaintance. He was
drawn so deeply into the exuberance of that gathering
that he imagined that he was back in his parents' home,
as in his childhood. He recalled the festive meal which
was prepared every *Yud-Tes* Kislev in his grandfather's
little *shul*. He remembered too the *seudah* which his
grandfather used to hold whenever he came home
together with his friends after a visit to his rebbe in far-
off Lubavitch. His grandmother used to fuss happily
over the preparations for that meal, and his mother and
aunts all shared in helping for the joyous occasion.

After quite some hours had passed, he finally went home. The first thing he did was take a long, long look at the two pictures in his library. Then he sat down and prayed the *Maariv* prayer with sobs that came from some spot deep within him.

Within a few days he had bought new dishes and had made his whole kitchen kosher, and was himself well on the way to becoming a new man.

◆§ Sharing a Memory

There once lived a chassid whose reminiscences were particulary treasured, for by his old age he had the probably unique distinction of having seen with his own eyes six successive generations of rebbes of the *Chabad-*Lubavitch dynasty, starting with the Mitteler Rebbe. This chassid was called Reb David Zvi Chen, the *rav* of Chernigov.

In 1894, at a gathering of chassidim presided over by Reb Shalom Ber of Lubavitch, he related the following.

✿　✿　✿

Once, after Sukkos, I made the journey to Homil in order to spend a few months studying under Reb Yitzchak Aizik, who lived there. That year *Yud-Tes* Kislev fell on a Friday. Before the evening prayers of *Kabbalas Shabbos* the table was set with strong drink and refreshments. After the Maariv prayers, Reb Yitzchak Aizik intoned *Kiddush* with the festive tune of Simchas Torah over a goblet of strong liquor, and after everyone else had also recited *Kiddush*, he announced that he was going to give us a gift: he would tell us all about the Alter Rebbe's first thanksgiving *seudah* for *Yud-Tes* Kislev held at Liadi in 1801.

Two months earlier, he told us, in Tishrei, the elder chassidim had sensed that something was afoot for *Yud-Tes* Kislev that year. On Shemini Atzeres and Simchas Torah the rebbe was exceedingly joyful, and on various occasions he had told his sons and the inner circle of older chassidim that for various spiritual reasons he had not accepted the suggestion made by his chassidim in 1798 to establish *Yud-Tes* Kislev as a day of public feasting and rejoicing. He had mentioned too that he himself had not yet made a *seudas hodaah,* a festive meal of thanksgiving, even though this would be reckoned a *seudas* mitzvah. At one of the festive meals of Simchas Torah he had taken up this theme again and had engaged his brother, Reb Yehudah Leib of Yanowitz, in a debate on the legal intricacies of the question: If a person had not held such a *seudah* of thanksgiving soon after the event which occasioned it, could he hold it after some time?

From all of this the chassidim gathered that without a doubt the rebbe would instruct them to conduct a festive meal of this kind when *Yud-Tes* Kislev came around, and that he would attend it himself.

At the beginning of Kislev, therefore, we young men from Homil and Bobruisk and the other towns in those parts put together whatever money we had. We hired a wagon, and bought a dozen pairs of *volikess* (felt-lined winter boots). We set off together by foot, except that from time to time we took turns to rest on the wagon. At Brohachov, Yachov, and Shklov we were joined by more people, who hired two more wagons. By Thursday of the week in which the Portion of *Vayishlach* is read, we finally arrived — all eighty of us — at Liadi.

That *Shabbos* was one of the most wonderful ever experienced by a group of chassidim. In the course of that one *Shabbos* the rebbe delivered chassidic discourses. The first of these was given before the prayers of *Kabbalas Shabbos,* and was based on the verse, "And Yaakov sent messengers ..."; we heard the second *maamar* some two hours before daybreak, on the verse, "Yehoshua said, 'On the other side of the river ...' "; the third discourse was late in the afternoon, after the *Minchah* prayers, and began with the verse, "And he took of that which came to his hand ...". The full-time local students as well as the guests reviewed the *maamarim* orally together, under the guidance of the *chozrim,* whose task it was to memorize the rebbe's discourses, lovingly preserving his every word for their listeners.

On Sunday and Monday people began to converge on Liadi from far and near — from Kiev, Tatarsk,

Chotemsk, Chaslavitch, Amchislav, Klimovitch, Pahar,
Pochip, Dubrovna, Orsha, Krupka, Tolchin, Barissov,
Babinovitch, Dobromishl, Lubavitch, Rodnia, Liozna,
and yet other towns and townlets in the regions of
Vitebsk and Polotzk. The townsmen of Liadi announced
that all the guests would receive meals without payment
for a whole week, until after the forthcoming *Shabbos*.
Even the gentile townsmen joined to a degree in the spirit
of hospitality that filled the air. Indeed, a few dozen of
them cleared their houses to make room for the out-of-
town guests to sleep. Most outstanding in this direction
was the manager of the estates of Count Liubemirsky.
He made it known in the Jewish community that every
day a consignment of food would be delivered to them
from the Count's estates, consisting of seventy-five *pud*
(one *pud* = 16 kilograms) of flour for bread, and three
cows and a number of calves for *shechitah*. In addition,
he would deliver a number of wagonloads of hay for the
horses of the travelers.

On Tuesday, the Nineteenth of Kislev, it was announced that after an early *Minchah* service everyone
was to assemble in the *beis midrash* which stood in the
large courtyard, where the rebbe would deliver a chassidic discourse. The packed synagogue was then shaken
by the mighty voice of Reb Shmuel Eliyahu *der
Heizeriger* ("the hoarse," so called in jocular reference to
his bellowing roar). He announced that the rebbe was on
his way. This was the cue for a husky band of broad-
shouldered young chassidim to plunge their way
through the crowd, leaving in their wake a broad path
from the door to the dais.

"As soon as the rebbe appeared at the door" (as Reb
Yitzchak Aizik clearly recollected), "we were overcome
by a dreadful awe." As he walked in, accompanied by his
sons and brothers, the rebbe sang alone to the words
צְאֶינָה וּרְאֶינָה, taken from the *Song of Songs*. As he
ascended the steps leading up to the *bimah*, he sang the
melody which he had composed to the words from
Psalms: קֵלִי אַתָּה וְאוֹדֶךָ ("You are my God and I will
praise You"). On the dais there stood a large table at
which the rebbe sat, and there he delivered a *maamar* expounding the verse in Psalms: פָּדָה בְשָׁלוֹם נַפְשִׁי ("He has

delivered my soul in peace ..."). When he completed his discourse (which was later published in *Torah Or* under the title וַיֵּאָבֵק אִישׁ עִמּוֹ), the entire gathering burst out in a jovial melody.

In the smaller *beis midrash* which was used for *yechidus*, a table had been set for a thanksgiving meal. This was attended by the rebbe, his sons and brothers, and a few selected elder chassidim. The rebbe's son Reb Moshe repeated for us, after many requests, the talks which the rebbe had given at that meal — but only on condition that we would not pass their content on to anyone. "For that reason," Reb Yitzchak Aizik told us, "I am unable to tell you all that was said at the table. One statement of the rebbe, however, I can tell you, and this is it.

"I have received a tradition from my *zeide* (for thus the Alter Rebbe used to call his spiritual grandfather, the Baal Shem Tov — his teacher's teacher) that ... foolishness, melancholy and a sense of one's own worthiness are counted by chassidim as transgressions explicit in the Torah. Likewise, intelligence (or 'sense'), joy — through perceiving in everything the element of goodness which brings joy — and alacrity tempered with deliberateness are counted among chassidim as commandments explicit in the Torah."

חנוכה

chanukah

◄§ Out of Your Own Egypt

There was once a man whose mind was severely troubled by persistent thoughts involving disbelief and idolatry. He called on a certain tzaddik in search of a remedy, but he was told: "I cannot help you, young man. I would advise you, however, to pay a visit to Reb Shlomo of Karlin. He will help you."

The man promptly took his problem to Reb Shlomo, whom he found reciting verses from the Book of *Psalms*, as was his custom, while lighting his Chanukah lamp.

When Reb Shlomo arrived at the verse, "And He delivered us from our oppressors, for His kindness is everlasting" — he slapped his visitor on the shoulder and said: "Do you believe that the Almighty can deliver a man from every impurity and from every *Mitzrayim?*" (For מִצְרַיִם, the Hebrew word for 'Egypt', also implies מְצָרִים — the restraints and constrictions suffered by the soul in an unspiritual body.)

At that moment the man was free of all this loathsome imaginings, and he left — a new man.

◄§ Leaving its Mark

Reb Shlomo of Karlin used to say (contrary to the accepted view) that wax candles were the best thing to light on Chanukah, for at the place where they are stuck to the wall an impression is made that sits throughout the year — whereas the house bears no mark of oil that is poured into a *Menorah*.

It once happened that he kindled wicks of oil in his *Menorah* and a fire broke out — just enough for the wall to be burned. Reb Shlomo was most pleased, for even though an oil *Menorah* is soon forgotten, this time the mitzvah had left its mark on the house.

◄§ Supplementary Budget

After lighting his Chanukah lamp one year, Reb Avraham Yehoshua Heschel (the Ohev Yisrael) of Apta walked outside, and having stood there for about a quarter of an hour came inside and sank into his chair in a state of obvious dejection. A little later he again went outside, but this time when he returned he sat down joyfully, and told the chassidim who were then in his house: "When I was out there the first time and looked over our little town of Mezhibuzh, I saw that the entire income which was apportioned on Rosh HaShanah for our townsfolk for the forthcoming year — has now already been consumed, by Chanukah! So of course I was sad. But then I thought it over, and decided to go out again and look up into the sky just in case I didn't see the truth the first time. And indeed the second time I saw that I had been right all along — except for one thing. You see, last year exactly the same thing happened, and nevertheless the Almighty provided them all with a livelihood for the whole year. So this year, too, no doubt in His mercy He will do the same thing all over again!"

◄§ Making Use of the Torah

Reb Yisrael, the Maggid of Koznitz, once recalled that when he was a child of about seven he studied in the yeshivah of the renowned scholar Rabbi Yechezkel of Ostrovtze. At night, after the formal studies were over, he would stay on in the *beis midrash* and study alone.

When Chanukah came around his father refused him permission to go to the communal House of Study at night for fear lest he join the other boys in the pastime of cardplaying, which has been customary on Chanukah in various periods and places. The child would have wanted to study instead at home, but his father was a poverty-stricken bookbinder, and the house boasted neither candles nor books. Young Yisrael therefore promised his father that he would buy a candle of the size that cost no more than three small copper coins, and would study in the *beis midrash* by its light until it went out. He would

then come home at once, and his father could thus rest חנוכה
assured that he had not stayed on to play cards. The
father agreed, and the boy went off to the *beis midrash* to
study.

But the angels in heaven found such pleasure in his
study that a miracle was performed for him, just like that
of Chanukah: the little candle burned on and on right
through the night. When his father saw that the
promised hour had passed and his son had not returned,
he became convinced that the child had acted against his
wishes and was no doubt playing cards with all the little
emptyheads in town.

Morning came, and Yisrael returned home and lay
down to sleep. His father, however, decided to administer discipline in the only way he understood — and
beat him soundly.

Recalling this incident, the Maggid of Koznitz commented that if he had told his father at the time that he
had studied all that night, he would have believed him,
for his father knew that he never lied. But he thought it
would be sinful to spare himself a beating by making use
of the honor of the Torah — and that was why he had
chosen to be beaten and bruised, in silence.

✍§ Soul Roots

R eb Zvi Elimelech of Dinov was the grandson of the
sister of Reb Elimelech of Lyzhansk, the author of
Noam Elimelech. A few months before his birth, his
mother went to visit her uncle Reb Elimelech to ask his
advice as to what name she should give the child.

"You will give birth to a son," said the tzaddik, "and
you shall call him 'Elimelech'."

The poor woman was aghast: did that mean that her
saintly uncle expected to die before she gave birth?

The tzaddik saw her plight and said: "If so, call him
'Zvi Elimelech'."

After she had given birth and named the baby as instructed, Reb Elimelech told her: "If you had called him
'Elimelech', he would have been entirely like me; now he
will be half like me."

In due course this child grew up to be renowned as a

scholar and a tzaddik, to whom thousands turned for guidance, and whose learned works have become classics — chiefly *Bnei Yissaschar*, on the festivals.

One day, while on his way to visit his rebbe, the Chozeh of Lublin, he began to ponder the question of which of the Twelve Tribes he descended from. "Why," he thought to himself, "as soon as Chanukah comes around, do I always experience a heightened measure of spiritual delight? Now it cannot be because I am descended from the Hasmoneans, for I am not a *kohen*. So where does this blissful sweetness come from?"

So he decided that when in Lublin he would ask his rebbe — for the "Chozeh" means "the Seer", and Reb Yaakov Yitzchak of Lublin, in the *ruach hakodesh* which enabled him to see from one end of the world to the other, would certainly give him the answer.

He arrived at his house, but before he managed to say a word the Chozeh said: "You should know that you are descended from the Tribe of Yissaschar. As to the question of why you experience what you do on Chanukah, that is because in the time of the *Beis HaMikdash* you were a member of the *beis din* of the Hasmoneans" — for this Tribe traditionally supplied the scholars who manned the rabbinical courts in Temple times.

And that is why Reb Zvi Elimelech entitled his learned book on the festivals — *Bnei Yissaschar* ("The Sons of Yissaschar").

∾§ Earmarked for a Mitzvah

All the utensils used in the household of Reb Yitzchak Aizik of Zhidachov were of cheap materials. He used silver only for objects used in the performance of mitzvos — a little *Menorah* for Chanukah, a few candlesticks for *Shabbos*, a large wine goblet for *Kiddush*, a spice-box for *Havdalah*, and in addition a small pocket-watch whose hours were marked in Hebrew letters, and which always stood on his table.

One day one of his wealthy chassidim won a small silver table in a lottery, and brought it to the tzaddik as a gift — but he declined to accept it. His son, Reb Eliyahu, contended that this too could be used for a mitzvah — as

a pedestal on which to place the *Menorah* on Chanukah. חנוכה
In fact such a use would accord with the well-known
teaching of the Sages, based on the verse זֶה קֵלִי וְאַנְוֵהוּ —
"This is my God and I will exalt him." The Hebrew word
וְאַנְוֵהוּ is interpreted in the sense of נָאֶה ("beautiful"),
whence comes the injunction: "Conduct yourself
beautifully before Him in the performance of the mitzvos."

The tzaddik found this argument convincing — but
just convincing enough to accept the table as a gift *to be
used on Chanukah.* Accordingly, for the other fifty-one
weeks of the year, it would stand in the house of his son.

ﺱ *In Mortal Danger*

During the period that the newly-married son of Reb
Yitzchak Aizik of Zhidachov was staying in the
household of his father-in-law, Reb Avraham of Stretyn,
he observed that his host spent a great deal of time singing all kinds of hymns after lighting the Chanukah candles every night. He began to wonder why his own
father somehow finished the whole process in a quarter
of an hour.

His father's answer to his question bore a dread allu-
sion to the propensity of a tzaddik's soul to seek so rap-
turously to cleave to its Source, that during the performance of a mitzvah it could even seek to leave its bodily
haven.

"My son," said Reb Yitzchak Aizik, "It is indeed a
miracle that when I recite a blessing over the Chanukah
lamps, I am not burned up together with them. Would
you have me stay near them for hours on end?"

ﺱ *The Rules of the Game*

Without any warning, Reb Nachum of Stefanesti (the
son of Reb Yisrael of Ruzhin) walked straight into
his *beis midrash* one Chanukah evening. Here he found
a number of men playing draughts (or Chinese
checkers), as some people are accustomed to do on
Chanukah. Needless to say, they were not a little embarrassed.

"Do you know the rules of the game?" he asked them. They remained silent.

And the tzaddik answered his own question — though predictably enough, relating it to the challenges and decisions that each man faces in the course of his lifelong mission of self-refinement.

"*I* will tell you the rules," he said. "You give one, in order to gain two; you must never take two steps at a time; you always move upwards, never down; and once you've reached the top, you can go wherever you like!"

ᴥ§ The Same Man

Reb Yitzchak Meir of Ger, the author of *Chiddushei HaRim*, once related at candle-lighting time that a group of chassidim traveled to Lublin one Chanukah to see the Chozeh. One of them handed the rebbe a *kvitl* which bore the name of a friend of his. The tzaddik took one look at the note, and spat. The same evening the visiting chassid decided to try once more to hand the note to the rebbe. This time, as soon as the clairvoyant tzaddik saw it, he said: "This man illuminates all the worlds!"

He then added: "At the time I first saw the *kvitl*, that man was playing cards; this time he's lighting his Chanukah lamp."

ᴥ§ Come Down to Our Level

In the household of Reb David of Tolna, the kindling of the Chanukah lights was a major event. The *Menorah* itself was of gold, and altogether an intricate piece of artistic craftsmanship. His chassidim would assemble in his house with due ceremony, and the air was soon filled with hymns and melodies.

On the first night of Chanukah one year, when the tzaddik, surrounded by his chassidim, was ready to kindle the lamp, he turned to one of them and said: "Look here. Your wife is short, isn't she? When you want to speak to her, what do you do? Do you bend over towards her, or does she raise herself up to your height?"

And without waiting for an answer, he recited the

blessings and kindled the *Menorah*. Needless to say, the חנוכה
man questioned was as baffled as everyone else present.

Now staying with the tzaddik at the time was his
brother's grandson, Reb Mordechai Dov of Hornisteipl.
He of course was present at the time, and when he saw
how puzzled the chassidim were, he said: "I will explain
to you what my saintly great-uncle said."

"As you know, the Talmud says: 'The Divine Presence has never descended lower than ten handbreadths
from the ground.' An exception to this rule is the
Menorah on Chanukah, whose place is ideally required
to be less than ten *tefachim* from the ground. The
Shechinah on this occasion does descend lower than ten.
And in the kabbalistic writings of the *Arizal* it is written
that this is the mystical concept that lies at the root of the
Talmudic dictum: 'If your wife is short, bend over and
whisper to her.'

"This was what the tzaddik wanted to make mention
of."

The next evening at candle-lighting time, Reb David
again made some puzzling comment to one of his chassidim. And immediately, though he had not been told of
the previous night's explanation, he turned to his
brother's grandson and said: "This time you will not
perceive as you did yesterday!"

פורים

PURIM

⊷§ The Thought that Goes With it

During the first year after Reb Avraham Yehoshua Heschel of Apta had accepted a rabbinical position in Jassy, the local townsmen sent him a number of gold coins on Purim as *Mishloach Manos*. Seeing his father playing with them, his son Reb Yitzchak Meir was amazed, for he knew him to be a man who loathed money.

"Father," he asked, "what has made you suddenly throw off your characteristic hatred of money?"

"Throughout the year," explained the tzaddik, "I treat gold with scorn. I don't value it in the least. But today's mitzvah obliges me to give gifts of money to the poor, *Mattanos LaEvyonim*. This means that I would be giving them something which in my eyes is worthless. I therefore decided today to make an effort to introduce the love of money into my heart. When that reaches a peak, *then* I will distribute it among the needy!"

⊷§ The Taste of Success

A poverty-stricken villager once came to the nearby town of Koznitz on Purim in order to hear the *Megillah* read in the synagogue. The Scroll was read by none less than Reb Yisrael, the celebrated Maggid of Koznitz, and as the simple fellow listened to the story he beamed with joy.

When the service was over the Maggid approached him and said: "Aren't you from the village over there, that is part of my region? So why didn't you bring me *Mishloach Manos*?"

The poor fellow did not know what to answer. At home there was not even enough bread for his half-dozen toddlers, so where was he to find the wherewithal for buying *Mishloach Manos* for the Maggid?

purim Reb Yisrael continued: "Look, today is Purim! Come along with me and have a little sip of something!"

With the help of the little sip and the refreshments that he was given in the home of the Maggid, together with the joy he felt at being privileged to be there in the company of the Maggid's disciples, he became daring of spirit. He went from there straight to the house of a wealthy wine merchant, where he knocked on the door and told the householder: "A happy Purim to you, sir! Would you be so good as to give me a bottle of choice wine on credit? Without a doubt I will pay you, but just in case I don't — isn't is Purim today?"

The merchant obliged; so off strode our villager to a nearby shop, where he said: "A very happy Purim, my friend! Two or three shiny apples, if you don't mind. It goes without saying that I will pay. But if I don't, — why, it's Purim today!"

Off he went, buoyant and carefree, to the Maggid.

"Rebbe, I've brought you *Mishloach Manos!*" he said, with the confidence of a man who knows the taste of success.

"Well done," said the Maggid. "And remember to bring *Mishloach Manos* every Purim!"

On his way out, cold reality hit him hard.

"My poor family are famished, and haven't the slightest inkling of today's Purim joy," he said to himself. "I'll have to do something about it!"

So he headed straight for the vendor of vodka, where he again used his tried and tested formula, and then used it once more for a hot loaf of bread and yet again for a few fat herrings.

With these luxuries under his arm he ran all the way home, kicked the door open, and announced as if he were the town crier: "It's Purim today! Purim today!"

His wife and children were hardly used to seeing him in such spirits. Perhaps his grinding worries had put him out of his mind, God forbid?

But he put their minds at ease by laying out the royal spread on their rickety table, and saying: "Eat, drink, and be merry, because it's Purim today!"

The ragged family ate their fill, and then, as if animated by a breath of life, they sprang up from their

places and danced around their cottage kitchen, singing **פורים**
lustily: "Today is Purim! It's Purim today!"

A thud on the door soured their idyll.

"Don't open!" whispered the villager to his wife. "It's most probably one of those gentile peasants who has come to disturb our Purim joy."

The gentile knocked repeatedly.

"Don't worry," said the villager's wife. "I think it's only old Ivan who always comes around wanting to sell potatoes."

Opening the door, she was shocked to see the state old Ivan was in — beaten and bruised, and bleeding on all sides. Feeling sorry for him, they gently washed and dressed his wounds, and raised his spirits by letting him share their ration of bread and vodka.

"You folk saved my life," he muttered. "There was only a hairsbreadth between me and death."

He went on to tell them how his only son had beaten him up and thrown him out of his own house. Had they not come to his help, he would surely have died of his wounds out there in the snow.

"Now listen here," he said after he had rested a while. "Since my only son has proved to be a cruel murderer, and you poor folk had pity on me, come along with me to the forest and I will show you a big treasure. It's the money I saved, and was going to give my son before I die. Now it's yours — a gift from me!"

The villager followed the limping gentile into the forest, where he was shown a certain tree under which, he said, the money was hidden. A few days later the gentile died as a result of his wounds. The villager later went out to the spot he was shown, dug near the tree — and was suddenly a rich man.

And every Purim after that he would call on the Maggid, and give him *Mishloach Manos* with an open hand and a glad heart.

◂§ Make Your Own Lawyer

An obscure Rumanian Jew called Mendel once moved to Kishinev, which was then part of Russia. Back in his hometown, a former friend turned enemy laid a false charge against him to the Rumanian authorities. According to his libel, while he was still in Rumania this Mendel had found a chest of gold coins which had previously belonged to the Rumanian treasury, and this was why he had suddenly decided to abscond.

The Rumanian government thereupon demanded that the Russian authorities hand over their former citizen for trial. Mendel in the meantime had received Russian citizenship, so his government therefore replied that if the Rumanian authorities had some claim against him, they could raise it in the Russian court situated in Kishinev, and could send an attorney and witnesses to the trial.

Poor Mendel set out at once to Shpola, where he told his whole miserable story to Reb Aryeh Leib, the Shpoler Zeide.

"Don't be afraid about the trial," said the tzaddik. "Just make every effort to have the trial postponed to Purim. And don't hire any lawyer, because I'll send along someone who will speak excellently on your behalf."

"How much will I have to pay that lawyer?" asked Mendel.

To this the tzaddik replied that there was an orphaned bride whom he was now trying to marry off, and for this he needed three hundred rubles. If Mendel would give him this sum, then the tzaddik would send the lawyer at his own expense.

He further instructed him to prepare a document of power of attorney for the lawyer whom he would meet in the courtroom. He would be able to identify the stranger by two agreed signs: he would be wearing a white hat and red gloves.

Mendel gave the tzaddik the three hundred rubles and set out for home. After considerable effort he managed to have the date of the trial fixed for the exact day of Purim. Four weeks in advance he received a notification which set out the details of the charge, and a summons to appear. The Rumanian authorities were likewise informed of the date. As the day drew near, Mendel sent a messenger with a *pidyon* to be given to the tzaddik, who would be in Shpola on Purim, as well as gifts of money

for the tzaddik to distribute to the needy on Purim as פּוּרִים
Mattanos LaEvyonim.

Now the Shpoler Zeide had his own characteristic way of dealing with situations of this kind involving the authorities. He would get together a group of masqueraders — Purim-*spieler* — who were no mean jesters, but men of intelligence selected from among his circle of followers. The matter under trial would be presented before them, as if in a court, and they would hand down a verdict according to the wishes of the tzaddik. Sometimes he arranged for a Purim-*rav*, and sometimes a Purim-king, complete with retinue of ministers and judges. There were times when even he himself joined the masqueraders. This was not a light-hearted piece of play-acting, but a mystical tactic with ideological basis in the Kabbalah. Remarkable feats were achieved through it, for the benefit of individuals and communities.

On Mendel's fateful Purim the Shpoler Zeide instructed his men to dress up as judges and court officials, so that they would be ready to conduct Mendel's trial in the tzaddik's house in Shpola. He asked the local *rav* to dress up as the chief justice, and appointed two other townsmen to sit as judges on the same bench. Another man's face was blackened: he was to be the prosecutor representing the government of Rumania. Everyone in the room made fun of the poor fellow, and laughed at his every word. The Shpoler Zeide himself dressed up as the defense attorney, not forgetting to cover his *shtreimel* with a white silk scarf and to put on a pair of red gloves. One more townsman had to be the informer, and another stood in for the defendant, Mendel. The last two took up the guise of witnesses. Their task was to tell the court how they had once seen the informer brazenly approaching Mendel with an utterly unfounded demand for money; when Mendel had refused, he had threatened to take his revenge.

These people only were in the room: no one else was allowed to enter.

The trial began. The chief justice read the document which stated the case against Mendel. He was followed by the representative of the Rumanian government, but whenever he opened his mouth to speak, he was laughed

PURIM out of court. The informer was next to be summoned to the bench, and he now repeated his calumny. It was then the turn of the two witnesses who testified as to the vengeful background to the whole trial. Finally, the judges called on the venerable attorney to speak in Mendel's defense.

In a masterful piece of courtroom eloquence, the Shpoler Zeide now stated the case for acquittal. He elaborated on the motivation behind the charge; proved that the story of the chest of gold coins was fabricated; and demonstrated by legal arguments that even if this charge were true, the government of Rumania was not entitled to any claim on the find.

His speech completed, the judges now handed down their verdict. Mendel was declared innocent, and the man with the blackened visage was pushed out to the bathroom to wash his face.

The Shpoler Zeide and his associates then adjourned to the waiting tables, where they conducted the festive *seudas* Purim together with a bustling throng of jovial chassidim. And that same night a telegram arrived from Kishinev with the good news that Mendel had been pronounced innocent, and was on his way to Shpola.

A few days later, the celebrity himself arrived. He walked straight into the *beis midrash* of the tzaddik, and told the exuberant chassidim there that he had had a first-rate defense attorney. What a speech he had delivered! He went on to give them all the details of the arguments — but could not fathom why they all looked more and more stupefied as he continued with his story. For to them it was incredibly familiar ...

Mendel went in to see the tzaddik.

"*Nu*, Mendel," he asked, "were you pleased with the lawyer I sent you?"

"Why," said Mendel, "a first-class defense attorney, that's what he was! Everyone in the courtroom hung on his every word — and look, I came out with my innocence proved!"

"My young man," said the Shpoler Zeide, "that defense attorney was an angel from heaven who was created out of the *tzedakah* money that you gave me to marry off an orphaned bride. If you are found worthy of

it, you may yet be privileged when the time comes to see פורים
that attorney in the World Above — for when you are
one day summoned to give an account of your doings in
This World throughout your lifetime, that attorney will
speak up in your defense!"

⊰§ How Not to Read the Megillah

There is a passage in the Mishnah dealing with the
reading of the *Megillah* which says: הַקּוֹרֵא אֶת הַמְּגִלָּה
לְמַפְרֵעַ לֹא יָצָא. In its plain meaning this tells us that if a
person reads the Scroll of *Esther* out of order (לְמַפְרֵעַ, lit.:
"retroactively"), he has not discharged his obligation.
Interestingly, though, as we shall see, this key word
(לְמַפְרֵעַ) has other connotations as well.

❋ ❋ ❋

After the reading of the *Megillah* one year a certain
well-to-do citizen sent Reb Baruch of Mezhibuzh a considerable sum of money for *Megillah Gelt* — as
it is customary in some places for the one who reads the
Scroll in the synagogue to be given a gratuity in return
for his trouble. The tzaddik declined to accept the gift,
and explained his reason to the messenger who had
brought it.

That day, he said, while reading the *Megillah*, a novel
interpretation of the above words from the Mishnah
came to mind — that the word לְמַפְרֵעַ implies פֵּרָעוֹן,
which means "payment". Hence: a person has not fulfilled his obligation to read the *Megillah* if he does so in
the hope of soliciting payment thereby ...

❋ ❋ ❋

On Purim, Reb Baruch of Mezhibuzh was fond of
quoting a well-known dictum from the *Haggadah* of
Pesach: "In each and every generation a man is obliged
to regard himself as if he personally came out of Egypt."

In the same way, Reb Baruch would say, a person is
obliged to understand that in each and every generation
there is a Mordechai and a Haman, and in his own life to
relive the lessons of the Purim story. If, however, a
person reads the *Megillah* only לְמַפְרֵעַ — "retroactively",

פורim as a record of *a miracle that belongs only to the past* —
then he has not fulfilled the mitzvah of reading it.

✥ Just a Plain Mitzvah

To hear Reb Shalom of Belz reading the *Megillah* was
a rare spiritual experience, and year after year the entire assemblage in *shul* would be electrified by the awe of
Him Whose Name is written between its lines. Once
when he was still a very young man, a disciple of Reb
Yaakov Yitzchak (the Chozeh) of Lublin, his rebbe gave
him the honor of reading the *Megillah* in *shul*. When it
was over his rebbe commented to someone: "This story
I've heard many times, but the way this young man tells
it — never."

It once happened that his sons, Reb Yehoshua and
Reb Elazar, were traveling not far from home, but when
the Fast of Esther came they were obliged for some
reason to stay in an inn in a village, and to hear the
Megillah read there. Reb Elazar was disappointed and
distressed that he had to hear the reading from the
mouth of a plain ordinary householder, and that he had
thus not experienced the spiritual delights of upliftment
that came from hearing his father's reading. His brother,
however, reacted otherwise.

"On the contrary," he pointed out, "I am more than
happy. This evening I was privileged to fulfill the obligation of hearing the *Megillah* without any self-serving
motivation at all. For when I hear it every year from our
father, my mind is not exclusively intent on the fulfillment of the mitzvah *per se*, for every word he utters is
sweeter than honey and richer than gold. But this year
when I heard the *Megillah* from an ordinary Jew I had no
other motivation for listening at all but simply to fulfill
the mitzvah."

✥ Under My Own Steam

At the festive *seudas* Purim one year, Reb Noach of
Lechovitch announced to the chassidim around his
table: "It is written that on Purim, 'Whoever stretches
out his hand for alms is to be given!' Therefore, if there

is anyone who would now like me to give him a gift in פּורים the area of divine service, I can give it to him."

Various chassidim snapped up the bargain and asked their rebbe to grant them help in cultivating the love of God, in praying selflessly, or whatever else they happened to be working on. One man sat silent — Reb Moshe of Kobrin, who was one day to succeed Reb Noach as rebbe.

"And what is *your* request?" Reb Noach asked him.

"I don't want any free gifts," said his disciple. "I want to be a soldier, and work my way up through my own efforts."

◦§ Too Much Money

In Kobrin there lived a good-hearted simple fellow called Yekkele Rashes who earned his living by sewing for the local squires. On his first visit to Reb Noach of Lechovitch, the tzaddik asked him what he did about the custom of *yittur* (Hebrew: "leaving remnants") — for there were tailors in those days who took their clients' measurements in such a way as to leave themselves remnants of material by way of unproclaimed baksheesh.

Yekkele answered that he did what many tailors did ... The tzaddik thereupon explained that this was no petty sin, and from that day on Yekkele never succumbed to the habit of his profession again. Instead, he told his clients that he had learned a new style of tailoring which enabled him to cut the fabric more economically, except that he asked to be paid a little more for his work during the time that he was mastering this new art.

Once he spent Purim with the rebbe at Lechovitch, and when early the next morning, on Shushan Purim, he went to pray in the rebbe's *beis midrash*, he saw people buying firewood. Being always charitable with his income, he was puzzled by this sight, and thought to himself: "How could it possibly be that people have that much money so early in the morning? Didn't they give away all their money yesterday as charity to the poor?"

He decided that this was a queston for the rebbe. The tzaddik listened, and replied: "Don't you realize, my friend? The people out there buying firewood are those

PURIM who *received* charity yesterday. That's why they've got money today ..."

⋖ﾞ *Governor for a Day*

It used to be the custom in the good old days for each community to appoint some local wit as their *rav*, whose tenure would last for the duration of Purim; and likewise any number of judges, or policemen, and whatever other functionaries they fancied. One year, in the days of Reb Zvi of Zhidachov, the townsfolk chose Reb Koppel, the tzaddik's lively nephew, to be the provincial governor, a position whose incumbent in real life was empowered to enact and repeal statutes. He in turn chose a retinue of advisers from amongst his usually sage and sober colleagues, and they all showed him the respect that is due a potentate.

Masqueraded gaudily, this whole motley band danced and tottered their way into the household of Reb Koppel's uncle, the tzaddik; and it goes without saying that in that whole itinerant legislature there was not one man sober. The tzaddik treated his nephew like a king, and entreated him to issue a decree repealing the legislation which that same year had in fact imposed the infamous candle tax and meat tax on the Jews of the province. The provincial governor was kind enough to oblige. The tzaddik then proceeded to ask his nephew to repeal the ordinance conscripting Jews to the army — but the tipsy young man flatly refused. The tzaddik tried both scolding and entreating, but to no avail. His chassidim too tried to help out — some by threatening, others by imploring — but the young man's mind was not to be changed. The tzaddik thereupon left the room in anger, and all day would not look him in the face.

The next day, when the effects of the wine had evaporated, the young man was asked by his fellow chassidim: "What on earth came over you yesterday, that you defied the rebbe's wish?"

"I solemnly swear I haven't the foggiest recollection of what went on here yesterday," he declared — and indeed the poor fellow could hardly believe the whole story.

❀   ❀   ❀

That year the provincial authorities in fact repealed **פורים**
the legislation which had imposed the anti-Semitic tax on
candles and meat — but the cruel conscription order
remained in force. The chassidim now realized that on
Purim they had witnessed something beyond their comprehension: their rebbe had not been playing games.

◆§ Practical Jokers

R eb Yitzchak Aizik of Zhidachov once related the
following episode involving the learned tzaddik Reb
Avraham of Ulianov to the latter's son.

Reb Avraham was head of the rabbinical court in
Ulianov, and the *rav* of the entire province. One of the
townships under his jurisdiction was Rodnik, whose *rav*
was Reb Chaim, later to become famous as Reb Chaim of
Zanz. Another citizen of stature in that little town was
Reb Melech, the saintly grandson of Reb Elimelech of
Lyzhansk.

Now in those regions the custom was that since,
"When Adar begins, joy is to be increased", the townsfolk would get together and appoint — just for one rollicking day — an officious Purim-*kahal* (community
council), presided over by a duly pompous Purim-*rosh-
kahal*; a quick-witted Purim-*rav*, who was fussed over
by a witless but loyal Purim-*shammes*; and so on.

In Rodnik one year such a Purim-*kahal* was duly
elected. Its first official act was to send off a letter to Reb
Avraham, the provincial *rav*, informing him of the
names of the newly sworn-in office-bearers. They
enclosed a gift of money in honor of the forthcoming
festival, and added a letter — just for fun, of course — informing him that the members of the Purim-*kahal* of
Rodnik hereby ordered him, the celebrated *gaon* of
Ulianov, and the revered doyen of the rabbinate of that
entire region, to appear in their hamlet on Purim the
fourteenth of Adar, together with all his material possessions, right down to the last shoelace. All the worthies
and unworthies of the Purim-council signed this document. Moreover, some of the more serious members of
the community also joined in the prevailing spirit of
harmless fun, and so it was that Reb Chaim and Reb

Melech likewise appended their signatures. The letter went off, being expected to provoke no more than a smile.

The fourteenth of Adar came as expected. In the morning the townsfolk of Rodnik were streaming out of their little gabled weatherboard shul for the sheer joy of Purim. Then one after another they looked up in horror, for one by one, creaking their way over the hill towards them crawled half-a-dozen wagons, loaded to the clouds with beds and basins, *kapotes* and books. And bearing up the rear, in a modest carriage all alone, they beheld the venerable presence of the rabbi in person!

When he descended, he was quick to put them at ease by explaining himself: "Among the signatories are eminent scholars. And does the Talmud not teach us, that it is a mitzvah to heed the words of sages? So here I am!"

The townspeople of Rodnik were ashamed no end, and repeatedly begged his forgiveness. This he countered by asking *their* forgiveness, for he confessed that in violation of their summons, he had left his *sifrei Torah* at home.

⊷§ A Generous Reward

Reb Menachem Mendel of Kotsk once made the following comment to his chassidim about his son-in-law, Reb Avraham of Sochatchov, the author of *Avnei Nezer:* "Do you know why the *rav* of Biala was privileged to be granted a son like that?

"One Purim it so happened that all the tzaddikim and scholars were engaged in the mitzvah of eating their festive Purim *seudah.* That meant that there was no one anywhere studying Torah — except for the *rav* of Biala, who sat alone and studied. Heaven was well pleased with this, for if not for him the whole world at that moment would have been void of Torah study.

"And that is why they granted him this gift — a son who would illuminate the whole world."

◆§ Clothing the Naked

For some twenty years on end, Reb Menachem Mendel of Kotsk lived in seclusion, declining even to receive his chassidim in audience.

Reb Yechiel Meir of Gostynin was once in Kotsk for Purim during this period. He approached the unopened door and took the liberty of knocking on it, hard.

The Kotsker rebbe opened the door and asked in amazement: "What's this?"

The other replied: "In the Shulchan Aruch it is written that on Purim, 'Whoever stretches out his hand for alms is to be given!' Rebbe, I am naked, and seek to be clothed. *Teach me!*"

"Then come in," said the Kotsker.

Reb Yechiel Meir entered, the door was closed behind him, and the two tzaddikim spent long hours together. And from that time on the chassidim of Kotsk regarded the guest from Gostynin with the utmost reverence.

◆§ Working Conditions

At *seudas* Purim one year, Reb Aharon (the son of Reb Mordechai) of Chernobyl spoke as follows: "Master of the Universe! We learn in the mystical writings that the Day of Atonement (*Yom HaKippurim*) is like Purim (*yom ke-Purim*). That means that just as on *Yom HaKippurim* we are obliged to repent, so too are we obliged to do *teshuvah* on Purim. The only trouble is that the bodies of Your People are weak, and a livelihood is hard for them to come by, and the yoke of the Exile weighs heavily upon them — so that we haven't got the peace of mind that one needs in order to do *teshuvah*.

"But I assure You, *Ribbono shel Olam*, that if all Israel were strong and healthy, *and* were freed of this Exile, *and* if they had a little money in their pockets, *and* some peace of mind — then for sure they would all repent wholeheartedly. For it is written in the *Megillah*: 'The Jews fulfilled and accepted upon themselves.' And on this verse the Talmud comments: 'They now fulfilled what they had accepted at Sinai.' Now when Your People received the Torah at Sinai, we learn in the Midrash that all the sick were healed; everyone was healthy. They lacked nothing, for they had just recently been given all the wealth of Egypt and their booty at the Sea. And of course they were free of bondage. Without any question their minds were happy and free — so much so, that we have learned that the merest maidservant at the Sea saw a loftier revelation of Your power than even the Prophet Yechezkel saw in his visions. And in that state they received the Torah.

"I therefore assure You, *Ribbono shel Olam*, that if You give us all those conditions today, then without a doubt we will fulfill the Torah today just as we did at Sinai!"

מגלת אסתר
esther

✺§ Fatherly Vigilance

The first chapter of the *Megillah* closes by recording the decree of Achashverosh "that every man should rule in his own house" (לִהְיוֹת כָּל אִישׁ שֹׂרֵר בְּבֵיתוֹ).

שֹׂרֵר בְּבֵיתוֹ
Rule in his own house (1:22)

When Reb Shmuel Abba of Zichlin used to read the *Megillah*, he would pronounce the word שֹׂרֵר, meaning "rule", as שׂרֶר, meaning "look" — for this is one of the connotations which this Hebrew verb bears. His intention in so doing was to remind his listeners that every man should look closely and constantly at the tone of what goes on in his household.

✺§ Basic Training

In the time of Reb Shneur Zalman of Liadi, the author of *Tanya*, it was the custom among chassidim not to visit the rebbe for their first private interview until they had first spent a certain time in studying the teachings of Chassidism and had been given guidance in their divine service by elder chassidim. Thus it was that Reb Yitzchak Aizik of Homil prepared himself for two-and-a-half years, and only then set out to visit the rebbe for his first *yechidus*. On his way he passed through the township of Kazan, near Polotzk, where he called on a certain chassid of his rebbe called Reb Shaul.

שִׁשָּׁה חֳדָשִׁים
בְּשֶׁמֶן הַמֹּר
Six months with oil of myrrh (2:12)

"I heard the following," said Reb Shaul, "from the earliest chassidim from Vitebsk. When our rebbe established the *Chabad* way of divine service he once said: 'It is written, שִׁשָּׁה חֳדָשִׁים בְּשֶׁמֶן הַמֹּר וְשִׁשָּׁה חֳדָשִׁים בַּבְּשָׂמִים — *Six months with oil of myrrh and six months with per-*

fumes. Six months should be spent *with oil of* מֹר, that is, in the kind of meditation that brings on מְרִירוּת אֲמִיתִּית. (In the writings of Reb Shneur Zalman this term signifies uncompromising but purposeful self-scrutiny.) Six months should then be invested *with perfumes*, that is, in cultivating one's spiritual sensitivity apprehending manifestations of Godliness. All this should serve as a preparation for one's *yechidus*.' "

Reb Aizik heard these words and decided to wait another twelve months — and only then to undertake his *yechidus* with his rebbe.

⋙ Do Yourself a Favor

וְאַתְּ וּבֵית אָבִיךְ
תֹּאבֵדוּ
And you and your father's house shall perish (4:14)

Before Reb Yosef Yitzchak of Lubavitch set out once on a journey, his father Reb Shalom Ber asked him to endeavor to do a certain favor for one of the chassidim, a businessman, who was in need of help.

When he returned he told his father: "I did everything you told me to do, and the favor to that man I did punctiliously."

"You err," said Reb Shalom Ber. "You did a favor to yourself, not to him. It is the Almighty who did a favor to him, by arranging for agents through whom the will of Divine Providence could be realized. Here, listen to a story.

"In 1888, when anti-Semitism was rampant here in Russia, and in many provinces our enemies incited the local citizens to rampage through Jewish townships, my father, Reb Shmuel, set out for St. Petersburg to see what he could do for our people. My father had many working connections with high-ranking officials, and within days of his arrival there he already found ways of having the ardor of the *pogromchiks* suppressed. However, in order to set the matter up on an official basis, the senior officials with whom he spoke advised him that an impressive delegation should call on the Minister of the Interior and on the President of the Senate. This delegation should be broadened to include men of means and the most prominent *maskilim*, the advocates of the 'Enlightenment' movement.

"When he returned from the capital, my father called

a meeting in his home of magnates and *maskilim*, proposed a mode of procedure, and suggested that they choose from among their number a team of dignitaries who would join with him in making up the delegation. However, since my father commonly ignored the opinions of people of their kind in public affairs, they were somewhat peeved at his present proposal. In fact one of them put it this way: 'We are not lumps of wood to be moved around like pawns. If we are important in our own right, then we should be taken notice of at all times. If not — then we can be dispensed with now too!'

"My father answered: 'In the *Megillah* we read Mordechai's warning to Esther:*For if you remain silent at this time, then relief and deliverance shall arise for the Jews from elsewhere, but you and your father's house* (וְאַתְּ וּבֵית אָבִיךְ) *shall perish. I am certain,'* my father went on, 'that *relief and deliverance will arise for the Jews*; if you do not choose to participate in it, then it will come *from elsewhere.* But then, *you and your father's house shall perish*, that is, you will have missed your opportunity.' "

"A man should always keep in mind," continued Reb Shalom Ber after having finished his story, "that whenever he does a good deed he is doing a favor *to himself.* A man needs to remember with simple and trusting faith that *relief and deliverance will arise for the Jews*; if not through himself, then *from elsewhere*; but then *you and your father's house shall perish.* In the Kabbalah, the word for *you* (וְאַתְּ) represents the reflection of the soul in the body, while the words for *and your father's house* (וּבֵית אָבִיךְ) signify the soul's root and source in heaven. The real elevation of them both is dependent on the divine service which a person performs in actual practice in *This* World, and a person should therefore see to it that neither should lose the noble privilege of being the agents of the Almighty in doing a favor to a fellow Jew."

⋅§ Such a Hilarious Sight!

וַיִּמָּצֵא כָתוּב
אֲשֶׁר הִגִּיד
מָרְדְּכָי

*And it was
found written
that Mordechai
had told
(6:2)*

As any old-timer will tell you, Pinsk and Karlin are so near each other that they can almost be regarded as one town.

During the period that Reb Levi Yitzchak of Berditchev was *rav* of Pinsk and the surrounding regions, there lived in the neighboring town Reb Shlomo of Karlin, who died the death of a martyr in 1792. One day Reb Levi Yitzchak asked that Reb Shlomo be called to him. Reb Shlomo duly arrived, and for a few hours they sat together, their faces ablaze with holy fire. Not a word did they exchange. After a long time they both broke out in uproarious laughter, and Reb Shlomo returned soon after to his home in Karlin.

This whole strange scene was witnessed by Reb Levi Yitzchak's attendant, who was so puzzled by it that he asked the rebbe to explain.

"All the Jews of our entire region," said the tzaddik, "were under the threat of a fearful verdict that was being considered in the Heavenly Court. The local gentile aristocracy had been consulting on the imminent expulsion of the Jews. They had therefore decided to call a meeting at which they would all sign a proclamation which would bring this into effect. I prayed with all my might that the evil decree be rescinded; I received no answer. One day I implored with all the intensity of *mesirus nefesh*, and I was told from Above that Shlomo the son of Yuta would be able to help out in this case, because Eliyahu the Prophet visits him frequently. I therefore asked to have him come here at the exact hour for which that fateful meeting had been called.

"Reb Shlomo arrived, and it was then that we saw that every single nobleman there was giving his assent to the proposed decree! We were so seized by terror that we could not utter a word.

"Now according to their procedure, any single one of them can veto a proposal. At this point, then, we saw Eliyahu the Prophet walk in and join their meeting in the guise of an elderly squire. He took his seat among them, and when the document reached him for his signature,

he insisted loudly that he would never agree to such an מְגִלַּת
edict. In fact, he would withhold his signature. This אֶסְתֵּר
shattered their unanimity, and in the fracas that followed
between their rivalling factions the document itself was
torn to shreds.

"This was such a hilarious sight that we broke out in
laughter. Imagine: a whole assemblage of fools allowing
an utter stranger to upset their plans!"

⋖§ They Live Forever

A strange phenomenon surrounds the handwriting of כְּתָב אֲשֶׁר
Reb Shlomo of Radomsk, the author of *Tiferes* נִכְתָּב בְּשֵׁם
Shlomo: until the present day the ink has not faded. הַמֶּלֶךְ
Anyone reading a document of his would be certain that *Writing that*
it was written and signed that same day. Several letters *was written*
are extant that were written by a different hand, and *in the name*
only signed by his. Their ink has either faded or peeled *of the king*
off — but in each case his signature stands fresh and *(8:8)*
clear.

Chassidim used to comment that this bears witness to
his purity and holiness, for, as the Psalmist says of him
who fears his Maker, "his righteousness endures
forever". In fact there are those who found a hint of this
connection in the Scroll of *Esther*. There it is written
(albeit with reference to Achashverosh, a king of flesh
and blood): "For writing that was written in the name of
the king, and sealed with the king's ring, cannot be
revoked."

That is to say: words written or signed in a state of
holiness, in the name of the King of the Universe, cannot
be revoked. *They live forever.*

⋖§ Inside Job

And honor: This alludes to the mitzvah of וִיקָר
tefillin (Talmud, Tractate Megillah). *And honor*
(8:16)

R eb Yisrael of Ruzhin had passed away, and his sons
had to divide up his vast estate. Their first thought
was that each of them should write down what he would
like as his share, and put his note in an envelope. This

they did, but for some reason the idea was dropped at this point, and they agreed instead to apportion the inheritance by drawing lots. The share that was drawn by Reb David Moshe of Chortkov, who at the time lived in Potik, included the most prized treasure of all — the *tefillin* that their father had inherited from his father, Reb Shalom, who had received them from his father, Reb Avraham "the *Malach*," who had received them from his father, Reb Dov Ber, the Maggid of Mezritch.

After the division was completed one of the older brothers, Reb Avraham Yaakov of Sadigora, said: "It would interest me to see what each of us had intended to choose for himself."

Sure enough, when they came to the envelope of Reb David Moshe they found a note that stated that he was willing to forgo his whole share in the estate — in exchange for the *tefillin*. The thought that no doubt crossed their minds at that moment is expressed thus by the Psalmist: רְצוֹן יְרֵאָיו יַעֲשֶׂה — "He fulfills the desire of those who fear Him."

❦ ❦ ❦

The following episode was related by Rabbi Meir Shapira of Lublin.

About two year after the passing of Reb Yisrael of Ruzhin, his son Reb Avraham Yaakov of Sadigora was sitting with a group of his disciples after kindling the Chanukah lights, sharing chassidic insights with them.

He remarked in passing: "I envy my brother Reb David Moshe; while praying he wears the *tefillin* of our great-great-grandfather, the Maggid of Mezritch."

At these words, two of the young men in that company grew instantly pale. Finally one of them mustered the courage to say: "Rebbe! I must air my old sins. Once, when my friend here and I saw how dearly you would have liked to use those *tefillin*, we decided to take it upon ourselves to get hold of the parchment scrolls that lay inside them, and to put those *parshios* into your *tefillin*. And indeed, we got as far as to take out the *parshios* from the *battim* of your brother's *tefillin*, and to replace them with kosher but ordinary scrolls. All this time we have been watching for an opportunity to tell you what we had done so far — but our minds were not at ease

about our whole plan, because we began to suspect that מְגִלַּת
perhaps we had not acted properly. Now, rebbe, that you אֶסְתֵּר
have mentioned the *tefillin* again, we have revealed our
secret, and we will now bring you the *parshios*."

A restrained tremor shook the little crowd of listeners.
In the first place they were amazed that the two young
men had dared to even contemplate such an escapade.
Secondly, was it not disconcertingly strange that Reb
David Moshe had not sensed that the *parshios* of the
Maggid had been subtracted from his *tefillin*?

Anyway, as soon as the two young men brought the
parshios, Reb Avraham gave an order that the matter
was not to be talked about, nor was it to be com-
municated to anyone not then present. He further instructed the group of chassidim then with him to prepare
themselves for a journey to Potik immediately after
Chanukah.

The day after their arrival in Potik, Reb Avraham
entered the room in which his younger brother Reb
David Moshe used to pray. On the table he found two
pairs of *tefillin* — the priceless pair inherited from the
Maggid, and another pair. Reb David Moshe now joined
him, approached the table, took up the Maggid's *tefillin*
in his hand, sighed, and returned them to their place. He
then picked up the other pair and donned them in the
usual way, on the bicep and above the forehead.

"Brother!" asked Reb Avraham Yaakov. "Why don't
you use the *tefillin* that became yours through the lottery?"

"I'll tell you the truth," replied Reb David Moshe.
"Not once in these two years have I donned those holy
tefillin. You see, every time I pick them up I feel that I
am unworthy of them. So I put them down again with a
humbled heart, and use these others."

Reb Avraham Yaakov could not remain silent: "No,
my dear brother! It is not that you are unworthy of using
those holy *tefillin*. The reason is quite different. You do
not sense their special sanctity because the Maggid's
parshios have been removed from them! Now here they
are. Return them to their place, for you are worthy indeed of using them!"

esther During the First World War, when the Cossacks burned down the *beis midrash* of the tzaddik of Chortkov, and pillaged all of its contents, these *tefillin* disappeared. However, in due course they were traced, identified by incontrovertible evidence, and restored to the hands of his only son, Reb Yisrael.

Glossary

All terms are Hebrew unless otherwise indicated.

AHAVAS YISRAEL: the love of a fellow Jew

AMORA (pl., *amoraim;* Aram.): authority quoted in the *Gemara*

APIKORES (pl. *apikorsim):* freethinker

ARENDA (Pol./Yid.): lease on inn or other source of livelihood commonly held by East European Jews; the leaseholder was called the *arendar*

AV BEIS DIN: chairman of a rabbinical court

AVODAH: the service of God, whether in sacrifice, prayer, or self-refinement

BAAL TESHUVAH (pl., *baalei teshuvah):* a penitent

BAR-MITZVAH: religious coming of age on a boy's thirteenth birthday

BATLAN: impractical fellow; clumsy no-hoper

BEIS DIN: rabbinical court of law

BEIS HAMIKDASH: the Temple (First or Second) in Jerusalem

BEIS MIDRASH: communal House of Study

BERACHAH: blessing, benediction

CHACHAM: sage

CHALLAH (pl., *challos):* braided loaf baked in honor of the Sabbath

CHANUKAH: eight-day festival commemorating the Maccabee's rededication of the Temple

CHANUKAH GELT (Heb./Yid.): pocket money traditionally distributed to children at that season

CHASSIDIM: Movement within Orthodox Judaism founded in 18th-century Eastern Europe by Reb Yisrael, known as the Baal Shem Tov. Stresses emotional involvement in prayer; service of God through the material universe; the primacy of wholehearted earnestness in divine service; the mystical in addition to the legalistic side of Judaism; the power of joy, and of music; and the collective physical and moral responsibility of the members of the informal brotherhood, each chassid having cultivated a spiritual attachment to their saintly charismatic leader — the rebbe or tzaddik.

CHAZZAN: cantor

CHEDER: elementary school for religious studies

CHEVRAH KADDISHA: voluntary burial society

CHIDDUSHEI TORAH: novellae; i.e., innovative interpretations of Talmudic or halachic subjects

CHILLUL HASHEM: desecration of the divine Name

CHUMASH: the Pentateuch

CHUTZPAH: nerve

DARSHAN: preacher

DAVVEN (Yid.): to pray

DAYS OF AWE: the New Year period of judgment, from Rosh HaShanah to Yom Kippur

DAYYAN: judge

DERASHAH: a sermon or discourse

DERUSH: exegetical or homiletical interpretation

DEVEIKUS: the ecstatic state of cleaving to the Creator

DIVREI TORAH: discourse or conversation on Torah subjects

DREIDEL (Yid.): four-sided spinning top used on Chanukah

ERETZ YISRAEL: the Land of Israel

ESROG (pl., esrogim): the citron fruit used in the festivities of Sukkos

FARBRENGEN (Yid.): gathering of chassidim for mutual edification and comradely criticism

GABBAI: (a) attendant of a tzaddik; (b) master of ceremonies in synagogue

GALUS: exile; the Diaspora

GARTL (Yid.): belt worn in prayer

GEFILTE FISH (Yid.): traditional Sabbath delicacy

GEHINNOM: purgatory

GEMARA (Aram.): that portion of the Talmud which discusses the Mishnah; also, loosely, a synonym for the Talmud as a whole

GEMILUS CHASSADIM: the mitzvah of doing good deeds

GET: a bill of divorce

GOY (pl., goyim): gentile

HAFTARAH: the passage from the Prophets read in the synagogue after the Pentateuchal reading

HAGGADAH: the order of service for the domestic Passover evening ceremonies which recall the Exodus from Egypt

HAKADOSH: "the holy" — traditionally suffixed to certain names

HAKKAFOS: circuits made around the bimah (dais) in the synagogue on Simchas Torah (and in some congregations on Shemini Atzeres as well), with sifrei Torah in hand, and accompanied by the singing of verses from Psalms, and dancing

HALACHIC (Eng. adjectival form): referring to the Halachah, the corpus of Torah law

HALLEL: a bracket of Psalms (113-118), framed by berachos and recited or sung on festive occasions

HAMOTZI: blessing pronounced over bread

HASKALAH: the 18th cent. "Enlightenment" movement which sought to introduce Western culture into traditional Jewish circles

HAVDALAH: the Saturday evening ceremony by which the sanctity of the outgoing Sabbath is separated from the workaday week

HOSHANA RABBAH: the seventh day of the festival of Sukkos

ILUI: prodigy; genius

KABBALAH: the body of Jewish mystical teachings

KAPOTE (Yid.): black frockcoat, worn usually in honor of the Sabbath

KAVANAH: devout intent

KIDDUSH: blessing over wine, expressing the sanctity of the Sabbath or a festival

KIDDUSH HASHEM: sanctifying the Divine Name, especially through self-sacrifice

KITTEL (Yid.): white gown worn on certain solemn occasions

KOHEN (pl.: *kohanim*): priest;

KOHEN GADOL: High Priest

KOPEK (Russ.): small copper coin

KOSHER: ritually fit for use

KREPLACH (Yid.): pastry delicacy with cheese or other filling

KVITL (pl., *kvitlach;* Yid.): note handed to tzaddik, bearing name of supplicant and his mother's name, and the nature of the request

LAMDAN: scholar of repute

LASHON HARA: lit., "the evil tongue"; slanderous talk

LECHAIM: lit., "To Life!" — greeting exchanged over strong drink

LULAV: palm-branch used in ceremony on festival of Sukkos

MAAMAD: regular contribution made by chassid for maintenance of his rebbe's household

MAAMAR: chassidic discourse

MAGGID: preacher

MALACH: angel

MASHIACH: Messiah

MASKIL: (pl., *Maskilim*): adherent of the Haskalah movement

MATTANOS LAEVYONIM: gifts of money presented to the needy as one of the mitzvos of Purim

MATZOS (pl. of *matzah*): unleavened bread eaten on Passover

MAYSES (pl. of *mayse;* Yid.): story; anecdote

MAZEL TOV: greeting of congratulation

MECHUTAN: the parent-in-law of one's son or daughter

MEGILLAH GELT: (Yid.) gratuity offered the reader of the Scroll of Esther on Purim

MELAMED: schoolmaster or tutor

MELAVEH MALKAH: Saturday evening meal which farewells the departing Sabbath Queen

MESIRUS NEFESH: self-sacrifice

MIDRASH: (a) classical anthology of the Sages' homiletical teachings on the Torah; (b) a particular passage therefrom

MIKVEH: pool for ritual immersion

MINCHAH: the afternoon prayer service

MINYAN: quorum of ten men required for communal prayer

MISHLOACH MANOS: the sending of food gifts to friends on Purim

MISHNAH: (a) the germinal statements of law elucidated by the *Gemara*, together with which they constitute the Talmud; (b) any paragraph from this body of law (pl. *Mishnayos*)

MISHPACHOLOGY: mythical word of hybrid etymology signifying family relationships as a study or preoccupation

MISNAGED (pl., *misnagdim*; adj., *misnagdish, -er*): opponent of the teachings of Chassidism

MITZVAH (pl., mitzvos): a religious obligation; loosely, a good deed

MOTZAEI SHABBOS: the time of the departure of the Sabbath; i.e., Saturday night

MUKTZEH: something set apart and forbidden for use on *Shabbos* and festivals

MUSAF: prayer added to the service in honor of Sabbaths and festivals

NE'ILAH: concluding service of the Day of Atonement

NETILAS YADAYIM: ritual washing of the hands

NIGUN: melody, usually wordless

PARITZ: local squire in Eastern Europe

PARNAS HACHODESH: communal functionary, in office by rota for a month

PASUK (pl., *pesukim*): Biblical verse

PESACH: the festival of Passover

PIDYON (or *pidyon nefesh*): the contribution for charity which accompanies a chassid's request to his rebbe

PILPUL: involved legalistic dissertation

POSKIM (pl. of *posek*): decisors; rabbis whose legal decisions are authoritative

RAV: rabbi

REBBE (Heb./Yid.): (a) a tzaddik who is spiritual guide to a following of chassidim; (b) a Torah teacher

REBBITZIN: wife of a *rav* or a rebbe

RIBBONO SHEL OLAM: Master of the Universe

ROSH CHODESH: New Moon; i.e., one or two semi-festive days at beginning of month

ROSH HASHANAH: the New Year festival

ROSH YESHIVAH: head of a Talmudic academy

RUACH HAKODESH: divine inspiration, and the extra-sensory gifts accompanying it

SABBATH QUEEN: the Sabbath personified

SANDAK: person who holds infant at circumcision

SCHLEMIEL (Yid.): something like a *batlan*, but more so

SEFER TORAH: Scroll of the Law

SEGULAH: spiritual remedy; talisman

SELICHOS: penitential prayers

SEUDAH: meal, especially a festive one

SEUDAH SHLISHIS: the mystic Third Meal held at sunset on the Sabbath

SEUDAS MITZVAH: meal held in celebration of a religious obligation

SHABBOS: the Sabbath

SHACHARIS: the morning prayer service

SHALOM: greeting — "Peace!"

SHALOM ALEICHEM: (a) greeting — "Peace be upon you!" (b) Friday evening hymn of welcome to ministering angels

SHAMMES: sexton in synagogue or beadle in attendance on rabbi

SHAVUOS: the festival commemorating the Revelation at Sinai

SHECHITAH: the ritual slaughtering of meat for kosher consumption

SHEMA YISRAEL: opening words of the Jew's declaration of faith

SHEMINI ATZERES: festival at end of Sukkos (celebrated in *Eretz Yisrael* for one day and outside *Eretz Yisrael* for two days, the second of which is called Simchas Torah)

SHEMONEH ESREH: prayer which is the solemn climax of each of the three daily services

SHIDDUCH: a matrimonial match

SHOCHET: ritual slaughterer

SHOFAR (pl., *shofaros*): ram's horn blown on Rosh HaShanah

SHTREIMEL (Yid.): fur-rimmed hat worn on Sabbath and festivals

SHUL (Yid.): synagogue

SHULCHAN ARUCH: the Code of Jewish Law

SIDDUR: prayer book

SIMCHAS BEIS HASHOEVAH: "the Rejoicing of the Water-Drawing" — festivities held on Sukkos in commemoration of the service in the Temple

STENDER: moveable lectern

SUKKAH: booth lived in during the festival of Sukkos

SUKKOS: seven-day festival marked by living in a *sukkah*

TACHANUN: prayer requesting forgiveness, omitted on festive occasions

TACHLIS (lit., "destiny"): in Yiddish usage signifies brass tacks, especially as regards financial self-sufficiency

TALLIS: shawl worn in prayer

TALMUD: the basic compendium of Jewish law, thought, and Biblical commentary; comprises Mishnah and *Gemara*; Talmud Bavli — the edition developed in Babylonia; Talmud Yerushalmi — the edition of the Land of Israel

TAHARAH: purity; specifically, the ritual washing of a body in preparation for burial

TANNA (pl., *tannaim*; Aram.): authority quoted in the Mishnah

TASHLICH: riverside ritual of atonement on Rosh HaShanah

TEFILLAS GESHEM: prayer for rain

TEFILLIN: small black leather cubes containing parchment srolls inscribed with *Shema Yisrael* and other Biblical passages, bound to the arm and forehead at weekday morning prayers; phylacteries

TEHILLIM: the Biblical Book of *Psalms*

TENAIM: betrothal agreement

TESHUVAH: repentance

THIRD MEAL: see *Seudah Shlishis* (above)

TIKKUN: (a) refreshments for *Farbrengen*; (b) the task (pl., *tikkunim*) of uplifting the universe by revealing its hidden sparks of spirituality

TIKKUN CHATZOS: midnight lament over the Exile of the Divine Presence

TISH (Yid.): lit., "table"; ceremonial Sabbath meal or inspirational gatherings conducted publicly by a chassidic rebbe, characterized by spontaneous Torah discourses, and singing by all present

TISHAH B'AV: the ninth day of the month of Av; fast day commemorating the Destruction of both the First and the Second Temple in Jerusalem

TREFAH: ritually unfit for use; opposite of kosher

TZADDIK: (a) a saintly individual; (b) specifically, a chassidic rebbe

TZEDAKAH: charity

TZITZIS: the fringes worn at the corners of the *tallis*

VIDUI: the confession recited on the Day of Atonement, and during the final stocktaking of a lifetime

VORT (Yid.): lit., "word"; a quotable and insightful morsel of moral teaching or Biblical interpretation

YAHRZEIT (Yid.) anniversary of the passing of a near relative

YECHIDUS: private interview at which chassid seeks guidance and enlightenment from his rebbe

YEITZER HARA: the Evil Inclination

YESHIVAH: Talmudic academy

YICHUD: a union in the spiritual spheres, effected by devout divine service in This World

YICHUS: distinguished lineage

YOM KIPPUR: the Day of Atonement

YOM-TOV: festival

ZAL: suffix — "of blessed memory"

ZECHUS (pl., *zechuyos*): the merit of a good deed, especially as deserving a spiritual reward

ZEIDE (Yid.): grandfather

ZOHAR: the basic work of the Kabbalah